Beyond
Fund Raising

The NSFRE/Wiley Fund Development Series

BEYOND FUND RAISING
NEW STRATEGIES
FOR NONPROFIT
INNOVATION AND
INVESTMENT

Kay Sprinkel Grace

JOHN WILEY & SONS, INC.

NEW YORK / CHICHESTER / WEINHEIM / BRISBANE / SINGAPORE / TORONTO

Library of Congress Cataloging in Publication Data:

ISBN 0-471-16232-9

Printed in the United States of America

10 9 8 7 6 5 4 3 2

DEDICATION

This book is dedicated to all who encouraged me, but especially to my husband, Geoffrey Beaumont; our children, Michael and Liza, Andrew and Florence, Greg, Alison and David, and Catherine; to my parents, Robert and Marian Sprinkel; and to my friends, Joanne and Al Tisch, who encouraged me at every stage of my professional career. It is also dedicated to those thousands of individuals who, over the years, have enriched my understanding of the vitality and importance of the nonprofit sector.

Special acknowledgment is given to the profound influence of two towering individuals in the field of philanthropy and fund raising: Robert L. Payton, first Executive Director of the Center on Philanthropy at Indiana University; and Hank Rosso, founder of The Fund Raising School. They have been mentors, friends, and guides.

The NSFRE/Wiley Fund Development Series

The NSFRE/Wiley Fund Development Series is intended to provide fund development professionals, volunteers including board members, (and others interested in the not-for-profit sector) with top-quality publications that help advance philanthropy as voluntary action for the public good. Our goal is to provide practical, timely guidance and information on fund raising, charitable giving, and related subjects. NSFRE and Wiley each bring to this innovative collaboration unique and important resources that result in a whole greater than the sum of its parts.

The National Society of Fund Raising Executives

The NSFRE is a professional association of fund-raising executives which advances philanthropy through its more than 16,000 members in 138 chapters throughout the United States, Canada, and Mexico. Through its advocacy, research, education, and certification programs, the Society fosters development and growth of fund-raising professionals, works to advance philanthropy and volunteerism, and promotes high ethical standards in the fund-raising profession.

1995–1996 NSFRE Publishing Advisory Council

Preface

When I first started telling people what I planned to title this book, the response was delightful. Board members and other volunteers, who comprise the majority of my workshop and consultation clients, were relieved and encouraged to know there is "life beyond fund raising." They could hardly wait for the book to be published. Their professional counterparts—the scores of development professionals and nonprofit administrators with whom I work annually—were equally anxious to find out just what it means to go beyond fund raising.

BEYOND FUND RAISING: WHAT IT MEANS

Because this book is written for volunteers and staff people working in a sector that is based on the measurable success of its fund raising, the title may seem odd. The principle is simple: To go beyond fund raising, organizations must do more than raise funds.

- They must believe and practice the principle that development is a comprehensive process of which fund raising is a pivotal part.
- They must understand that development is the series of deliberate activities by which we involve and retain funders in a donor-investor relationship with our organizations.
- They must give up the view that "development" is just an unlinked series of approaches to prospects and donors (direct mail, phone appeals, fund raising events, fall campaigns, winter campaigns) which yield revenues and donors from year to year. That is not development, it is fund raising. And, it is not enough.

A GROWING NEED

The need for the nonprofit sector to go "beyond fund raising" and to understand and apply development principles is growing. Increased competition among funders and a higher level of sophistication among donors have changed the nature of philanthropy, development, and fund raising.

Once viewed as needy institutions to which people contributed out of a sense of obligation, nonprofits now find they are being evaluated against different and tougher criteria based on their own financial and community performance and their capacity to meet donor needs. This shift in expectations requires organizations to practice the longer term process of development; to go beyond fund raising.

PUTTING AWAY THE TIN CUP: THE ORIGIN OF BEYOND FUND RAISING

This book has been writing itself for a long time. Its principles and strategies have formed the basis of my workshop, "Putting Away the Tin Cup" which, since 1987, has been given for boards of trustees, other volunteers, and staff members of hundreds of not-for-profit organizations in the United States, Canada, Australia, the United Kingdom, and western Europe.

The primary purpose of "Putting Away the Tin Cup" workshops is to raise the comfort level of board and staff members as they raise money for their nonprofit organizations. It is a program based on innovative strategies that challenge and change old notions about fund raising. The workshop introduces new concepts and new ideas which enable organizations to position themselves more positively in their communities. These same ideas have also guided my consultation with scores of organizations. They have grown out of and informed my teaching with The Fund Raising School and other organizations, and they are the basis of this book.

Over the years, my insights have sharpened to reflect the experience and needs of the thousands of volunteer and staff leaders with whom I have worked. These leaders have represented many places and institutions: a children's services agency in Oregon, a university in England, a library in Paris, a Leukemia Foundation in Australia, a Catholic university in Minnesota, a technical institute in New Zealand, a preparatory school in Seattle, a medical center near Los Angeles, a children's hospital in Canada, a church organization in Australia, opera companies in New York and San Francisco, orchestras from across America, and museums in New Mexico, Colorado, and France. Although these organizations differ, and the volunteer and staff roles vary, the concerns expressed by clients and participants in "Putting Away the Tin Cup" workshops have many common threads:

- Fear of rejection and reluctance to be viewed as beggars —principal reasons for discomfort with fund raising;
- Worry about asking too often, and the need for strategies to make asking more effective;
- Weariness of the relentless cycle of fund-raising activities needed to generate revenue, and desire to know how to cultivate and retain donors;
- Enthusiasm about organizations and the capacity to make a difference in the community;
- Eagerness to learn how to position organizations in the community as constructive, vital, and important.

PRINCIPAL CONCEPTS

The principal concepts in this book are the "ahas" that have emerged from these common ideas and have been tested in workshops and consultations. To put away the tin cup and go beyond fund raising, nonprofits must:

- Position themselves as organizations that meet needs, not as organizations that have needs;
- Focus on program results, not just on financial goals;
- Remember that the process of asking and giving is based in shared values;
- View nonprofit organizations, and encourage others to perceive them, as vital agents in communities whose services and enhancements must be balanced and strong;
- Engage nonprofit leaders and donors at all levels in a process that will convert them to donor-investors, committed to long-term relationships based on shared values and vision;
- Position all contributions to nonprofit organizations as investments in the communities those organizations serve;

- See the process of revenue generation and constituency involvement as a much larger, inclusive, and energizing process called development.

THE BREAKTHROUGH INNOVATION

Organizations persist in trying new fund-raising practices, and do not see they still lack the development framework that will create a lasting base of donor-investors. They seek innovative strategies for increasing revenues: the event no one has tried, the cleverly (or emotionally) crafted mailing that will survive the 15-second initial exposure test and result in a first-time gift, or the hiring of the best possible "fund raiser" (as they persist in inappropriately calling development professionals). None of these strategies is enough to bring a consistent and stable base of funding to an organization without the principal innovation that goes beyond fund raising and inspires development.

The innovation that has the most singular impact on all organizations with which I have worked during my years as a consultant and teacher to the philanthropic sector is this: an innovation in attitude about the entire fund raising process, one which properly puts it into the larger context of development and philanthropy. Only then can true innovation occur and attitudes shift. One person wrote, after a particularly rigorous workshop, "I will now feel proud to ask for money for our college."

Innovation requires a willingness to set aside old ideas. A certain entrepreneurial spirit must prevail; there must be a willingness to take risks. Courage is fundamental and confidence is critical. The enviable mystique that surrounds those who are successful at fund raising is nothing more, in my experience, than the attitude those individuals have about the process:

- They know it is hard work, but it is worth it.
- They are passionate about the causes for which they are raising money.
- They come not as beggars, but as individuals offering others rare opportunities to invest in the future of their communities.
- They are the catalysts for converting citizens to donor-investors in the organizations whose values they share.
- They find the process to be satisfying and gratifying.
- They see it as a way of involving people known and unknown to them in organizations that are making a difference in their communities.

For those who have made the attitudinal breakthrough, an invitation to provide or ask for funds for an organization is an invitation to invest themselves or ask others to invest. Each act of giving and asking is an honor, a privilege and a trust. We can measure the impact of gifts by the results the organization achieves.

I have watched as board members, other volunteers, staff members, and the curious who are not yet involved with philanthropy realize that asking for money is an invitation to invest. I have heard their stories of the transforming nature of both asking and giving, and listened as they related their increased stakeholder roles. I have seen what happens to attitudes about fund raising when people realize that the investment goes beyond the organization: that an investment made in a not-for-profit organization is an investment in the community.

These are powerful realizations. They help combat attitudes shaped by the media, which still portray the nonprofit sector as one which must beg for funds to continue its existence. Years ago, one of the high-circulation American news magazines did an article on major university capital campaigns under way at the time. They titled it, "America's Top Universities Go Begging in High Style." We must go beyond that image. We do not come from weakness. We have no need to beg. We come from the strength of our convictions and values. That is why we must go beyond fund raising if we are to achieve the level of organizational stability our communities require.

A BOOK OF TESTED IDEAS

The principal ideas in this book shape and guide my training and consultation with more than 50 organizations each year. They are tested daily. My professional development work, which began in 1979, was seeded and continues to be greatly enriched by my uninterrupted years, since 1961, as a volunteer for a wide variety of organizations. That perspective has also greatly influenced this book.

My passions about the not-for-profit sector are many. They inspired a growing sense of professional urgency to write this book. These passions include ethics, values, professionalism, board participation, pride in the sector, partnerships at all levels of an organization and in the community, and a keen sense of mission and vision. They are governed by an absence of cynicism and an abundance of enthusiasm. Conveyed to workshop participants, this enthusiasm has stimulated requests over the years for a book to use with their organizations and for themselves.

A BOOK FOR VOLUNTEERS AND STAFF THROUGHOUT THE WORLD

This book is for both paid and unpaid leaders and servants of the not-for-profit sector throughout the world. Its principles are universal. Many philanthropic practices and strategies, long a part of the American tradition, are now being implemented with care and success in countries throughout the world. Cross-cultural adaptations must be made by those in other countries implementing American ideas—even by close neighbors in Mexico and Canada—but the kernel of each strategy is sound.

As my work has expanded globally in recent years, so has my perspective and understanding of both common and divergent practices.

Certain ideas and issues have distilled with force and clarity. While the primary focus of the sector will always be on ways to generate more revenue, it is a persistent conclusion that fund raising is not enough. Experienced organizations know this is so. In practice, unfortunately, they too often ignore this crucial truth. They do not take the time to do the kind of planning and relationship building that is indispensable for long-term development. Even if they cultivate their prospects well—building relationships as a prelude to asking for the gift—they often fail miserably at stewardship.

Stewardship is more than diligent monitoring of the way in which a person's gift is invested or used. Stewardship is the process of involving and appreciating donor-investors, and bringing them into a deeper relationship with the organization after the gift is made. Stewardship is the most critical development practice. It encourages long term investment in our sector. The importance of stewardship weaves its way through this book, and there is an entire chapter devoted to it as well.

As nonprofits take their place with business and government as an increasingly vital segment of a healthy society, they must provide both initiative and response. The philanthropic sector has an opportunity to build stronger communities through boldness, innovation, and new models for action that are based on results, not needs; investment opportunities, not institutional financial urgency.

As observer, counselor, teacher, constructive critic, and confidant, I have been privileged beyond expression to work with staff and volunteer leaders who are truly making a difference in the health and stability of our society.

This book is for them, and for all those who wish to implement nonprofit innovation and investment to strengthen their communities.

Contents

CONTENTS

Introduction

The steady retreat of government funding from support of community-based cultural, social and human services, medical, educational, and arts organizations in the United States and throughout the world has led to a variety of responses—from panic to problem-solving—by nonprofits. The rush to fund raise has led to confusion and resentment by those who are asked repeatedly to support a variety of causes. These potential funders feel they are approached too often, and frequently by organizations that position themselves as desperate to raise funds to protect their organization's stability during a time of dramatic change.

It is time to re-engineer the nonprofit sector, to infuse it with innovation and investment strategies that will develop long-term relationships with funders and volunteers. These relationships must be based on an understanding between organizations and their donor-investors of their mutual responsibility to provide essential community enhancements and services.

It is a relationship based on partnership, respect, and vision.

Beyond Fund Raising is a blueprint for building new donor-organization relationships and strengthened communities. It is for nonprofit volunteers and professionals who want to go "beyond fund raising" to values-based philanthropy, development, and a fresh approach to fund raising. It is based on these key principles:

1. Donors do not give to organizations because organizations have needs: they give because organizations meet needs.

2. Fund raising is less about money than it is about relationships: in the words of a Stanford Centennial Campaign volunteer, "Fund raising is a contact sport."

3. Philanthrophy is defined by Robert L. Payton (1988) as a participatory and democratic process which involves giving, asking, joining, and serving. It is *not* "multiple choice." In a vigorous society, people must engage in each aspect of the process.

4. There are three levels of involvement and practice for staff and volunteers: philosophical, strategic, and tactical. Successful organizations operate at all three levels.

5. There is no such thing as a "quick fix" in the philanthropic sector. Organizations that experience immediate or unexpected success still must create the systems and structures that will endure over time. Otherwise, they will find they have built a roof without creating a foundation or walls.

6. Based in values, philanthropy is the context for values-driven development and fund raising.

7. Stewardship is a neglected and misunderstood function. It must be practiced as diligently for the donor as it is for the donor's gift.

8. The process of asking for contributions to a nonprofit organization should be one in which the asker feels the pride of inviting investment and in which the donor feels not pressure, but release.

Those who reflect on these ideas and implement the strategies presented in this book will contribute substantially to the health of nongovernment nonprofit organizations around the world. In so doing, they will help ensure a safe passage for institutions through these chaotic times and into a restructured society whose shape they will have influenced through their involvement.

It is a quintessential role to play.

Values: The Context For Philanthropy, Development, and Fund Raising

Philanthropic behavior is motivated by values. Board member commitment to serve and ask, volunteer enthusiasm, and a funder's sense of satisfaction in giving are based in an implicit search for ways to act on their values. Matching volunteer, funder, and institutional values is a critical practice of successful nonprofit organizations.

PHILANTHROPY DEFINED

New definitions of philanthropy, developed by the Center on Philanthropy at Indiana University, position it as much more than giving money. Philanthropy is voluntary action for the public good, and it is based in values (Payton 1988). Voluntary action includes giving, asking, joining, and serving.

People do not engage in philanthropic community activities on behalf of organizations whose values they do not share. The values of our constituencies, when they are consistent with those of our organizations, can predict the level and intensity of the response a donor or volunteer will have to a cause.

In their quest for true innovation and long-term donor investment, organizations in the nonprofit sector must define and apply their values base. They should organize their internal systems and community outreach to maximize the understanding of, response to, and impact of those values. Only then will these organizations achieve full intersection with supporters, and engage them in a lasting and mutually satisfying relationship.

THE ROLE OF VALUES IN THE NONPROFIT SECTOR

Complex and passionate values are often present at the creation of nonprofit organizations. Wishing to act meaningfully on those values, people create and help sustain organizations that meet a variety of community needs:

- Parents whose son or daughter dies of a drug overdose channel their grief into constructive options for other young people by creating a counseling program at the local high school.
- Because she values independent living and the dignity deserved by all individuals, the grandmother of a developmentally disabled young adult helps create a center for her grandchild and for others with similar disabilities.
- The American Library in Paris is founded by the father of an American poet-soldier killed in the First World War.
- The families of leukemia patients in Queensland, Australia, help create an apartment building where they can stay while loved ones receive hospital treatment.

Other motivations may be less personal, but are no less values-driven.

- In America, the movement to keep local and regional symphonies strong and accessible is based in values: community leaders realize that live musical performances enhance the attractiveness of their communities, that children and adults need opportunities to appreciate and learn about music, and that local musicians need to play together.
- In Prague, a museum of modern art turns to the private sector for financial support and additions to its collections.
- Public school districts in California and other parts of the United States, reeling under reductions in tax revenues, create private foun-

dations to raise money to support jeopardized school programs. They are the invention of parents motivated by values of quality and opportunity in education.

- In Slovenia, citizens ensure the creation of a children's services agency to replace vital healthcare programs previously provided by government.

Throughout the world, communities are responding to changes in traditional sources of services and revenue by creating and sustaining museums, schools, social and human service agencies, and other vital institutions. Motivated by the values they hold and the values of their communities, nonprofit leaders are taking on new roles as community builders.

Inspired by America's globally unique nonprofit leadership, international philanthropy is emerging. This philanthropy is driven by values, and is the context for the related processes of development and fund raising.

DEVELOPING A VALUES-BASED APPROACH

Successful systems and structures that attract volunteers and funding rely on the identification of common values. These values become the foundation of all outreach and operations. This basis for philanthropy is often intuitive or subconscious. The understanding that values are at the core of voluntary action sometimes must be prompted. Board members, other volunteers, and staff may know instinctively why they are committed to an organization or to the voluntary sector, but most have not articulated the values that attract them. Nonprofit leaders, who may be stymied in their ability to convey a fresh or convincing message asking for community support, benefit from revisiting the core values of their organizations. The results of such an exercise are heartening. Renewed motivation is often immediate, and reaffirmation of founding or sustaining principles occurs. They take the first step toward values-directed outreach to the community that can result in revitalized support.

Whether an organization is long-established and looking for a current perspective, or new and looking for a solid basis on which to construct its outreach, the identification of values is a significant step.

Identifying Values

Values orientation is outward. It requires organizations to replace their windows with mirrors and identify those aspects of their beliefs and practices that will link with the needs of the community and the values of their existing and potential constituencies. In organizations that are evolving from a focus on the needs they have to an emphasis on the needs they meet, this is sometimes a difficult step. They are used to conducting community outreach and raising funds based on internal financial needs; they require some coaching to transcend old habits and focus on the core values that can attract and retain like-minded people.

Values will vary among organizations and donors. Some examples of core values expressed by organizations in discussions designed to increase their understanding of the philanthropic context of the development process and fund raising are:

- *A YMCA:* youth, leadership, families, community, and health;
- *An arts education organization:* creativity, expression, learning, opportunity, and family involvement;
- *A children's services organization:* safety, health, care, concern, families, and healing opportunities; and
- *A medical center:* healing, continuum of care, excellence, and compassion.

Detractors from these somewhat altruistic expressions suggest that the values which drive some people to support highly visible organizations, and major arts institutions in particular, are self serving: recognition, opportunity to mingle with the rich and famous, or prestige. These motivations are real and valid, and should be viewed without criticism as opportunities for exploration of other values. A person's motivation for giving an annual or capital gift, as long as it is within the ethical and values framework of the recipient organization, should be the starting point of a relationship. Over time, the initial WIIFM (What's in it for me?) motivation can be converted to a desire to work together with an organization to make a difference in an area of mutually perceived importance.

Organizations that position themselves as facilitators rather than judges can unleash opportunities to bring people into a larger understanding of the impact of their involvement. Most volunteers and professionals are wise enough to know when donor motivation is inconsistent with the mission of the organization and could lead to a compromise of the institution's values. Such instances are quite rare, and these gifts are almost always rejected.

EXHIBIT 1.1 Interrelationship of Values-Based Philanthropy, Development, and Fund Raising

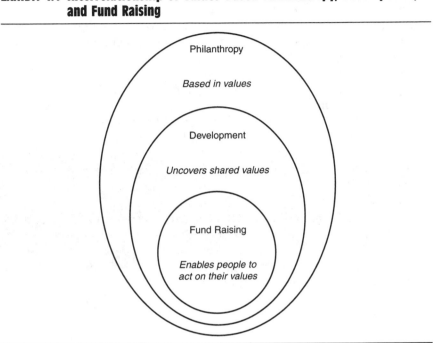

The identification and nurturing of the values people bring to their first interaction with an organization are the first steps toward going beyond fund raising.

A MODEL OF VALUES-BASED PHILANTHROPY, DEVELOPMENT, AND FUND RAISING

Mastery of the interrelationship of values-based philanthropy, development, and fund raising is a critical achievement for organizations seeking innovative and powerful ways to position themselves in their communities. Exhibit 1.1 shows how these three functions operate as one seamless context for constancy and donor development by nonprofit organizations. The integration of these functions is the primary premise in going beyond fund raising.

7

UNDERSTANDING THE MODEL

The largest element of this model is philanthropy, as redefined by Payton and others. It is the context in which development and fund raising must be set.

Most nonprofit volunteer and staff leaders, introduced to the larger interpretation of philanthropy as voluntary action for the public good, immediately grasp its role as a philosophical framework in which to plan and set priorities. The challenge to old ways of thinking comes more forcefully in understanding the difference between development and fund raising. In a survey administered as part of a workshop series by the National Center for Nonprofit Boards, the majority of participants indicate that "development" is just a "nicer way" of saying fund raising.

This three-part model, which distinguishes between development and fund raising, challenges that belief and places these functions as outgrowths of philanthropy. It separates the process of development from the activities of fund raising, and assigns each a different function within the values-framed structure.

The model has these three elements: Philanthropy, Development and Fund Raising.

Philanthropy: Based in Values

Philanthropy is the largest part of the model, and it is based in values. The research of Payton and others has verified this conclusion. We do not give to, ask for, join, or serve those organizations whose values are inconsistent with our own. At the most altruistic, this motivation draws people into selfless involvement with organizations that are advancing and strengthening basic community and individual values. At the other end of the continuum, there will be those whose initial motivation is the WIIFM (What's in it for me?). This initial motivation, as discussed previously, can be grown over time into a deeper understanding of mutual benefits for donor and organization.

Because core values are broad (e.g., dignity, independence, excellence, compassion, quality of life), they permit access to organizations by a wide range of donors with differing needs and perceptions. Messages can encompass all or one of these values. The values also cross boundaries from one organization to another. Those who value families, health, or safety will find several organizations in a community in whose philanthropy they can participate. This reduces the sense of competition among organizations, and focuses instead on the importance of fulfilling a values-centered community mission, which may be acted on by several institutions.

Two Institutions, One Campaign: Common Mission, Common Values

In one community, two separate organizations working with women and their children who had experienced domestic violence combined their efforts in one community campaign. An emergency shelter and a transition housing/job training program conducted a joint fund-raising campaign one year under the mutual banner of "breaking the cycle of violence." An advertising agency provided excellent quality pro bono print and electronic public service promotional materials, and a highly-respected county supervisor was the keynote speaker at the campaign kick-off. More than $75,000 in contributions were shared by the two organizations from the joint campaign. Each organization also conducted its own fund-raising activities that year, separate from the joint campaign but reflecting the common mission. Community awareness of the issue of domestic violence was heightened by the joint campaign, and response to the individual agency campaigns reflected this as well. The PSAs (public service announcements) were timeless in their production and appeal, and are still seen on the local television station. The two organizations attracted new donors who identified with their shared values, and renewed existing donors who saw with fresh clarity the importance of breaking the cycle of violence.

Translating Philanthropy: In Conveying Values, The Mission is the Message

The invitation to participate as a donor-investor or volunteer in values-based philanthropy is best extended through a mission statement that reflects those values. Many nonprofit organizations have succumbed to the pressure of people who are uncomfortable with values statements and have created "corporate" mission statements, describing *what* the organization does, rather than *why*.

To embark on successful values-based philanthropy, development, and fund raising, it is very important to have a mission statement that states why the organization exists. It may also say what the organization does, but the function should be a response to the purpose.

What Mission Statements Should Say and Do

Nonprofit organizations exist to fulfill community needs. People don't give time and money to organizations because organizations have needs; they give because organizations meet needs. This is a key premise for going beyond fund raising. Mission statements that describe only the function of an organization need to frame that function with the purpose: why does an organization exist? What need is being met? While some values are present in a statement of what an organization does, the core values that will ignite interest are more boldly expressed in a statement of why the organization exists. The Fund Raising School, a program of Indiana University's Center on Philanthropy, has generated the seminal work in values-based mission statements. Its basic course materials include numerous examples of statements that answer the question, "Why does your organization exist?"

Two Examples of Values-Based Mission Statements

Over the years, certain organizations have framed and used mission statements that are powerful invitations to invest. Vector Health Programs of Eureka, California, which specializes in procedures for repairing severe injuries to hands, has one that is stunning. Its executive director, Karen Angel, prepared it as part of a workshop exercise. Her initial mission statement, a description of Vector's services, was challenged as lacking an expression of core values. She wrote the following in response to the question, "Why do you exist?" *"Next to the human face, hands are our most expressive feature. We talk with them. We work with them. We play with them. We comfort and love with them. An injury to the hand affects people personally and professionally. At Vector Health Programs, we give people back the use of their hands."* The statement went on to describe how Vector restores the use of people's hands. The board chair, on hearing this statement the first time, was moved to tears. She said she had not realized, until then, just why she was involved. The mission statement had intersected with, and exposed, her values.

In another example, Yale University School of Medicine positioned this values-based mission statement as the lead to its case materials for a capital campaign conducted nearly two decades ago: *"We are in the midst of one of the most profound intellectual revolutions of all time, the revolution in the biological sciences. Its implications for understanding life processes and for combating disease are boundless. Yale is in the forefront of this revolution."* Succinct and potent, this brief statement reflects values of excellence, innovation, and involvement, and invites those who share those values to participate in the campaign.

Getting Comfortable with Expressing Values

It is not enough to have values: they must be expressed. If organizations are reluctant to present a values-based mission statement to an increasingly critical and pragmatic public, they should still go through the exercise of identifying their core values. The statement they develop may be for internal use only, but its presence will serve to inspire and motivate those who must engage others in institutional advancement.

Organizational reluctance to create and publish a values-based mission statement is puzzling. A look at most American and international advertising shows how emotions and values are used for commercial gain. Makers of automobiles, soft drinks, food products, cleaning products, insurance, health plans, and other consumer goods are not at all reluctant to press on values in their marketing. A nonprofit's mission statement is not an advertisement, but it *is* used to attract potential donors and volunteers in the way an advertisement is used to convince the consumer to purchase. As reflected in the two mission statements quoted above, there is room for modest expression of emotion in nonprofit mission statements. This emotion is anchored by values, and is never excessive or offensive. Most nonprofit organizations have an emotional basis to their origin: to deny this in a mission statement or other materials seems oddly contradictory to purpose.

An advertising executive offered himself as a constructive critic of his alma mater's series of fund-raising mailings. He cited an overintellectualism which did not ignite any memories or emotions for him. He admonished the university's development staff to evoke nostalgia-stirring images among alumni: the smell of a campus grove after a rain, the sound of the stadium at a football game's halftime, the taste of coffee hastily drunk with friends between classes. His ideas were incorporated into the next year's mailings, with positive results.

Creating a Values-Based Mission Statement

Creating a mission statement is a difficult but necessary step. The embodiment of values in a mission statement can inspire other materials, including mailings and proposals. It can be a talking point when recruiting volunteers, and the core of speeches and presentations. A mission statement cannot be written by a committee, but it will benefit from an initial idea-generating session involving key constituents. An exercise to identify core values is the first step.

In a meeting with board members, other volunteers and staff, each person participating in the session writes down what he or she believes to be the three core values of the organization. The facilitator then asks each person to state one value from his or her list, going completely around the room. After the second round, participants are asked to state any that are not yet on the master list. Duplications will occur by the second round, which is why it is important to request just one value from each person at the outset. A benefit of this process is the participants' awareness of the common views they hold of the organization's values.

Once these values have been identified, the same participants are asked to complete this sentence: "(Our organization) exists because. . . ." They should be coached that the statements are not to be written in the infinitive form of the verb (to inform, to educate, etc.), but rather as a statement incorporating the values just identified and expressing the reasons why the organization exists. This instruction was the inspiration for the mission statement about hands from Vector Health Programs.

These "why" expressions, and the lists of core values, provide the raw material for shaping the first draft of a mission statement. Assign the writing task to an individual with proven writing skills and a command of institutional history and priorities. Establish agreements regarding the review process and the extent to which the statement will be edited before the writing begins. Many fine, nimble, evocative, and inspiring statements turn into clumsy, inclusive, meaningless, and rambling paragraphs because too many people are given opportunities to whittle and alter the first or subsequent drafts. In one organization, a whole board meeting was devoted to the subtle yet substantial difference between "social injustice" and "social injustices" as contained in the draft mission statement. The group was divided irreconcilably over the nuance of these phrases, and the mission writing process was blocked.

Once a draft has been approved internally, organizations can benefit from circulating the statement to a select group of donor-investors. This may include former board members, major donors, and others whose interests will be solidified by including them in this "insider" communication. One organization, testing concepts derived from its mission for use in a capital campaign, received valuable feedback that led it to shape its campaign materials in a slightly different way. The modification created a more broadly appealing message and resulted in participation by a constituency that might not otherwise have been involved.

Accepting and Using Values-Based Mission Statements

Some values-based mission statements, reflective of organizational values and the need the organization is meeting, may never receive endorsement by boards or staff. Instead, leaders may approve and publish a more corporate statement of the organization's functions. While almost always uninspiring, these statements satisfy the need people have within and outside an organization for a mission statement that more closely matches those written for corporations or law firms. It is still prudent, however, to have an expression of the institution's values on hand.

A values-based mission statement may not be immediately welcomed or accepted. Sometimes it will be adopted later, or integrated into materials not as a mission statement, but as a framework for expressing the organization's purpose. On numerous occasions, organizations have turned to values-driven expressions of their mission when making tough decisions about their future. An organization that operated summer camps for a large religious organization found itself turning toward a statement of values and purpose at a decisive moment in its history. The development director, who had participated in a workshop in which he was asked to create a mission statement, had negative reception for the statement on his return to his organization. He kept what he had written, feeling there might be use for it some day. There was. At a board-staff retreat, the participants were at loggerheads about the direction in which the organization should be heading. Hours of debate created acrimony and dissent. A proposed action was outside the mission according to some; to others, it was the next logical step. The development director saw this as the moment to provide his values-based mission statement to the group. When he finished reading his statement, there was no longer any question about what direction they should take. He had affirmed for each of them the basic purpose of the organization, and had redirected their focus onto the need they were committed to meet.

Another key aspect in writing a values-based mission statement is to position the values or the need being met as the primary or opening phrase. (See the Vector and Yale statements, above.) In this way, people of like values are attracted prior to being introduced to the name or function of an organization. By starting with a description of the need that exists and continuing with succinct and powerful words that tell why meeting the need is critical, people who share similar concerns and values are alerted to a deeper purpose. When organizations begin their mission statements with the name of the organization or its principal function, some listeners or readers may "tune out" before the values or purposes are revealed. When that happens, the opportunity to draw people into the organization's mission may be delayed or lost. The perceived need must be identified first.

It is perhaps apocryphal, but there is a story from Black and Decker that sums up this approach. It concerns the Black and Decker drill, and the way in which sales associates are trained to sell it. They are asked, "Why do people buy a Black and Decker drill?" The answer most immediately given is, "Because they want a drill." That is the wrong answer. The reason people buy a Black and Decker drill, the trainees learn, is "Because they want a hole." It is the same with nonprofit organizations. People need to see what need we fulfill before they will invest in what we do. Just as they only buy a drill if they want a hole, they only invest in our organizations if what we provide is something they see as important to themselves and/or the community.

The philosophical mission statement, expressing the institutional values, is a fundamental tool for creating a solid constituency and donor development program. It can convey a message that moves people to action and communicates the impact the organization has in the community. It is a fundamental building block for *development*.

Development: The Process of Uncovering Shared Values

The second element of the model is development, which resides in the larger context of philanthropy. Development embraces, but is not synonymous with, fund raising. Often considered a euphemism for fund raising, development is much more. Philanthropy is based in values, and development is the process of uncovering shared values. This process includes the identification, nurturing, and reinforcement of shared values. It is a process driven by the importance of providing potential and current funders with opportunities to explore and apply these values on behalf of our organizations.

The full potential of the development process is seldom realized by organizations. These are the significant insights that can be gained with a more inclusive view of development:

- Development is the series of deliberate activities by which organizations involve and retain funders in a donor-investor relationship.
- Organizations that realize the power of the development process regard their new knowledge as seminal to the revitalization of their development and fund-raising practices.
- Development is understood as a much larger, and more patient process, concerned with initializing, nurturing, and maintaining relationships.
- Development is how nonprofits bring their potential and existing donors into an understanding of the impact of their investment on the organization and the community.

- Development is the process of creating *donor-investors*, individual and institutional funders who seek and receive a dynamic relationship with an organization.
- Development is based on the premise that all giving is a form of investment, the return on which is the knowledge that those values that the organization and the donor-investor share are being acted upon.

Why Development Must Be a Priority

Development is the process on which nonprofit organizations need to spend their time if they are to be successful. When development is planned and pursued as the sensitive and important process it can be, then funding stability can grow within organizations.

Those organizations which implement long-term strategies for identifying and developing the match between donor and institutional values are able to withstand change. They survive, and benefit from, shifts in the economy, evolutionary funding patterns, pendulum political changes, and other forces that mar the capacity of some organizations to retain donors. Organizations that practice development—universities, hospitals, visual and performing arts institutions, social and human services agencies—are adept at mounting successful annual campaigns and required capital and/or endowment campaigns.

But, for every organization that meets this description and is admired as a pace setter locally, nationally, or internationally, there are too many others whose annual campaigns flounder and whose capital campaigns, when attempted, are either extended repeatedly to ensure financial success or wither into obscurity without reaching their goal.

The problem is simply this: when development is not a firm and deliberate practice in an organization, when human and financial resources are not deployed toward this vital function, then fund raising ultimately falters.

Defining Development

Development consists of those often subtle, frequently intangible, and not immediately measurable acts which draw donors and volunteers closer to the organization and more deeply into an understanding of shared values. These include:

1. A prospect identification and qualification process which engages board, other volunteers, and staff in the regular and willing generation and screening of lists of potential donors and volunteers;

2. Development of strategies for involving potential and existing funders through a series of actions based on volunteer-staff partnerships and donor needs;
3. Cultivation of prospects and donors through a planned series of activities, mailings, and opportunities gauged to heighten interest and build relationships;
4. Solicitation of gifts using a process that results in the transformation of prospects into donor-investors;
5. Stewardship practices directed toward the donor in a way that is desired and acceptable by the donor and which strengthen the understanding of shared values; and
6. Promotion of overall community visibility of the impact the organization is making in the community.

Implementation of development practices is the necessary prelude to successful fund raising, and is the key to going beyond fund raising.

The exposition and application of development practices form the heart of this book.

Fund Raising: The Process of Enabling People to Act on Their Values

Fund raising, within the model presented here, is the persistent and vital function that is linked to development and philanthropy and nests within them. The three elements are interdependent. Successful fund raising is an outcome of philanthropy and development. Philanthropy and development, which require healthy nonprofit institutions in order to thrive, are dependent on the success of fund raising.

Fund raising, in this model, is the process of enabling people to act on their values. If all that we do in development, and all that we understand about philanthropy, is values-based, then fund raising is a values-related process as well. Viewed this way, fund raising becomes a less formidable and frustrating act. It is viewed with less apprehension by volunteers and staff, and its potential as a transforming act for asker and donor-investor is clear.

With this new definition of fund raising, the tin cup can be put away. If the act of asking for a gift is seen as a way to permit potential donors to act on the things they value, then asking no longer feels like begging.

Asking as Release, Not Pressure

Instead of a process implying *pressure* on the potential donor, asking is understood as a process involving *release*. If a prospect has been developed appropriately, and brought into a relationship with the organization based on shared values and an emphasis on program results, not just financial needs, then the act of asking becomes a positive experience for both asker and prospect.

This way of asking is a values-based transaction. The values of the asker and the prospect are fulfilled when an organization receives a gift that advances, preserves, and protects those programs and results that the asker and the donor value. This is a relatively simple realization, but one that is new for many volunteers and staff who may perceive fund raising as an uncomfortable process. It is also a reaffirming realization for those who have not minded the task of asking for money, but appreciate a broader understanding of the impact of their action.

Fund raising, as presented in this book, is based on these ideas, and on the integration of fund raising with philanthropy and development.

A PARADIGM SHIFT: INTEGRATING PHILANTHROPY, DEVELOPMENT, AND FUND RAISING

The three-part model is best implemented when its elements are integrated into a unified and seamless program. Values-based relationship-building in an organization is based on a theory that prospective funders move from philanthropy to development to fund raising.

This theory has some variations in practice. Funders will self-identify first through fund raising (direct mail, special appeal, memorial/in honor, special event, phone appeal) and then be brought into a relationship with the organization that explores the basis for development and philanthropy. Determination of values and interest comes after the initial gift and inspires future gifts. This is one reason why early and personalized stewardship is critical to the development process (see Chapter 7).

It is important to see the model as flexible, and as applicable to relationship-building practices whether donors self-identify with an initial gift or grow gradually into a relationship that results in a gift.

Successful integration of the three parts of the model requires two basic institutional decisions, both of which indicate a major paradigm shift for most organizations:

- To market the values-based model internally to board members and other volunteers and to program, administrative, and development staff;
- To allocate human and financial resources within the organization to *development* as well as to fund raising and to reflect a commitment to development in the institutional plan and budget.

Internal Marketing

Internal marketing of the development function as a values-based process is a strategic management practice. Well-advised internal communication regarding the importance, impact, and values basis of development can make a major difference in the extent of institutional support for development. This support is critical to getting broader involvement in development by volunteers and all staff.

Internal marketing is always important, but never more than when an organization is repositioning itself with a newly integrated and inclusive model for development and fund raising. One key way to accomplish this is through the involvement of the entire team of staff and volunteers in promoting development. Because the emphasis in values-based development is on results, not needs, pride is instilled. Program staff and volunteers, encouraged to convey these results to those with whom they interact, become willing advocates for the organization and champions of the development process.

Another important technique is to promote internally the impact of development on the organization: the increase in volunteer and funder involvement, and the implications of new or increased financial support for programs. One organization, determined to market the importance of development among staff who were skeptical and critical of a process which seemed cost-intensive, were persuaded of the importance of development by a "Good Newsletter" which appeared weekly in employee mailboxes. The "Good Newsletter" summarized community outreach activities, site visits by potential funders, board activities on behalf of the organization, successful foundation and corporate proposals, and regular reporting of revenues from direct and planned gifts. The staff began to see that many positive program changes were the direct result of resources and contacts generated by development activities.

Budget Allocations for Development

Budget allocations for development, not just fund raising are critical to implementation of the model. The activation of consistent cultivation and stewardship practices requires allocation of funding for staff, materials, outreach, and analysis. Advocates for development may find at first that these budget allowances are difficult to obtain. Fund raising costs, which are measurable and easily understood because of their short-term return, must be complemented with expenses allocated for development. Otherwise, fund raising costs will spiral. Without donor retention and growth of donor-investors, the only recourse is increased activities designed for donor acquisition (direct mail and special events). These are the most costly of the fund raising functions and, while they will always be necessary in a balanced fund raising program, they can only be offset by the growth in larger donor-investors and the involvement of volunteers who will be partners in the development process.

SUMMARY

The power of the three-part model is in its implementation. The elements are interdependent, and each is strongest when integrated with the others.

The chapters that follow are designed to encourage and instruct nonprofit leaders in the implementation of the model, and to help build the capacity to go beyond fund raising.

Putting Away The Tin Cup: Changed Attitude, Changed Practices

Adoption of the three-part model of values-based philanthropy, development, and fund raising, described in Chapter 1, can move organizations beyond fund raising into a much deeper process of donor and institutional development.

The model will only be implemented successfully, however, when volunteers and staff let go of the idea that fund raising is a begging process based on the needs of the organization, and view it as an investment process based on the needs the organization is meeting. Organizations must believe that asking for funds is not begging for money, but an invitation to invest; not holding out a tin cup, but offering opportunities to work together to meet community needs.

Even those who view philanthropy and development as values-related processes in which they can participate with comfort and pride may balk when asked to fund raise. Whether it is the engagement of a prospective donor in a one-on-one ask, participation in a phone appeal, selling tickets to an event or writing a letter, volunteers and staff will still confess to an uneasiness and a feeling they are carrying a tin cup. It is fundamental to going *beyond* fund raising that organizations first get comfortable with fund raising.

WHY THE TIN CUP ATTITUDE PERSISTS: ASKER, FUNDER, AND INSTITUTIONAL REASONS

1. Why the Attitude Persists for Askers

The tin cup attitude is acutely bound into the fear of rejection. This fear is the root of most discomfort with the asking process. Volunteers and staff slip into apologetic and begging asking patterns because they fear they will be rejected and they want to cushion themselves for the inevitable response. Subconsciously, they frame their request in a hesitant or apologetic way that conveys a lack of confidence on their part that this is a good investment. ("You probably don't want to give, but I have been assigned. . . .") Subsequently, once or twice rejected, askers feel as though the entire effort is a pointless foray into an arena where they will be refused. They procrastinate when they receive their assignments. Their resistance to getting involved in fund raising mounts.

This fear of rejection is, without exception, the most voiced impediment to comfort in fund raising. Skilled lawyers, accountants, community volunteers, media specialists, and bankers, each of whom bring talent and experience to boards and committees, readily confess that, when it comes to fund raising, they fear rejection. The signature cartoon for "Putting Away the Tin Cup" workshops shows a Teddy bear sitting on a sidewalk with a tin cup by his side and a sign that reads, "Dumped by a six-year-old for a computer. Please help." Most participants identify strongly with that Teddy bear, confessing that is the way they feel when they ask for money. They lack confidence that people will want to give, and end up positioning the ask (see Chapter 5) in such a way that it is easy for those being asked to say no. This reinforces the reality of rejection and confirms people's fears.

Six Keys to Overcoming the Fear of Rejection

Very few people say they look forward to asking for money. Some say they steel themselves for the process but actually end up enjoying it. They are a curiosity to others. When probed, they cite these reasons for feeling comfortable asking for money. They are all key strategies for overcoming the fear of rejection and feeling comfortable with fund raising and development:

1. Understanding of the importance of the need the organization is meeting and the impact a gift will have;
2. Passion for the organization or project;
3. Adequate information about the organization to feel capable of handling objections;
4. Adequate information about the prospect to feel knowledgeable about interests and concerns;
5. Training in how to ask; and
6. Support from staff or volunteer leadership, including appropriate materials, research and resources.

These six essentials help overcome the fear of rejection by raising confidence, and thus enable volunteers and staff to ask from a position of strength, not weakness. Focus is placed on the need that is being met by the organization, not the organization's needs; it is also on the donor's needs to see their values acted on by a successful organization. Asking becomes a negotiation and an exploration of how donors and organizations can combine their efforts to accomplish goals that are important to the community.

Training Volunteers and Staff to Feel Comfortable With Fund Raising

All six of these strategies for overcoming rejection can be addressed to a major extent through appropriate training, and reinforced by one-on-one coaching. Training for board and staff members in the appropriate development and solicitation process is essential. Even if a board member says, "I know how to do this. Just give me my assignments," or a new staff member says, "I've been doing this for years. Just let me get started," it is important that everyone receives the same messages. This is particularly true when shifting to a values-based development process. Some very experienced volunteers are heavy-handed with the tin cup or other less effective methods of asking. Whether a staff, board, or outside facilitator is used for the session, there should be enough new information each year about the organization and the constituency to make the training valuable. Several hours is usually enough time: some organizations conduct an extended board meeting for this purpose. Sessions should focus on:

- The community needs the organization has met (results) and the needs it will continue to meet (impact projected for revenue generated by current fund raising);

- Organizational priorities (vision and goals);
- The profiles and motivations of key prospects (treating such information with discretion and confidentiality);
- Objections that will arise and appropriate responses (both general and specific to the organization); and
- Specific techniques for making the ask (detailed in Chapter 5).

Fast-paced and challenging, training sessions should be energizing and informative. And, they should be fun. People should leave a training session feeling like they want to go right out and make their calls. Good training can curb procrastination. Be sure to time the session so that prospect assignments are ready. People forget the strategies and lose the excitement if there is too much lag time between training and asking.

Why Training is Essential

Reluctance to participate in development and fund raising is often based on the ignorance a person feels about the process itself. Insecurity about saying the right words, asking for the right amount, closing effectively, following up appropriately, or dealing nobly with defeat can prevent volunteer involvement and effective staff support. No matter how professionally talented in their own fields, board members (with few exceptions) need to be educated in the fundraising process. This is as true for annual campaigns as it is for capital drives.

A training session need not always be called a training session. Experienced volunteers and staff may consider themselves beyond the point of needing a skills session. Some labels attached to training sessions include refresher session, kick-off, campaign orientation, leadership orientation, and retreat. One organization, where training sessions are exceptionally well-attended by staff each year, refers to the weekend program as its "round up." Its staff comes from all over the United States and internationally for a true refresher course. The course reignites staff members' enthusiasm and sharpens their skills.

Whatever it is called, the training session should have three basic ingredients:

- Inspiration
- Information
- Motivation

Inspiration

Inspiration is provided by bringing board, other volunteers, and staff closer to the mission. This "product demonstration" at training sessions is a key factor in helping askers feel passionate about the cause. A report from a program staff person is not enough. To inspire volunteers and staff, connect them directly with the process and impact of the programs. This can be done through:

- A facilities tour to observe the program (if appropriate and possible);
- Personal witness or testimony from someone who has benefited from the program.

Inspiring through first-hand presentations. Many organizations organize their training sessions or retreats around presentations by those who have been involved as clients or recipients. One organization had particularly powerful results from using this technique. A community organization, whose primary purpose and activity had been the awarding of scholarships from funds provided by another foundation, found itself challenged by that foundation to raise $3 million in matching funds for child care scholarships. They were very apprehensive about their ability to raise that amount of money, and most of the board members felt very uncomfortable about asking. The energy for development and fund raising increased only slightly over time, although new board members, who had experience in fund raising, were recruited.

The turning point came at a board retreat. Three parents, who were recipients of the kind of scholarships to which the matching funds would be directed, were invited. As the board, other volunteers, and staff watched and listened to these parents the true mission became apparent. A young mother with two children explained how assistance for child care had enabled her to finish school and start her own business. A young man who had left south central Los Angeles with his son in search of new opportunities said he was able to go to college because he had after-school care for his son. His nine-year-old son told of his pride in his father, adding that he and his dad were both "getting A's in school." An older woman, formerly a domestic worker and now a bank teller, described how the scholarship funds had provided care for her children so she could return to school. The inspiration provided by these first-hand stories exceeded anything the staff could have provided with descriptions of success. Suddenly, the impact of the child-care scholarship program was apparent, not only on these individuals, but on the community. The campaign stepped up its pace with new commitment.

Information

Information also builds confidence in volunteers and staff. Inspiration ignites, but information sustains. While it is important to engage the heart, it is just as important to satisfy the left-brain needs of those who will ask, or be asked, for support. Information should be clearly presented, documented with statistics, and include financial as well as program material. The use of visual aids to understanding budgets, income sources, program demographics, community involvement, program impact, and other key "talking points" is important. Some people, when confronted with budgets, annual reports of income and expenses, campaign reports or other financial data, respond with the "MEGO" syndrome: "Mine eyes glazeth over." Help these people internalize this information by providing visual aids. Pie charts and bar graphs can explain a great deal. For some, a narrative is also helpful: "Last year, boosted by the gift from the community foundation, we increased our service units by 27 percent and were able to attract 42 percent more funding from other community funders."

Types of information. Information is more than financial. Program information gives people something to talk about with their prospects. Be sure it is accurate, easy to understand, free of jargon, and accessible. Fact sheets are good tools. Print them in 14-point type so they can easily be glanced at during a presentation in person or on the telephone. When preparing the information for a training or orientation session, the organizer should be familiar with the prospect base and anticipate what information will be requested. There is nothing more discouraging for a volunteer than receiving a series of questions from a potential donor for which no answers have been provided. It is helpful to equip askers with a list of possible objections and an appropriate response for each.

During the information segment of a session, the steps in the actual solicitation process are introduced, reinforced, and either demonstrated by several willing volunteers or practiced by everyone at the session. These steps are presented in Chapter 5.

Motivation

Motivation is the third element of training. What motivates people to be advocates for an organization is a feeling of confidence that their efforts will be valued, appreciated, and make a difference. This part of the training is locked in when program or administrative staff convey to the development staff and volunteers how critical their efforts are to the capacity of the organization to meet community needs. For example, with hospital foundations, CEOs can have a tremendous impact on the volunteers by just being at the training session. If they also provide a "state of the medical center" presentation and show the impact of contributed income on certain programs, it is particularly effective. Hearing that news from the CEO reinforces staff and volunteers and therefore is highly motivational. The same is true for all organizations: those responsible for development and fund raising are motivated most strongly by the impact of their efforts on program delivery.

Each of these three elements of training sessions is important. They can be blended, alternated, and fashioned into a smoothly sequenced program that is appropriate to the organization, the time frame, and the skills and expertise of those attending.

While training will not entirely cure the tin cup tendencies of those who are asked to ask, it will contribute substantially to their understanding of the value and importance of their role. They will begin to develop a new attitude toward the process. (See Chapter 6.)

2.   Why the Tin Cup Attitude Persists for Funders and Institutions

In spite of work with volunteers and staff to help overcome their concerns about asking, tin cup fund raising is still practiced regularly by organizations around the world. This attitude within organizations is based in the belief that organizations have needs that individual and institutional funders must meet if the organizations are to survive. While this is true in the strictest sense, there is a dangerous indication: that nonprofit organizations are involved with these funders in a more or less one-sided relationship, and that fund raising requires a supplicant posture. This has two problematic implications:

- It can lead to a belief by nonprofits that giving is a moral obligation, and there is no need to develop dialogue or relationship with donors. That approach may work for a while, but it does not build a long-term sense of loyalty, involvement, and investment.
- It can lead to a belief by funders that nonprofit organizations should always appear "needy" rather than successful: that it is somehow appropriate to have inadequate administrative facilities, inferior office equipment, budgets that do not permit donor development activities, and other visible or subtle symbols of continuing institutional needs as the basis for giving.

These outcomes block synergy between organizations and communities that enables them to continually grow and address changing needs. The benevolence of funders, if conveyed as a one-sided handout relationship in which the funders are strong and the organization is dependent, becomes a block to the natural maturing of the nonprofit and its potential for being perceived as an agent of change in the community.

A Paradox

Ironically, one-sided donor relationships are encouraged by one of philanthropy's kindest motivations, the desire for people to help those who are in need. The need to put away the tin cup is often challenged by this paradox: *can* we put away the tin cup, or do funders *want* the nonprofit sector to continue to present itself as an array of needy organizations dependent on community support (Grace 1991)? Much donor education is required if the nonprofit sector is to be perceived differently.

There is also a connotation of the word "charity" which tends to perpetuate this problem. Rooted in biblical heritage, charity has evolved as a concept applied to the nonprofit sector which to many implies a handout and an image of the wealthy helping weak organizations survive. This is not the image the sector should perpetuate.

Funders must come to view nonprofit organizations as vehicles for accomplishing efforts of mutual purpose. They must see nonprofits as successful, sturdy, and progressive institutions that act on their behalf. They must see institutions as good investments for the stability of the community.

WHY INDIVIDUALS AND INSTITUTIONS MUST CHANGE

When fund raising is positioned as begging, both the asker and the organization lose credibility in the eyes of the potential donor. Desperation replaces dreams as the focus of the transaction, and the excitement of investing in an organization whose services are fundamental to the quality of the community is lost.

If we are to go beyond fund raising, we have to assume a posture of pride regarding our organizations as worthy investments. Then, if requests for funds are turned down, it is *not* the rejection of the asker, it is the rejection of the need the organization is meeting. It is not a current priority for the person being asked. This leaves the door open for repositioning the need as an eventual priority for the prospect, or identifying another interest or motivation of the prospect that will provide better access for presenting the funding opportunities.

A NEW VIEW OF FUNDERS: DONOR-INVESTORS

The model on page 29 conveys the difference between the ideas inherent in contribution and donation and the power of investment. While organizations will continue to use the first two words to describe donor support, both have subtle implications that can lead to a passive relationship. Only investment conveys the dynamism that organizations should seek in donor relationships.

Organizations that are strategic innovators know the importance of putting away the "tin cup" attitude and embracing fund raising as the logical outgrowth of solid philanthropic and development practices. The key to this is found in the way these organizations view their prospects and donors and their responsibility to them. They bring their donors into a dynamic relationship beginning with their initial gift. It is a relationship based on values and characterized by continual communication of the "return" on their investment. Their practices are based on the implicit belief that donors are really donor-investors, and that there are two "bottom lines" in the nonprofit sector.

1. The first is the *financial return* bottom line which reflects solid administrative, program, and fund-raising performance and sound management of earned and contributed revenues.
2. The second is the *values return* bottom line which conveys the impact the organization is making in solving problems, providing services, or improving quality-of-life opportunities in the community.

Conveying these two bottom lines to potential and current donor-investors is one of the best ways to cure the tin cup attitude. Pride grows from a review of the organization's accomplishments and frames the message. Initial or increased investments are sought based on the acknowledged impact the programs have or will have on those served. Focus shifts away from the internal fund-raising goal and on to the impact of each investment and the value of the programs in the community. Donor-investors are invited to be participants, not just part of the donor base. Their role is dynamic, not passive, as Exhibit 2.1 reveals.

EXHIBIT 2.1 Model: Gift Contribution/Donation vs. Investment

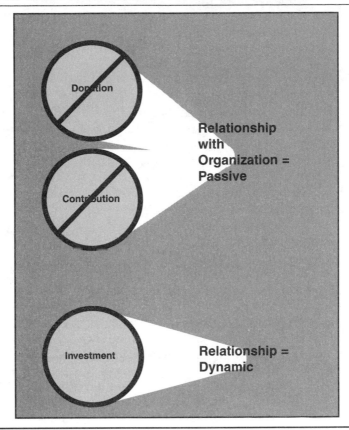

THE INVESTOR RELATIONSHIP

In seeking and engaging donor-investors, organizations are making a commitment to communicate regularly regarding the "return" on their investment: the impact of the gift, the stability of the organization, and the continuing importance of the need the organization is meeting in the community. They are also making an implicit commitment to continue to uncover the values, interests and needs of their donors. They are making a commitment to stewardship (Chapter 8).

Some organizations are reluctant to move from a passive to a dynamic relationship with their donors. They cite inadequate resources (time, money, people) for maintaining donor relationships. They perceive donors as the result of fund raising, not the reason for development. And, they may also be comfortable with a passive relationship because they believe it is what their donors want.

Understanding Prospect and Donor Motivation

There are three principal attributes that we must identify and develop in our constituencies: *connection, concern, and capacity*. It is important to uncover these during the initial development process, because they are the reservoir of values. It is equally important to continue to unfold them as the relationship matures. When a gift is made as the result of a relationship, organizations are already somewhat aware of the depth and direction of these attributes. When a gift is made as the initial action toward an organization, the strength and dimension of each of these attributes must be verified.

1. *Connection.* This is the strongest factor in determining the potential gift and involvement. Often called "linkage," it is the emotional connection an individual or institution has with an organization. A grateful patient gives to a hospital; an appreciative surviving spouse contributes to a hospice; a symphony receives support because its educational outreach was appreciated by the donor's children; a university receives a gift because of the impact of meeting old friends at a reunion. It is fundamental to values-based development and fundraising that these connections be identified, cultivated, and nourished. Emotional connections cannot be taken for granted; nor should they be treated with any but the highest regard. The values return for donor-investors is closely tied to their connection with the organization. Organizations must be very diligent in their efforts to keep the connections strong and vibrant. In connection, the inherent motivations are usually inspired by closely held and strong values.
2. *Concern.* Concern is intellectual or thoughtful. A person can be concerned about an organization's mission without being emotionally linked to it. Concern about the hungry or homeless in communities is evidenced among those who have never experienced those conditions. A corporation or individual invests in the local arts programs not out of passion for that particular art form, but in recognition of the importance of having a balanced community arts program for its employees. Values inherent in concern are more intellectual in their root than the values embedded in connection, but they are no less strong.

3. *Capacity.* This is the most obvious, but weakest, denominator when assessing a funder's inclination to give. Too often, it is the only focus when preparing a list of prospects. Those who are wealthy are sought out every day, most often by organizations whose mission is unknown by or inconsistent with the values and vision of the people to whom they are reaching out. If capacity were the strongest motivator for giving, then organizations could simply take the *Forbes 400* or the *Fortune 500* listings and write each of them a letter saying, "You've got it, we need it, let's make a deal!" A young woman who worked as an appointments secretary for one of America's wealthiest families reported they received, at home, hundreds of requests for donations each *week.* This, despite the fact that family members had a well-publicized foundation with a different address at which they received a similar number of requests. Few if any of these requests were from organizations with any connection to the family, and the vast majority of the inquiries fell outside the family's stated areas of concern. Capacity is a difficult attribute to measure. Very visible wealth may not be liquid enough to permit major investment in an organization. Often, truly great wealth is very quiet, manifesting itself occasionally and dramatically in gifts that have a huge impact on the community. Organizations need to balance the capacity factor with connection and concern. Capacity predictably informs some very strong donor values regarding the financial performance bottom line of an organization. For many donors whose capacity is great and for whom the requests are many, it also influences the kind of values return they seek overall from an organization: quality, excellence, pride, and satisfaction.

Volunteers and staff who are increasingly comfortable with values-based donor development will find that both connection and concern intensify as relationships develop. And although nonprofits can do little to increase a potential donor's absolute capacity (e.g., income, net worth), they do have an opportunity to increase relative capacity: the share of wealth a donor will consider giving to an organization.

Understanding donor motivation is essential to fund raising and development, because it is pinned so tightly to values. It is also a helpful tool in raising confidence in asking and putting away the tin cup. A knowledge of donor motivation, when coupled with increasing comprehension of the organization's value and performance, can take volunteers and staff a long way toward becoming more comfortable about asking for money. The two factors combine to develop a new attitude, one that enables institutions to go beyond fund raising.

CONVEYING A NEW ATTITUDE

It is imperative that nonprofit organizations transfer the focus of philanthropy from organizational needs to community needs. They must position fund raising as a process of investing in successful institutions which are solving societal problems or providing fundamental enhancements to the quality of community life. Donors then perceive the importance of their gifts not from the standpoint of annually rescuing organizations in need, but of continually providing support for those in the community who benefit from programs and services.

Messages, from mission statements to newsletters, can convey this new positioning. People can be overwhelmed by needs; they become excited about results (especially when those results are attributed to the impact of their investment in an organization or program).

Analyze the content of an institutional newsletter and what it conveys. Does it focus on community impact (how many were helped, or are doing something they could not do before) or only on the organization (fund raising event, capital needs campaign, management changes)? Is there an overemphasis on the social side of the organization's volunteer activities, with too many photographs of people holding wine glasses? It is far better to keep that kind of reporting to a minimum, and focus instead on photographs of volunteers doing program-related work and on patrons or clients benefiting from services.

Choosing Words that Work

An extremely successful human services organization reflects just the right balance in its newsletter. The lead article is always an in-depth piece about the impact of one of the organization's programs on a family or individual. Information is presented (statistics and statements from leading spokespeople) about the need the organization is addressing in its local community and how that relates to national trends and programs. Donor listings are provided quarterly and news about volunteers and staff are kept to an interesting minimum. There is also a strong emphasis on spotlighting the ways programs are making an impact while costs are contained. The newsletter itself is appropriately designed and produced for the organization. It is never glossy or burdened by excessive or inappropriate photographs and its writing conveys just the right tone of substance and authority. Over time, this newsletter has done a great deal to position this organization as a prudently managed community asset. A capital campaign for a new program and administrative center was hugely successful, exceeding even the most optimistic projections. Part of its success was due to the image of stability, strength, and service promoted over the years through the newsletter and by the portrayal of its overall outreach to the community.

A community arts education organization increased its return from a year-end mailing by 70 percent over all previous results when it removed the negative "tin cup" language from the letter and substituted a lively description of its many accomplishments during the previous year. The letter invited the community to participate in its continuing music education programs, and conveyed the good news of a foundation challenge grant that community giving would help the organization meet. In the letter's first draft, the focus had been entirely different: the overwhelming sense was desperation to meet the challenge. The second and final draft repositioned the focus from a simple plea for money to an explanation of why contributing would be a great investment in the future of music education in the city.

CHANGED ATTITUDE, CHANGED PRACTICES: THE TRUE INNOVATION

It takes encouragement and training to help volunteers and staff put away the tin cup and to bring an organization's development team to the point where it considers gifts as investments and the asking process as not one of pressure but of release. It also requires funders to be educated to let organizations retire the tin cup. However, even the best encouragement and training will fail, and fund raising will persist in being an exhausting, unfulfilling, and only moderately successful activity, if:

- The attitude persists internally and is conveyed externally that fund raising is driven primarily by the organization's need for money instead of by the needs it is meeting in the community through its programs and services.
- Fund raising is conducted without the benefit of the strategic acts of development and the philosophical framework of philanthropy.

Both of these underpinnings to successful repositioning are attainable if certain key management and organization steps are taken.

GETTING ORGANIZED FOR VALUES-BASED DEVELOPMENT AND FUND RAISING

Part of the attitudinal shift comes from getting organized for values-based development practices. The creation of internal systems for managing the development process is driven by a vision for institutional and development achievement. Borrowing a phrase from athletics, it is vital to "keep your eye on the prize." The prize, in the nonprofit sector, is a stronger community, people who are better served through the sector, and the donor's feeling of fulfillment when their values are acted on through their investments. Capacity to achieve these results is eroded through organizational disarray and a failure to secure the entire management structure to a foundation of broadly involving development activities. If there is chaos within the organization, it will be difficult to focus on a community-based mission. Likewise, if there is no sense of a values-based mission, the organization will quickly deteriorate (Chapter 3).

SUMMARY

How Development Practices Help Organizations Put Away the Tin Cup

In the previous chapter, the relationship between development and fund raising was drawn and the need for internal marketing of the development process was set down as a requirement for implementation of the three-part model.

These are basic understandings for organizations wishing to put away the tin cup. Once an organization adopts an attitude toward development that positions its needs as opportunities for community investment, change occurs. Fund raising and volunteer recruitment materials reflect results and success, and people want to buy in. Volunteers, drawn into a process of development, find there is a way for them to be involved that is both comfortable and constructive.

People who participate in donor development and relationship building grow in their willingness to play a role in fund raising. They see how potential donors, and current donors with greater potential, derive pleasure from involvement with the organization. As the relationship grows, staff and volunteers move naturally to the next step:

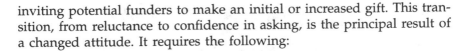

inviting potential funders to make an initial or increased gift. This transition, from reluctance to confidence in asking, is the principal result of a changed attitude. It requires the following:

1. *Pride in the achievement of the organization.* Communicate accomplishments and surround them with information about what resources are required (human and financial) to further strengthen the programs and services.
2. *Involvement and communication.* Board members, other volunteers, and program staff need to be kept informed about accomplishments and concerns, and be invited to participate in celebrations and problem-solving.
3. *A belief that the donor, not the organization, is the center of the marketplace.* The donor's and the community's needs, not the organization's, are paramount. Their interests, enthusiasm, attachments, and concerns, must be the focus in determining the potential relationship.
4. *An overriding conviction about the value and impact of services.* Overall, this is the key to confidence in the organization and the process of development and fund raising. It is the key to innovation and changed practices.

The tin cup attitude can and must disappear as organizations are increasingly positioned as investments that reflect donor and community values. A passive donor-institution relationship will not provide the active partnership needed within our communities. The dynamic donor-investor relationship must be created.

Preventing Mission Drift: The Leadership Imperative

A nonprofit's mission, as described in Chapter 1, is its compass and rudder. It guides and stabilizes through changes and helps the organization stay on course.

Respect for the mission is basic to good management and is the heart of effective development and fund raising. A mission statement that says why the organization exists attracts leaders and maintains donor-investors. As the expression of the organization's core values, it must be continually validated and carefully protected. The leadership imperative for nonprofit volunteers and staff is to prevent mission drift: to adhere to the mission and keep the organization on course.

MAINTAINING A STRONG ORGANIZATION AND A STRONG MISSION

Nonprofit leadership is a balancing act for boards and staff. Complex organizations require extraordinary leadership. Leading and managing any organization is difficult; the many constituencies and community-entrusted mission of nonprofits produce even more challenging situations. To ensure dynamic values-driven support, development and fund raising must focus on the needs an organization meets, not on the needs it has. All community outreach must purposefully emphasize external impact, and deemphasize the organization's internal needs. The mission must be the message.

The principles and practices of leadership given in this chapter are expanded throughout the book. This chapter focuses on the ways in which effective leadership prevents mission drift.

DEFINING MISSION DRIFT

Mission drift is a condition, either long-term or temporary, in which an organization becomes so consumed with its institutional issues that it loses sight of its mission. A popular cartoon several decades ago showed a man, with only his head visible, being sucked into quicksand and surrounded by alligators. The caption read: "When you are up to your neck in alligators, it's hard to remember that the original mission was to drain the swamp."

The most common source of mission drift is a deterioration of leadership which leads to a crumbling of systems within the organization. The organizational focus shifts from strategies for meeting community needs to tactics for controlling internal problems. Symptoms indicating mild to severe mission drift are:

- Board meetings in which there is little or no mention of the programs or services except in the financial report.
- Board members who refuse to get involved with the organization except at board meetings and make little or no financial commitment.
- Leaders who fail to encourage leadership growth and succession.
- Battles for control between board and staff.
- An approach to organizational priorities that ignores the needs of constituencies and changes in the marketplace.
- A shift from the passionate commitment that characterizes board membership in an organization at its founding or early stages to an overly pragmatic view often found among board members in organizations with greater maturity.

Any of these symptoms is dangerous and can damage an organization's capacity to enroll others in its mission and stay financially stable. Each should be addressed as it arises, and dealt with decisively. All detract from the required emphasis on mission, and can overly divert attention to organizational issues rather than program accomplishments. Uncontrolled, these problems can become so consuming that the organization ends up getting in the way of the mission.

AVOIDING MISSION DRIFT

Leadership is the primary anchor against nonprofit mission drift. Without strong and consistent leadership, an organization falters in times of difficulty and cannot move smoothly ahead in times of calm.

Leadership in the nonprofit sector has a dual structure: it is the responsibility of both board and staff. Board or staff members in organizations which manifest one or more symptoms of loss of focus on mission too often descend into blaming each other for the problem. This is not only counterproductive, it is inappropriate. In no other sector is the responsibility for leadership as interwoven between an internal leadership/management team and an externally elected or appointed board. The nonprofit sector is disciplined by partnerships within its organizations and its constituencies. The power of partnerships, explored in Chapter 4, begins with leadership that is perceived as a shared responsibility. The fundamental partnership in nonprofits is that between board and staff. Strategies for building effective boards are detailed in Chapter 9.

PRACTICES OF ABLE NONPROFIT LEADERS

Able staff and volunteer leaders demonstrate their strengths in numerous ways, each of which helps to stabilize an organization and keeps it tough and resilient. They provide or encourage the following:

1. *An emphasis on mission and purpose at all board and/or committee meetings and in all institutional decisions.* The tone and tempo of meetings convey a great deal about an organization, particularly to a new or prospective board member. Leaders ensure that agendas are well drawn and adhered to, that time is provided at each meeting for a testimonial or presentation by a program participant or recipient, that timeframes are respected but meetings are not "railroaded," that discussions are well-guided, and that tough decisions are made using a process that includes exploration of the facets of issue(s) relative to the mission and purpose of the organization.
2. *A commitment to passionate pragmatism throughout the life cycle of the organization.* Those involved in the leadership of nonprofit organizations are aware of the ways in which the board's role changes as an organization matures. From hands-on involvement during the early stages to functioning as a corporate oversight board as the organization approaches and achieves maturity, these changing roles require board members to keep their passion and pragmatism operative.

In the beginning, when the ideas that inspired the organization's conception are fresh and bold, there is no lack of passion among board members. They are living the mission. This passion, which arises out of common vision and shared values, propels and characterizes board behavior. Boards move swiftly to decisions, act boldly on opportunities, and take risks based on their dedication to the mission. Seizing the day, board members extend themselves into the community as ambassadors, fund raisers, and advocates. The communication of the leader's vision and the organization's mission is steady and intense. Pragmatism is sometimes in short supply.

As organizations grow, they rightfully begin to focus on systems and structure. Passion can wane. Board members are recruited who were not present at the creation and who may not even know the founding members. These new board members must be given the big picture: they must not be recruited only for the professional expertise (legal, financial, marketing) they provide. Otherwise, they will view the organization narrowly, have little passion, and the mission can drift as they focus on specific issues in the absence of a larger institutional context. Passion must be injected to inspire the pragmatism. Throughout the life of an organization, it is essential to keep these two dynamics in balance.

3. *Leadership succession planning, including enforcement of board member evaluation and limits to years of board service.* No matter how effective or valuable a board member or officer may be, wise leaders will enforce bylaws that limit terms of service or office. Terms should not be automatically renewable if board member attendance or participation has been poor. Healthy boards provide space for new people who bring a fresh balance to governance tasks. Most bylaws have provisions for allowing board members to be reelected after a year or more off the board. A person with expertise that is vital to the organization can always be placed on a committee during the off year(s). Leaders who are good succession planners are constantly looking at the board members and other volunteers and thinking how people might be used more effectively within the organization. They also provide opportunities for people who are new to the organization to get involved. Board succession planning is covered in greater detail in Chapter 9.

4. *Regular evaluation of the Executive Director/CEO.* A function related to board self-evaluation and leadership succession is regular evaluation of the executive director. A requirement for all boards, this is an often-neglected task. Executive directors can go for years without receiving an evaluation. Leaders encourage leadership: the board's executive

committee should provide an annual evaluation for the executive director, one which provides motivation, validation, and feedback for growth.

5. *100 percent financial participation by the board in all fund-raising campaigns.* Leaders do not accept the response: "I give my time; I do not have to give money." By their own example, they inspire others to give at an appropriate level, and they also convey the importance outside funders place on 100 percent board giving. Board participation in annual and capital campaigns is requisite for inviting the participation of others.

6. *100 percent participation by the board in donor and fund development activities.* Because development is the process of uncovering shared values in potential donors, and involves much more than fund raising, all board members can and should be involved. Strong organizational leaders create opportunities that motivate all board members, even the most reluctant, to get involved in development. Not everyone has to participate in face-to-face solicitations, but everyone should be involved with one or more of the other steps in the development process or with other kinds of solicitations (letters, telephones, special events).

7. *Early and thorough attention to budding program or people problems (board, other volunteers, or staff), which could grow and overwhelm the focus on mission.* Strong leaders are problem solvers. They know at what level a problem should be solved within the board or staff or between board and staff. They bring only the most critical problems to the board, preferring to solve others within the structure of the personnel, executive, or other committee. They have mastered and used techniques for fair and objective problem-solving, and they try to hear all sides of an issue during the process. Decisions, and the reasons behind them, are communicated openly and in a timely fashion. Conflict is not allowed to escalate. If the leaders cannot solve the problem, outside professional help is brought in before the problem overwhelms the organization.

8. *A focus on solutions, not problems.* Hand-wringing consumes energy and accomplishes little. Leaders see beyond the issues to how they can be resolved. In the problem-solving process, they thoroughly isolate and examine the problem but emphasize solutions. Leaders get people involved in the implementation of solutions, and use their delegation skills in ways that tap into the creativity and interests of board, volunteers and staff. Leaders welcome evaluation of ideas and implementation, and are willing to make changes if an original course of action is not working.

9. *Respect for staff, board, and other volunteers as partners who share a mutual dedication to the organization and the mission.* Leaders trust and

respect those with whom they work. They understand the unique contribution each person can make, and they encourage and respect, through their words and practices, a mutual focus on mission.

These practices, while not unique to nonprofits, are basic requirements for effective leadership of our sector.

SPECIAL CHALLENGES TO NONPROFIT LEADERS: BALANCING MISSION AND ORGANIZATION

Balancing a strong organization and a strong mission provides unusual challenges:

- Two bottom lines for which we are accountable to our donor-investors: financial performance, and values-based program results;
- Overlap and confusion about the roles of board and staff;
- Inevitable turnover among development staff; and
- The need for volunteer leaders who must balance the nonprofit's demands against their full-time jobs or other commitments.

Two Bottom Lines

Managing two "bottom lines" is the greatest challenge, and the greatest opportunity, for leaders who want to prevent mission drift. It is a *challenge*, because the importance of the financial bottom line, examined without benefit of the values bottom line, may result in decisions that curtail the organization's capacity to act on its mission. Reduction in staff or program, which may seem prudent relative to the financial bottom line, can diminish the availability of vital programs and services in the community and result in reduced opportunities for investment by those who share the organization's values.

The *opportunity* presented by the two bottom lines is the capacity to develop donor relations and fund raising practices based not just on financial information but on values-based results. This opportunity can be the countervailing force against harsh reductions in staff or services. It can be turned into a strong motivation for potential funders to make increasingly larger investments in order to ensure the continuation of programs that are needed in the community. It is imperative that a balance be maintained between the two bottom lines so that the strength of one supports the results of the other. Only then can appropriate decisions be made.

Overlap and Confusion About Board and Staff Roles

Defining board and staff roles is a nonprofit leadership challenge of the first order because of our unique dual leadership structure. It is also one of the principal contributors to mission drift. The challenge can be met by determining and conveying expectations. Leadership by expectations is a powerful approach. Executive directors, boards, committees, and volunteers with other assignments benefit from having expectations conveyed to them either individually in special sessions or in an annual discussion or retreat. People are evaluated daily by the expectations others have of them. Most often, these expectations are not revealed until problems arise. Clarity regarding board, committee, and other volunteer and staff roles helps maintain organizational strength and prevents mission drift. When roles are understood and carried out, internal communication improves. An increasing number of organizations are placing a priority on expectation-setting as part of their annual retreat. This process, which should be guided by a facilitator, has three required exchanges:

1. Executive director (and staff) convey to board members and other volunteers their expectations of volunteers;
2. Board members convey to executive director (and staff) their expectations of staff leadership; and
3. Board and staff convey to each other what they expect of themselves.

The value of this process is significant. Following one such session, a former executive director, who was filling in as business manager while the new executive director hired other staff, said to the board: "If I had known this was what you expected of the executive director, I might still be here." We cannot lead by expectations if we do not convey them. When we fail to let people know what we expect, we continue to evaluate them against standards they may not know about. Tensions arise, communication crumbles, and energy that should be given to tasks is diverted to worry or quarreling about relationships and responsibilities. Exchanging expectations may be a threatening thought for some board or staff members, but the process encourages organizations to be fair and frank in their delineation of board and staff roles. The result is a stronger organization which can focus more fully on mission.

Inevitable Turnover Among Development Staff

While experiencing considerable improvement, particularly at the higher levels of management, mid- and entry-level development officer tenure is still averaging about two years. This is an inevitable pattern in the nonprofit sector as people enter from other professions and/or seek more professionally or financially rewarding positions in other organizations. As compensation for development staff has improved, thanks to efforts by the various organizations serving the profession, there will be further improvement in longevity. Management and compensation is a continuing area of study and action for leaders of the National Society of Fund Raising Executives (NSFRE) and other similar professional organizations (Association for Healthcare Philanthropy, AHP; Council for the Advancement and Study of Education, CASE).

Efforts placed toward retaining good development staff have a high payoff. The effect of development staff turnover on nonprofit organizations is considerable. Everything we know about development indicates it is a process that takes time and requires continuity in communication and stewardship. Turnover on the development staff disrupts this continuity. Leadership among board members and other volunteers, especially those on the development committee, must see that development managers and staff are compensated adequately and given regular evaluations and appropriate feedback for their accomplishments. They must advocate for the development director to be included as part of the management team in budgeting and other policy matters. At the same time, to keep the organization stable when changes do occur, board and executive leadership must ensure that development systems are so well established that changes in development staff do not substantially disrupt the development program.

Handling Turnover

The executive director and board chair, faced with the resignation or necessary removal of the development director, must make sure that the transition is managed as smoothly as possible. Likewise, capable development directors must handle turnover on their staffs smoothly and quickly, exercising personnel management skills and networking capabilities to find the best person possible in the most reasonable amount of time. In the case of the removal or resignation of the person in charge of development (development director or vice president for development), the executive director and board or development committee chair must:

- Communicate the decision openly and promptly to all key leaders and constituents, including major donors and fund-raising volunteers;
- Prepare and implement a plan for transition: search strategy, interim work load distribution, anticipated timeline;
- Convey confidence that work will continue uninterrupted and be handled with skill and professionalism;
- Keep important constituencies informed regarding the progress of the search and the continued progress of development activities;
- Involve key board and development committee members, and select major donors in the search process;
- Create an opportunity, shortly after the person is hired, for the new development officer to share vision and expectations with the board and development committee;
- Support the new development officer in every way possible, including regular evaluations with constructive feedback, and ample reinforcement to maintain energy and enthusiasm.

Turnover among development officers is often attributable to the pace, intensity, and complexity of managing the development function. Burnout is common, and there are those who leave the profession temporarily or permanently. Prevention of burnout is critical: key maintenance factors for development officers include support from board and other volunteers, clarity of expectations, direct and honest feedback, and appreciation. Strong development officers are dedicated to making volunteers look and feel good. Development staff do the majority of the background work and position the volunteer to be successful and visible. A successful solicitation for a major gift, or the production of an outstanding event, are usually partnerships between volunteers and staff in which the volunteers receive the community recognition. It is very important for executive directors and board leaders to remember the role development officers have played in such successes. A handwritten note, a bouquet of flowers, special recognition at a board meeting: these techniques work for keeping volunteers involved and they work for keeping development officer burnout to a manageable minimum.

The Need for Volunteer Leaders Who Must Balance the Nonprofit's Demands With Their Full-Time Jobs or Other Commitments

Volunteer involvement is a basic component of the nonprofit sector's capacity to respond to community needs. Because volunteers represent the community, they provide the insights and perspective that nonprofits must have to shape their programs and outreach appropriately. Volunteering is a form of philanthropy (Payton). While gifts of time must be balanced by gifts of money for philanthropy to be complete, the satisfaction derived from a volunteer experience often intensifies the willingness to make a financial commitment.

Reciprocal appreciation helps volunteers stay involved. Just as board members and other volunteers have a responsibility to provide feedback and support to development staff, staff members who work with volunteers have a tremendous duty to ensure the quality of the volunteer experience. Every executive director, development officer, and development or program staff person should find time to volunteer at another organization. In this way, they never forget the demands on their own volunteers, and they maintain a sensitivity and respect for the volunteer's time. Volunteers want to feel their time is valued, makes a difference, and is well-spent. Like donors, volunteers are looking for an exchange with the nonprofit: skills, values, opportunities, recognition, and opportunities to act on their values.

Appreciation should be accompanied by clear standards. Nonprofit organizations that succeed in retaining valued board members and other volunteers do the following:

- Provide written job descriptions, including expectations, for all board, committee, and other assignments;
- Set high standards for volunteer involvement: attendance at meetings, timely completion of assignments, quality of work;
- Ensure that staff members also adhere to these standards;
- Consult volunteers on key decisions and review drafts of materials the volunteers will be using (case statements, brochures, and letters for community mailings);
- Develop and follow enlistment (and de-enlistment) policies and procedures for all volunteer positions, including board membership;
- Value the volunteer's time by making sure that all meetings and assignments are necessary and important;
- Offer appropriate appreciation and recognition;
- Communicate regularly regarding the progress or results of projects in which volunteers are involved;
- Provide special opportunities for volunteers to be involved with the mission of the organization through interaction with program staff and/or clients (as possible and appropriate);
- Make assignments that fit the motivation and needs of the volunteer;
- Provide all support necessary for the volunteer experience to be successful and rewarding.

THE ROLE OF LEADERS IN MAINTAINING EFFECTIVE SYSTEMS

Effective management, development, and fund-raising systems undergird all highly productive nonprofit organizations. Systems provide a reliable framework in which leaders stay focused on the achievement of the mission. When created and guided by strong leadership, systems are among the primary preventers of mission drift.

Systems provide structure to an organization. Systems are the policies and procedures that have been developed by the organizational leadership to guide its principal activities: by-laws, articles of incorporation, board policies, personnel policies, institutional and development plans, and other written or understood rules. Systems guide; systems liberate (Grace in Rosso 1991). When well-designed and agreed upon within an organization, systems can stabilize the structure. Effective systems ensure that routine and predictable activities can be handled with relative ease, allowing organizations to spend time on program and donor development, and on other creative or strategic activities.

Basic nonprofit systems include:

- Development and institutional plans
- An internal communication system
- Board recruitment and development procedures
- Policies that support values-based development and fund raising
- Acknowledgment, recognition, and stewardship practices
- Appropriate computer systems to support donor and financial development

LEADERSHIP IN TIMES OF CHANGE

Change is the most consistent aspect of the nonprofit sector's environment. Successful nonprofits anticipate and initiate change through sound institutional planning. They retain their stability when buffeted by unanticipated changes. Their systems gird their mission, and permit leaders to deal more effectively with the unexpected. The most admired organizations are those that are able to implement and constantly adjust their practices to meet the challenges of change.

Because they exist to meet community needs, nonprofits are constantly buffeted by the unexpected. A natural disaster calls them into action. A previously undiscovered illness becomes an epidemic. Voters curb tax spending for schools, and citizens rally. A nationally funded European museum suddenly needs private endowment funding to survive. Change requires organizations to continually adapt their internal practices and programs to meet emerging external challenges. A suicide prevention organization fails financially and a family counseling organization is asked to absorb its services. Two hospitals merge, along with their foundations, creating new opportunities but eliminating others. A library responds to needs for after-school programming by increasing its young adult collection and supervisory staff.

The response of leadership to change determines how well systems will respond. If change is perceived as opportunity, and responded to creatively, it leads to growth. If change is perceived as a threat, and responded to with fear, it leads to decay. Leaders make choices when they react to change. They can implement responses that freeze the organization's initiative and impair its growth; or they can rebound with options that will position the organization more strongly than before.

Four Leadership Attributes That Can Help Prevent Mission Drift

Organizations cannot go beyond fund raising towards values-based development if their missions drift. The mission is the message, and leaders are in place to convey and explain it. This places an imperative on board and staff leadership to reflect qualities that will help ensure the organization's continued role as a sound community investment.

There are four qualities of nonprofit leaders which contribute to the strength and stability of the organizations they serve: courage, confidence, creativity, and commitment.

Courage

If people are to lead, especially in the nonprofit sector whose structure and function is still misunderstood by so many, they must have courage and they must *en*courage. Courage is a key element in values-based development and fund raising. To *have* courage is a more commonly acknowledged attribute of leaders, but to *en*courage is equally important. To prevent mission drift, leaders must maintain their own courage, and that of others, by encouraging the heart, the mind, the passions, and the willingness to serve. They must encourage others to grow, excel, produce, and become leaders themselves.

Courage manifests itself in calculated risk taking that produces change and makes a difference in our communities, but it also is demonstrated internally by board and staff leaders in the direction they set for the institution and the way in which they implement planning. In various studies of corporate culture and its impact on organizations, one of the common threads among all researchers or observers is that "heroes" comprise a very strong part of organizational culture. These are people who were courageous in advocating for the organization, standing by their own beliefs in board or community meetings, taking an unpopular but ethical position on an internal or external issue, making a tough ask and doing it well, and/or having the courage to inspire others through their own perseverance and success. We don't talk much about courage among leaders, perhaps because we have seen so little of it. But when we do find it, we know and respect it. Leaders become more courageous when they master another quality of leadership—confidence.

Confidence

Confidence is derived from an understanding of the importance of the organization, the mission it is fulfilling, and the sector we serve. Confidence grows for board and staff in an environment where there is pride rather than apology for the development and fund raising process. That atmosphere of pride and shared success promotes confidence. Confidence in the organization and confidence in the sector are important in the encouragement of leadership.

Just as we build confidence through understanding the organization's impact and successes, and through a focus on results, we extend that confidence when we view the accomplishments of the entire philanthropic sector. A story that embodies both courage and confidence is illustrative. It was part of an article in the 19 December 1991 issue of *The Wall Street Journal* in which Peter Drucker spoke admiringly of the nonprofit sector's capability to accomplish much with little. In this brief article, he cited the activities of several organizations. But one story conveyed the message of courage and confidence most powerfully. In Royal Oak, Michigan, the "tiny Judson Center" had created a program to move single mothers and their families off welfare while simultaneously getting severely handicapped children out of institutions and back into society. The program replaced two government-funded programs that had shown little success: one for welfare mothers and the other for children institutionalized with disabilities. The Center trained carefully selected welfare mothers to raise in their homes, for a modest salary, two or three developmentally disabled or emotionally disturbed children.

The success rate for the mothers was close to 100 percent, with many of them moving into employment as rehabilitation workers. The impact on the developmentally disabled children was equally dramatic. Institutional confinement is now about 50 percent and, Drucker added, "everyone of these kids had been given up as hopeless." He summarized his viewpoint in this way: "The nonprofits spend far less for results than governments spend for failure." Such statements elevate the philanthropic sector in the eyes of the general public, and make those who work and volunteer in the sector feel good.

Confidence in the sector, and in its organizations, leads to self-confidence—the basis of courage. Self-confidence grows as apology recedes. When nonprofit support is approached from a position of service or strength, rather than weakness, self-confidence flourishes. People can speak with confidence about the organization's accomplishments and the pleasure of their involvement and advocacy. It is this self-confidence that can ease a difficult solicitation or rescue a cultivation interaction that is veering off course. Self-confidence is a strong quality of those who successfully generate and maintain values-based relationships within and for nonprofit organizations.

Creativity

Creative solutions, creative approaches, creative results: all are expected of nonprofit leaders. Creativity is a quality often overlooked in leaders. It manifests itself in effective problem-solving and containment of conflict in which new approaches or perspectives are identified, appreciated, and acted on. It is most obvious in the materials and programs of organizations, particularly those that are provided on small budgets and have high impact. One dance company, broadly supported in the community, has an artistic director who honestly tells donor-investors that he makes "one dollar do the work of five." His creativity, both on stage with his choreography and administratively with community investments, is a source of pride and satisfaction to staff, volunteers, and donor-investors. Creativity for board members includes bringing new ideas to the boardroom table, and new volunteers to events or meetings. Creativity requires a keen sense of opportunity and a willingness to be a leader in advancing new ideas.

Creativity and change are strongly linked. An organizational environment that endorses and rewards creativity usually responds more positively to change. Resilient organizations are those in which change, while not always welcomed, is accepted or initiated when required. The creation of several scenarios in response to anticipated changes in internal or external conditions contributes considerably to the avoidance of mission drift. When organizations become consumed with the imagined negative impact of change or loss of alternatives they lose sight of the positive new directions the change may imply.

Commitment

There are those who would argue this is the strongest quality of leaders. It certainly is essential and, when combined with courage, confidence, and creativity, can result in dauntless and innovative leadership. Commitment is seen in acts that nourish and support the organization: loyalty in time of crisis, willingness to give and ask, and enthusiastic advocacy for the organization that invites others to enroll in the mission.

Commitment is sustained passion. It manifests deeply felt and understood beliefs. It exemplifies values. Commitment is encouraged and sustained by effective leadership. It is kept healthy and fresh through constant reconnection to the values and mission of the organization. Commitment is reinforced when trustees grasp solidly not only what the organization does, but why it exists. Commitment grows from a respect for and a dedication to the mission and values of the organization and to the needs it is meeting in the community.

When trustees and other volunteers connect with the values in which the organization bases its existence, and with the value of the work it is doing in the community, commitment grows. Joy and energy override apathy. Development volunteers become compelling asker-advocates. Commitment is seen and felt in long hours volunteering in a child care center or cancer ward, involvement in the board-building process in an organization that is re-engineering itself, providing pro bono legal or financial service to nonprofits, and in countless other ways. Commitment is an elusive yet visible quality. In the development and fund-raising process, it is the aspect of the asker that is most convincing to the potential donor-investor. Commitment is shown through gifts of time and money, but also through willingness to participate in the full range of philanthropic behavior: giving, asking, joining, and serving.

Strong leadership, exemplified in these and other qualities, can prevent mission drift. The importance of avoiding mission drift cannot be overstated: when organizations veer away from their mission and become consumed with organizational issues they endanger their ability to sustain development practices that will enable them to move beyond fund raising.

Even if the mission drifts once in a while, it can be brought back in focus. Organizations whose missions drift can get back on course by reconnecting their boards, other volunteers, and staff members with the mission. This can be done in countless ways:

- Presentations and testimonials at board meetings;
- Facilities tours;
- Meetings with constituents and clients; and
- Occasional opportunities to immerse those closest to the organization in the outpouring of positive feedback about the impact of the services or programs on the community.

Messages to board members and other volunteers need to be balanced: include the good news with that which will create concern; focus on solutions, not just on problems; maintain optimism even in times of crisis; and let people know how valued their involvement is.

Organizations need both anchors and sails. They need pragmatism and passion to keep them on course. Leadership should reflect both.

SUMMARY

Leadership As Passionate Pragmatism

A focus on mission and values, presented in an environment in which courage, confidence, creativity, and commitment can flourish, can result in "passionate pragmatism"—a convergence of qualities that produces balanced decision-making and ensures that even as an organization matures, the passion of the founding is not forgotten (Grace 1995).

As organizations mature, it is essential that both passion and pragmatism be present if mission drift is to be prevented. In the early stages of an organization's development, pragmatists should be recruited to serve on the board alongside those for whom passion is the driving force. They can learn from each other. By balancing these qualities from the beginning, there will be less chance that at some later time in the organization's growth the board will overcorrect and end up disposing of the passionate in favor of the pragmatic. If both qualities are kept in balance, then even as the board's role changes, its commitment to mission can be sustained. For without passion—based solidly in pragmatism—commitment can waiver and the organization's growth may be uneven, chaotic, and marked by setbacks and confusion.

Here are 10 tips for maintaining passionate pragmatism and preventing mission drift in an organization. They can help both boards and staffs become more avid keepers of the mission.

1. Maintain a balance on the passion to pragmatism continuum even in the founding or very mature stages of an organization. Always recruit volunteers and staff with both, and let them blend to create and sustain a strong organization.
2. Infuse the mission constantly: believe it, live it, examine it, value it. Words are not enough. The creed behind the receptionist's desk is only believable if it is practiced.
3. Be sure board members give early and as often as they can, and encourage staff to give as well. Giving is a transforming act, in which the donor-investor becomes a participant. When there is appropriate and sustained stewardship of the board or staff member as an important provider of both time and money, a sense of belonging and involvement grows. This feeling of belonging translates to loyalty, which sustains passion while encouraging pragmatic and appropriate solutions to institutional issues.
4. Enroll board members as asker-advocates and encourage staff members to participate in solicitations when it is comfortable and appropriate. In taking the organization out to others, their own commitment is renewed.
5. Inspire and reward commitment. Board membership does not automatically bring deep commitment, particularly if an individual is brought onto the board because of a particular expertise or talent and is given a narrow view of his/her responsibilities. The same is true for staff with highly specialized assignments. Tie all board and staff recognition and rewards into the ways in which those who are recognized have advanced the organization's ability to meet critical community needs, and the ways in which those efforts improved the quality of life in the community.
6. Set standards for board participation and staff performance and maintain them. Passionate pragmatism is the result of commitment to the cause and awareness of what it requires to act on that cause. Passion for an organization is increased, not diminished, when standards are conveyed during enlistment of board members and hiring of staff. Evaluation and reward systems need to be in place. It is a singular truth of organizational behavior that having effective systems in place can actually preclude the erosion of the sense of mission. Systems liberate and permit staff and board to utilize their energies in creative pursuits that support the fulfillment of the mission.

7. Create a sense of ownership. Involve board and staff in planning (Chapter 11). It creates ownership among those who participate and provides greater support for decisions and change.
8. Keep the "product" on view all the time. Bulletin boards, newsletters, testimonials at board meetings, slide shows, videos, and people who can tell the story are all effective at keeping a passionate basis to pragmatic decisions. These "product connections" also inspire people to ask for money. At one kick-off of an annual campaign, a presentation by a staff therapist was more effective in inspiring the volunteers to go out and fundraise than the pep talk by the fund-raising consultant. The therapist let them know why what they were about to do was so important, telling them a success story about a breakthrough with an extremely troubled youngster. With that story in their minds and hearts, the volunteers felt their fund-raising efforts driven by the urgency and importance of meeting the needs of children, not just by the goals of the campaign: they could talk results with those on whom they were calling.
9. Encourage board and staff to attend local, regional, or national meetings of umbrella organizations (dance, music, social services, libraries, etc). By comparing notes with other board or professional staff people, they will gain a larger perspective. Their pride will increase for what their organization has accomplished, and they will learn from others.
10. Be honest. Passion turns to anger, and pragmatism into narrowness and control when boards and staff learn they have not been told the whole or true story about the financial or program status of the organization.

This decalogue of strategies, combined with knowledge of the symptoms of mission drift and the qualities and practices of able leaders, can help chart a course for nonprofits that will keep the mission firmly in place and avoid the kind of organizational mishaps that throw passion and pragmatism, mission and organization, out of balance. There is convincing evidence that staff and board connection with the mission stabilizes an organization through both unexpected and inevitable change. Organizations can and must protect and advance their missions through balanced and productive leadership.

4 ▼ Successful Development: Partnership and Process

The nonprofit sector is built on partnerships. We are partners with the community in solving problems and enhancing the quality of life. We initiate partnerships with funders for the mutual accomplishment of our mission, and with volunteers to help us leverage time and money in the most effective way possible. The dual leadership structure of nonprofits, in which board and staff share responsibility for the organization, is itself a preeminent nonprofit partnership. Partnerships, and the team work implicit in their formation and function, are a distinguishing aspect of excellent organizations.

The most successful development programs and fundraising campaigns are based on partnerships. From the outset, staff and community volunteers need to work together to create goals, materials, and strategies. They must establish the structure and systems that will enable them to work most productively.

PARTNERSHIPS FOR DEVELOPMENT AND FUND RAISING

Effective development and fund-raising partnerships are based on a shared understanding of the importance of meeting a critical community need. That understanding is enhanced by shared enthusiasm regarding the capability of the organization to address that need. Partnerships are strengthened through regular opportunities for honest and substantive communication, and reinforced by mutual trust based on that communication. Partnerships are powerful alliances of dedicated people working on behalf of an organization.

KEY OUTCOMES OF SUCCESSFUL DEVELOPMENT PARTNERSHIPS

To be effective, partnerships need to be understood, encouraged, and rewarded. This is particularly true with the development partnership—one of the most critical in any not-for-profit organization. The development partnership is defined as a cooperative and coordinated arrangement in which staff, board, and other volunteers work together in the development process to ensure five vital outcomes:

1. The attainment of shared financial and outreach goals including the engagement and retention of donors with capacity and willingness to make large gifts;
2. Involvement of board and other volunteers in development tasks that are appropriate, rewarding, challenging, and purposeful;
3. Mutually satisfying results, including enhanced donor relationships and better board-staff communication;
4. Strengthening of board and staff respect for each other and the unique roles each can play in the development process;
5. Realization, by funding partners, of their investment in an organization that enhances their community.

It takes full organizational support to build a successful development process. The full partnership will include all of these individuals or groups:

- CEO, President, or Executive Director and his/her staff
- Development Officer and his/her professional and support staff
- Development Committee
- Chair of the Board of Directors/Trustees and members of the Board
- Other volunteers engaged in program, administrative, or development support
- Program staff as resources for critical proposals and solicitations

Working together, these individuals can help ensure the future of the organization.

CREATING DEVELOPMENT PARTNERSHIPS

Establishing the environment in which partnerships flourish can be difficult and discouraging. It requires a great deal of internal marketing of the development process (Chapter 1): what it is, why everyone benefits when it works well, what is expected of each person relative to the process. Taking the time to do such marketing requires a leadership commitment to the importance of the eventual result. The creation of a donor and fund development program is a long-term systemic solution to the chronic and exhausting need to scramble for funds to meet ongoing or special needs. When people understand the value of the development process, and of the partnerships that support it, everything works better.

In theory, few would dispute the value of partnerships. In practice, they may be difficult to implement. All partnership-building requires shared institutional vision, coordination of human and financial resources, a spirit of cooperation, and a willingness to take the time to delegate tasks and empower leadership. For development, this means that organizations must initially rally board leadership and key staff into a common understanding of what the partnership entails, why it is important, and what impact it can have.

What the Development Partnership Entails

The development partnership is inclusive. At the outset, it involves key board, other volunteer, and staff leadership in planning and attainment of agreements regarding the goals and scope of the development and fund-raising effort. At its maturity, the partnership will involve the entire board, more volunteers, program staff (who will feel as though development is working on their behalf to ensure the funding of critical programs and services), administrative staff, and funders.

Why the Development Partnership Is Important

Partners are mutual stakeholders in an effort or enterprise. In development, this sense of ownership is vital to the commitment required to involve the community deeply and continuously in our organizations. If fund raising and development are seen only as the responsibility of the development staff and/or the development committee, it may discourage a widened sense of engagement and purpose that allows development to become the enhancing function it can and must be.

The gradual involvement of the entire organization in development is one of the most powerful processes in all of nonprofit leadership and management. When staff and board understand the essential role each member can play in the full development process, there is an elevated sense of pride and involvement. In one children's services organization, the program staff, previously not engaged at all in the activities of development and fund raising, became active participants in development. Through a series of brown bag lunch "funder forums" conducted by the development director, they were provided with information about potential foundation, corporate, and government funding opportunities and were encouraged to share pertinent program information with the development committee members and staff. Eventually, program staff were willing to help identify prospects from their program constituencies and be active participants in the preparation of proposals and in meetings and site visits with current and potential funders. A solid partnership had been forged.

Impact of the Development Partnership

A medical center received a major gift for the cancer treatment program from a woman who had undergone radiation therapy following her surgery. The story of that gift underscores how a development partnership can work. The head of the medical center foundation makes outreach to the medical staff a top priority. He goes on rounds with the physicians, attends medical staff meetings, and meets regularly with the various units at the medical center to let them know about the services of the foundation, what the fund and "friend" raising goals are, and how medical staff members can participate in identifying potential gifts among those with whom they work. He emphasizes that all referrals are handled discreetly and with the confidentiality of the patient's rights and records in mind. Further, the foundation does an excellent job of internally marketing the development function: how it works, who the involved community volunteers are, and what the impact has been over the years (this particular foundation raises in excess of $8 million annually for a wide variety of medical center programs).

The patient whose gift made such an impact on the cancer treatment program was identified to the foundation by the radiation therapist who, in the course of her compassionate work with the individual, had been told by the patient that she wished to do something for the hospital in gratitude for her treatment. The therapist notified the foundation, and discussed the particulars of the situation with the CEO. Foundation staff conducted research to identify whether the patient was a previous donor, was known to others on the foundation staff and board, or had made gifts to other medical centers. The foundation president and a volunteer then called on the interested prospect and found out more about her interests and needs and what size and type of gift she was interested in making. They showed her the plans for a proposed cancer treatment center, and arranged meetings for her with other key staff and volunteers over the course of the next several months. One of these subsequent meetings was with the radiation therapist who had referred the patient initially. Other medical center and foundation staff participated in the process by attending meetings, preparing information, or supplying financial data. When the gift was secured, all those involved experienced a sense of satisfaction: the donor, whose needs had been met with tact, skill, and consideration; and the medical center and foundation, which had put forth its best team in a true spirit of partnership.

STRUCTURING A SUCCESSFUL DEVELOPMENT PARTNERSHIP

The importance and potential impact of development partnerships cannot be overstated. To ensure the implementation of the development partnership, an organization should have the following:

1. *A solid plan for achieving development and fund raising goals.* This should be developed by board leadership and staff and be based on the reality of the previous year's (or campaign's) actual performance; the number of volunteers available, including board members, to be involved with each aspect of the development process; the environment for fundraising and volunteer enlistment; the vision and goals of the organization; and a current and objective assessment of the "marketplace"—a substantiation of the needs in the community. The plan must be linked to the overall institutional plan (see Chapter 11) and reflect the priorities of program and administrative staff in its funding goals.

2. *Adequate paid or volunteer staff to support the development program.* There is no point in creating a visionary partnership for development if there is no organizational framework to support it. It is more detrimental to excite volunteers about potential involvement in development and then give them no opportunity to act on your behalf than it is to delay the program until you are completely ready. In one major university capital campaign, solicitors were trained prematurely. Not enough prospects were researched and ready for cultivation, and staff was not yet ready to launch the program. The training, which had been historic in its thoroughness, inclusiveness, and motivational impact, had diminished value: the volunteers, enlisted care-

fully and trained expertly, had no immediate role to play. When the prospects were ready for assignment, many volunteers no longer had the time available for the campaign or, if they were still available, had to take a refresher course in solicitation techniques.

Lack of staffing keeps many organizations from forming development teams or partnerships. There are alternative management strategies. For start-up or transitioning organizations, in which there may be no paid development staff except the executive director, volunteer "staff" can be enlisted, trained, and given the responsibility and authority to manage the development process. These volunteer staffers may be one or more individuals from the board or development committee willing to coordinate the various development tasks under the executive director's leadership until paid staff is available. This can work well. When the organization matures to the point where it can afford to have paid staff, the phaseout of volunteer staff needs to be handled with sensitivity and appreciation for the hours and energy they have given to the organization. The development officer should learn as much as possible from these volunteers and keep them involved in a way that is newly-defined and appropriate, such as a development committee or advisory board or as solicitors.

3. *Specific job descriptions for staff and volunteer development workers.* This is essential. The development officer's job description should be part of a complete set of job descriptions for staff, all of which are related to the institutional plan and are revised annually to reflect changes in priorities or performance. Related to the development officer's job description are the job descriptions for the volunteers who will be required if the plan is to succeed. These jobs include chair(s) of the annual campaign, chair(s) of the capital or endowment campaign, volunteer solicitors for individuals, foundations, or corporations, team captains or other "administrative" volunteer jobs, phone volunteers, and annual mailing volunteers (signers, stuffers, labelers, baggers, etc.).

By having a compendium of job descriptions always ready, an organization can go about the important task of matching the right volunteer to the right job. Most critically, however, the volunteer knows from the outset what the job entails. Some organizations take this a step further and enter into an actual contract based on the job description with the volunteer (See Exhibit 4.1 and Exhibit 4.2). For every enthusiast of volunteer contracts there is a critic. Those dedicated to the volunteer contract say it provides a solid businesslike basis for evaluation and enlistment/reenlistment of volunteers. Those opposed to the formal contract say it is off-putting and violates the charitable and vol-

EXHIBIT 4.1 Sample Volunteer Contract

(Name of organization) and (name of volunteer) enter into the following agreement based on the attached job description for (name of volunteer job).

(Name of volunteer) agrees to provide the following volunteer services for (name of organization). (List comes from the job description.)

In support of these services, (name of organization) agrees to provide the following for (name of volunteer) in the fulfillment of the agreed upon tasks:

1. Requested information within mutually agreed time frame
2. Regular reports of progress and results
3. Staff support as required for carrying out volunteer responsibilities
4. Access to staff members or other volunteers whose participation or information is required for successful completion of assignments
5. Prompt return of phone calls or response to faxes/materials
6. (Others added as desired)

The completion/expiration date of this (task) (term of office) is (date). It is anticipated that the successful achievement of these responsibilities will require (number of days per month, hours per week, weeks per year). The volunteer agrees to commit this amount of time or to notify the organization if such time commitment is not possible.

Periodic review of (service) (progress towards completion of task) will be provided by (name of staff person(s) or volunteer leader(s) who will also serve as supervisor for this volunteer job). If at any time during the period of this contact either party wishes to terminate the contract, a face-to-face meeting will be provided to review the reasons. At that time, all unfinished assignments or materials will be returned to (organization or person) for reassignment.

(Name of organization) looks forward to working with (name of volunteer) in the productive fulfillment of this important volunteer assignment.

Signed and dated. One copy retained by volunteer; second copy for organization's files.

EXHIBIT 4.2 Sample Letter of Understanding

This may be used in place of a contract. It is sent following a face-to-face or phone meeting in which responsibilities have been reviewed and the volunteer has committed to undertake the task or office.

(Inside address)

Dear (first name, in most cases),

Thank you for agreeing to (name of task or office) for the (time period, completion date, or duration of office). We are looking forward to working with you on this important assignment.

The job description is enclosed. You will find that it reflects the points we discussed in our conversation. If there are any listed responsibilities which do not match your understanding of our agreement, please let us know as soon as possible.

It is our understanding that you have the time and the willingness to provide this volunteer service to us, and we are very pleased. If, during our work together, problems arise which will prevent you from completing your assignment, please let us know as soon as possible so we can make other arrangements. (Name of staff person(s) or board leader(s)) will be your primary contact person during this assignment. Please contact him/her if you have questions or concerns.

Thank you for working together with us. Your volunteer service is essential to the successful delivery of our programs into the community.

(Signed by appropriate volunteer or staff person.)

untary nature of volunteer participation. Organizations must decide for themselves what is appropriate for their culture, their needs, and their volunteers. If no formal contract is drawn, it is still extremely important to have a volunteer job description so the mutual expectations are clear. Likewise, it is often appropriate to share the scope of the staff job(s) with the volunteer as well. Volunteer expectations of staff sometimes exceed the staff person's job description, leading to unwarranted volunteer frustration and disappointment.

4. *A development plan that provides budget for both direct fund raising and indirect costs of donor development.* It costs money to raise money. Fund-raising budgets tend to focus almost entirely on the direct costs of fund raising (stationery, postage, development salaries, telephones, printing of brochures), forgetting that two of the key aspects of going beyond fund raising are indirect costs: cultivation and stewardship. If board members and other volunteers are to be involved with the full development process, there must be budget for refreshments for prospect review sessions, cultivation and stewardship events, extra postage for non-revenue producing mailings (thank yous, special mailings with "white papers" or newspaper clippings), special stationery for annual or capital campaign chairs who wish to write personal thank you letters, requested reimbursement of out-of-pocket volunteer or staff expense for cultivation lunches or dinners. These are critical costs that organizations should not necessarily expect volunteers to absorb. In many organizations, volunteers are more than willing to contribute these costs. However, that should not be the expectation unless it is communicated at the time of enlistment and reaffirmed before each event or activity. Also, an organization should consider its own program budgeting and how these costs are reflected even if they are covered by volunteers. It is important to keep realistic figures about the cost of fund raising—for purposes of accounting records and also for future planning. Be cautious about understating the costs of fund raising and development if, in fact, volunteers are funding certain activities which should be included in a total cost analysis. It is unwise to attempt to build development partnerships without clear communication of the financial implications of development and fund raising or an understanding of who is responsible for those costs.

5. *A willingness on the part of staff and volunteers to approach development and fund raising at all three essential levels: philosophical, strategic, and tactical.* In Chapter 10, these three levels are developed in depth. They are important to include, if briefly, within the required basic structure for development. The philosophical, or "soft," side of the development process is its true underpinning. It is the basis from which staff and key board leaders set the tone that will form the structure, commitment, retention, and success of the development partnership. A commitment to the philosophical basis of philanthropy in general and the organization's mission in particular will be reflected in the quality and dedication of both staff and volunteers.

    Our sector has a serious purpose, and an important one: to provide, in partnership with public and other private institutions, those programs and services which will meet the health, human services, cultural, artistic, educational, social, environmental, religious, and other needs of our communities. Those who keep their eye on this broader mission are more successful at keeping their own organization's mission in focus. This understanding, when coupled with knowledge of the community needs met by their particular organization, leads to a higher sense of the importance of the development effort itself. It is basic to "putting away the tin cup" and going out into the community to gain investors for organizations that are truly meeting community needs.

In recruiting volunteers, we tend to be shy about the philosophical side of our sector. Yet, because our philosophy is what distinguishes us from the corporate or business sector, it is that side of our organizations which appeals to prospective volunteers and donors. We are an alternative. We provide meaning and hope and joy. We offer people an opportunity to become involved with something that is purposeful and powerful. In the waning days of the Campaign for Stanford, the university's successful $326 million campaign in the 1970s, volunteer leaders were in need of a "booster shot." Those located in San Francisco gathered for an evening's "pep rally" with John Gardner, philosopher, humanitarian, business school professor, and great friend of Stanford. The volunteers were newly inspired to finish their campaign commitment when they heard from this busy and accomplished person how important becoming involved with something "bigger than himself" had been to his life. It was a keen philosophical principle that inspired volunteers to continue their efforts.

Organizations must also convey a sense of the strategic. They must indicate to their development partners that there is a clear strategy for the future. Intrinsic to this strategy is a commitment to consistent evaluation and modification of plans and practices. Organizations should conduct an annual evaluation of the long-range plan, a quarterly evaluation of the annual objectives, and a monthly evaluation of the budget. Such strategic practice and intent, coupled with a solid philosophical commitment to the sector and the organization, create an attractive opportunity for involvement by those whose thoughtfulness will be an asset to the organization.

No amount of philosophy or strategy can keep an organization moving forward if the people involved do nothing. This is particularly true with development and fund raising. Organizations with perfect mission statements and textbook institutional and/or development plans still fail at fund raising. The prevalent reason is the inability to perform at the tactical level. Inertia is a terrible organizational disease, easy to diagnose and difficult to cure. Tactical execution of the steps in development requires a workable framework.

The following 10-step process is a framework in which effective development and fund-raising partnerships can operate successfully to achieve donor and fund development goals.

THE DEVELOPMENT PROCESS: A PARTNERSHIP FOR DONOR AND RESOURCE DEVELOPMENT

The development process is a logical sequence which can be internalized over time by the participants in the development team. The following process, an amalgamation of several processes observed, taught, and implemented over the years, is intentionally detailed. Organizations must understand at the outset the intricacies of building relationships that will ensure an organization's ability to go beyond fund raising. As the framework is used and tested, certain steps may be combined or omitted depending on the needs of a particular organization. The goal with this process, as with any other with which the reader may be familiar, is to so well internalize the sequence of steps that their execution becomes seamless. The prospect should not be aware of traveling through the steps, and, eventually, the volunteer and staff team should be able to move through the process without stopping at each step. However, in the beginning, consideration of each step will help everyone on the development team feel more confident and comfortable about what they are doing.

THE 10-STEP PROCESS FOR DONOR DEVELOPMENT

1. Identify/Qualify
2. Develop Initial Strategy
3. Cultivate
4. Involve
5. Evaluate
6. Assign
7. Solicit
8. Follow-Through and Acknowledge

9. Steward
10. Renew

There are two critical ideas to remember when using this framework. First, every step in the process requires—and encourages—a partnership between board and staff and provides each with opportunities to be a resource, catalyst, and implementer. Second, only one of the steps requires asking directly for funds. This allows board members who are reluctant or lack confidence about asking—or who, for professional or conflict-of-interest reasons, cannot request funds (e.g., judges in certain communities are restricted from fund raising)—to play one of nine other key roles in the development process. These other roles are not "make work." They are vital to making the ask successful and retaining the donor as a renewing investor in the organization.

Be sure each step of the process involves those volunteers and staff who are involved in the development partnership. The effectiveness of the process depends on broad involvement.

1. Identify/Qualify

Identifying and qualifying potential prospects for initial, renewed, or major gifts is an easy partnership. At every board meeting and at every staff meeting, provide a regular opportunity and system for identification. At board and staff meetings, on the top of the agenda and materials, include a half or full sheet of paper which is headed: "Since our last meeting, I have met the following individuals or heard about the following corporations and foundations that might be interested in our work." Provide space for the name(s) and addresses (if available) and for the person filling out the form to indicate the next steps (please add to the mailing list, please see me, another contact person is __(Name)__ , etc.). Encourage people to write down the names even if they do not have the address or phone; those numbers can be obtained after the lists are submitted. The person filling out the list should sign his or her name so the staff person (or volunteer leader in charge of prospect identification) can follow up.

Then, check these names against the existing database and add new ones to the prospect files for further research. Those identified as appropriate to receive the newsletter (without a solicitation envelope) are placed on that mailing list. It is very important, when mailing out the first newsletter, to send it in an envelope with a cover note. If you have permission to use the recommending person's name, add a personal note: "At the suggestion of (e.g.) Roger Duncan, we are sending you a copy of our latest newsletter. He felt you would be interested in the work we are doing." You can also state what followup the prospect may expect: receiving the newsletter for six months, a call from the recommending person, a call from the board chair, and so on. If you cannot use the person's name, include a note that says, "It has come to our attention that you might be interested in learning more about our organization. . . ."

Silent Prospecting

As names are submitted by staff and board, collate them into a list for review by various staff and board groups. "Silent prospecting" is a discreet and thorough approach to qualifying prospects. In silent prospecting, each participant at a qualifying session is provided with an envelope with an identical list of names to review. The names are presented on a form and instructions are provided (see Exhibit 4.3). Each participant is asked to review the list silently, writing down comments. At the end of the session, lists are turned in to the staff or board person overseeing the session. Silent prospecting can be done as part of a board meeting or as a special session. It may also be done one-on-one with people who are unable to attend a meeting.

Silent prospecting is another opportunity for partnership. When reviewing a list that has been built over a period of months—which may also include some lapsed donors and/or some names from published lists of donors to other similar organizations (annual reports are a wonderful source for this)—care and confidentiality are essential. Those reviewing the list learn a great deal about the ethics and integrity of an organization from observing this process.

Silent prospecting involves one or more sessions to which board members, staff members, key community volunteers involved with the program, former board members, and others who have knowledge of the community are invited. Be sure the sessions are arranged at convenient times and places. Insist that people come to you; do not mail out lists for review. If people cannot attend a session, offer to take the list to their home or office and go over it with them. Because this list of potential donor-investors represents a great amount of time and involvement, regard it as one of your most valuable assets. This list of potential prospects should be guarded.

For an easy way to set up the silent prospecting list, run labels with the names and addresses of those you are wishing to qualify. Using the suggested form, set up a master list using the labels. Reproduce a copy of the master list and an instruction sheet for each session participant. Place in a large envelope and put a participant's name on each. Give verbal instructions as well, and let each person proceed through the list at his/her own speed. You may want to provide a brief opportunity for socializing afterwards, or conduct a board or committee meeting. A strategy that improves attendance at silent prospecting sessions is to offer several alternative times and places: breakfast at a centrally located board member's home; afternoon at another board member's home in a different area of the community; and an evening at the agency's offices. Participants can choose the most convenient time and location.

After all group and individual sessions have been held, appoint a board and staff prospect evaluation team to organize and analyze the responses. The silent prospecting form is designed so that each page can be cut or separated into three prospect evaluations. If a participant provided information on only one or two of the three names on the page, retain only the names on which information was provided. The blank forms can be discarded. Be sure the name or initials of the person providing the information is on each retained section of the form. Each name is handled separately, and multiple evaluations of the same person are grouped together. In this way, the body of information about a potential prospect is accumulated and can be analyzed for consistency and accuracy. This accumulated information becomes the basis for development of preliminary prospect profiles. These are used by the development committee for screening and rating prospects for the Key Prospect List (see Exhibit 4.4). This list must be kept confidential and should be free of any potentially damaging information. Don't write anything you would not want the prospect to read.

Silent prospecting works for organizations of all sizes and should be done regularly to keep the prospect pipeline full. It can be used for:

- Identifying potential capital campaign prospects
- Qualifying existing lists of members, subscribers, donors, parents, students, or other constituencies
- Providing an infusion of new names into a stalled annual or capital campaign
- Requalifying donor-investors who are thought to have greater capacity, connection, or concern

One very successful silent prospecting session occurred towards the end of a capital campaign. A performing arts organization, having "plateaued" in its fund raising for a new building, realized it had not

EXHIBIT 4.3 Sample Instruction Sheet for Silent Prospecting

Thank you for agreeing to participate in our "silent prospecting" program. This is a vital step in our ability to identify those individuals in the community who will have the greatest interest in our organization and be most willing to contribute through our giving programs. **The process is silent and confidential.**

The enclosed lists were drawn from existing and new lists put together for fund-raising purposes. They include current donors, likely prospects, and others who have shown interest in our organization. In each case, the name and address are noted, and opposite the name are boxes for you to check, and places to comment. **Each person participating in the process has the same list**.

1. We are asking you to evaluate each individual according to **connection** (do you know this individual, and how well (primary link); or does someone else (secondary link) know them who might be willing to contact them.) Also, please indicate whether you are willing to contact the individual.
2. We would also like to know (of course) your estimate of their **capacity** to give. We have set this up to make it easy for you—just circle a number opposite each name: (These will vary according to goal.)
   A–$10,000 or more
   B–5,000–9,999
   C–1,000—4,999
   D–less than $1,000
3. **Concern** or Interest is a big factor: choose from this checklist: (Suggestions for various organizations, e.g., arts education, historical societies, human services.)

Dance	Piano	Vocal
Preservation	Special Collection	Archives
Family service	Respite program	Childcare

A sample entry looks like this:

Mr. and Mrs. John Doe   Primary link?   yes/no
2222 Jackson Street   Secondary link?   yes/no
Hillsborough, CA Zip   Name of best contact:
Phone
                                        _____

                                        Known or suspected interest:

                                        _____

                                        Ability: A   B   C   D
I am _____ am not _____ willing to ask this person.
Comments:

Please work silently. If you have questions, ask a staff or board member for help. Be sure your name is on your envelope before you turn in your lists. Thank you so much. Please keep this process confidential.

(Continued)

EXHIBIT 4.3 *(Continued)*

By: Initials _____
PROSPECT:

Primary Link? YES No
Secondary Link? YES NO
Name of Best Contact: _____
Known or Suspected Interest:

_____

Ability: A B C D

I am _____ am not _____ willing to ask this person.
COMMENTS:

By: Initials _____
PROSPECT:

Primary Link? YES NO
Secondary Link? YES NO
Name of Best Contact: _____
Known or Suspected Interest:

_____

Ability: A B C D

I am _____ am not _____ willing to ask this person.
COMMENTS:

By: Initials _____
PROSPECT:

Primary Link? YES NO
Secondary Link? YES NO
Name of Best Contact: _____
Known or Suspected Interest:

_____

Ability: A B C D

I am _____ am not _____ willing to ask this person.
COMMENTS:

EXHIBIT 4.4 Key Prospect List

Name	Due Date	Primary Contact	Amount Requested	Past Activity	Current Cultivation	Comments	Amount Committed
STRATEGIC GIFTS— $100,000+	Tier One						
	12/1/9_		$250,000	Key major donor			
			$300,000	Special project support		Additional in-kind support—site review, project management and video tape	$300,000
	12/1/9_		$100,000				
	12/1/9_		$100,000	Special project support			
	2/1/9_		$100,000				
	12/1/9_		$250,000	Key major donor			
	12/1/9_		$300,000	Key major donor			
	open to follow corporate ask		$100,000	Key major donor			
	1/15/9_		$300,000				
	11/15/9_		$750,000				
	2/15/9_		$100,000				
	9/1/9_		$300,000	Key major donor		called on 9/28/9_. She said "everything looks good." Prelim. review 10/9_; decision 12/9_	

EXHIBIT 4.4 *(Continued)*

11/1/9_	$300,000				
12/1/9_	$100,000	Special project support in 1992–93			
12/1/9_	$100,000				
8/5/9_	$468,358	Key major donor	$150,000 pledged for 199_	Reapply for second year of funding—7/15/9_ deadline for 199_ funds	$150,000
12/1/9_	$100,000	Key major donor			
2/1/9_	$100,000	Special project support in 1993–94			
12/1/9_	$100,000				
12/1/9_	$100,000				
12/1/9_	$300,000				
1/15/9_	$200,000	Have asked to invite to site in 1/9_			
MAJOR GIFTS— $10,000+					
Tier Two					
11/15/9_	$25,000				
4/1/9_	$15,000				
4/15/9_	$50,000				

Tier Three names are usually included at the end of the Key Prospect List, but are not analyzed thoroughly until moved into Tier Two.

been moving prospects into the pipeline. In an all-out effort to infuse their prospect base with new names, they set up a meeting to which they invited a wide range of potentially helpful constituents: parents of students (and former students) in the training program, people who had participated in travel/study trips, current and former board members, staff people, and past and current funders. At moments the effort seemed chaotic: some lists circulated, the "silence" was often broken, people moved in and out as they completed their evaluations. However, it was fruitful and provided some new high-potential prospects as well as a somewhat daunting list of individuals and organizations needing more cultivation and/or research—all of whom had been previously overlooked. The eventual success of the campaign was partially derived from the results of that session.

In silent prospecting, success of the process is directly related to the comprehensiveness of the constituencies represented by those participating in the process. Organizations that cast their net broadly are rewarded by excellent information. Professional and electronic screening services for qualifying donors & prospects exist. The American Prospect Research Association (APRA) is an excellent resource.

2. Develop Initial Strategy

Based on the results of the silent prospecting sessions, certain prospects will emerge as those most likely to make a gift within the shortest period of time. They are the ones who have a clear connection to the organization, a known concern about the programs or services and those they serve, and capacity to make a gift at whatever level has been identified in the qualifying process. Others with known concern or capacity and/or connection will be identified, but will not have all three vital qualifications. Still others will be seen as great potential prospects, but too little information will have been generated during silent prospecting to make informed judgments about the next step in the relationship building process.

Creating a Key Prospect List

Priority prospects, and the strategies for their cultivation and solicitation, are organized into a Key Prospect List. The list is structured in three parts:

- *Tier One*—prospects about whom a great deal is known and with whom there is already a relationship. They may be ready for solicitation.

- *Tier Two*—prospects about whom some information is known, but with whom the relationship has not been established. They are ready for cultivation, and for further exploration of their connection, concern, or capacity.
- *Tier Three*—prospects about whom very little is known, who were identified in silent prospecting as perhaps having potential. They must be researched and cultivated.

The Key Prospect List is the strategic management tool for development, and the basis for monitoring progress. Preliminary volunteer assignments can be made for initiating the cultivation and solicitation steps with the prospects in Tier One—and a tentative figure and target date set for the ask. All strategy at this point is preliminary. The strategy may change several times depending on the actual readiness of the prospect to make a gift. In the process, the development partnership members may decide that another solicitor is more appropriate or that they have incorrectly estimated the capacity or concern of the individual. For purposes of getting the process rolling, however, the key prospect list should reflect preliminary solicitor assignment, target figure, and date by which the ask should be made.

Tier Two comprises those individuals and organizations who need more cultivation than those in Tier One. Usually, these are the prospects who need more connection to the organization. These are often potential funders whose concern for the programs and services of the organization are known because of the other funding they do in the community, and whose capacity is also known. The weak aspect of their potential as a donor-investor is their connection; fortunately, cultivation can build this.

Tier Three includes those about whom there is even less information. Frequently, these are people whose capacity is known because of their community position, income or investments, and gifts to other kinds of organizations in the community. Knowledge of the other two vital components, concern and connection, is missing. These two areas will require time, research, and effort. While there is a long-term priority for identifying values and building a relationship with those in Tier Three, principal energy is appropriately placed with Tiers One and Two.

In a well-managed prospect and donor development program, names in Tier Two will be moved into Tier One as those prospects are solicited. Tier Three prospects are moved into Tier Two for more focused cultivation if research reveals promising areas of their potential. Otherwise, the names may be dropped from the Key Prospect List and other names moved on to the list. In this process it is also vital to continually evaluate your key prospect list so that those in Tiers Two and Three, if they prove to have no potential as investors, can be moved off the lists entirely to make room for those identified in subsequent (usually quarterly or semi-yearly) silent prospecting sessions.

3. Cultivate

Planning moves into action with this step. Once again, the partnership is called upon. Staff choreographs and participates in opportunities for board members and other volunteers to meet and talk with prospective donors. While these are primarily prospects in Tier One, initial strategy setting may also involve some prospects in Tier Two who are connected to prospects in Tier One and might be responsive to an event or opportunity because of the presence of their friends. For this step to work, volunteers should make themselves available for regularly planned events (concerts, receptions, lectures, etc.) to which prospective donors will be invited and also for special cultivation activities (tours, lunches with the executive director) planned with a particular prospect (or prospects) in mind. For the cultivation process to work effectively, volunteers also need to provide feedback to staff regarding meetings they have held independently with identified prospects.

Here are two good rules to keep cultivation activities coordinated:

- *Any volunteer interaction with potential funders from any Tier in the Key Prospect List is communicated to staff.* To make this process easier, many organizations create and distribute an "Action Update" form (See Exhibit 4.5). These are used in capital campaigns, but also in the process of implementing the development process for annual gifts.
- *Any cultivation that takes place on behalf of an organization is coordinated with the staff.* The reasons for this are several. First, staff may have information that is critical to any conversation with the prospect (e.g., previous gifts, previous outreach). Second, the prospect may be "on hold" for another opportunity or time for a reason not known to the volunteer. Third, the prospect may have already been assigned to another volunteer and the duplicate effort would send a confusing signal to the prospect. Finally, the volunteer may benefit from special information about the organization which staff can make available based on what is already known about that individual's connection or concerns.

We tend to think of cultivation as parties and events during which we introduce potential donor-investors to the people and mission of our

EXHIBIT 4.5 Action Update Form

Action Update

Today's Date: _____

Volunteer's Name: _____

Prospect's Name: _____

Date of Action: _____

What Happened:_____

_____

_____

_____

_____

_____

Next Action Planned: _____

_____

By When: _____

Comments: _____

_____

_____

_____

Please fax to (number) or mail to the Development Office.

organization. While this is true, it is not the whole picture. Parties and events, without systematic follow-up based on a cogent cultivation plan, are ineffective. Follow-through is required. There is an important distinction between follow-up, which implies a renewed effort, and follow-through, which implies sustained effort. There is no relaxing of effort in our sector (news which comes as no surprise to anyone reading this book). After any kind of event or activity, a follow-through plan ensures a stronger connection with those who attended. Good follow-through techniques include immediate addition of names to the mailing list and thank you letters that convey the success of the event or program to those who attended. Personal phone calls from board members or event committee members to patrons of the event also make a huge impact. If some of those on your guest list are Tier One prospects, be sure a board member is assigned to look after those individuals at the event. Afterwards, have the board member file an Action Update form or meet with a staff member to plan the next steps. At cultivation or recognition lunches or dinners, assign a board member to each table (unless the table has been bought by someone for a group and is completely filled). Provide board members and other key volunteers with confidential lists and short biographies of those at their table. Where tables are hosted, a member of the board or dinner committee can circulate graciously at an appropriate interval among the seated guests.

The quality of the cultivation and the follow-through you provide has a major effect on the ease and success of the eventual solicitation. Those responsible for monitoring the cultivation of key prospects must recognize signs that a prospect is getting close to the point where he or she can be asked for a gift. Cultivation, because it is pleasant and painless, can easily become a consuming activity. Continuing cultivation staves off the inevitable—asking for the gift. You must learn to recognize ripe fruit *before* it drops to the ground.

The Role of Information in the Cultivation Process

Not all cultivation involves the kind of personal interaction just described. Providing information is another way to cultivate prospects. Your newsletter is a form of cultivation, and can be used very effectively for this purpose. Evaluate your newsletter and be sure it is conveying the message you most want your readers to receive. Does it convey the impact and results of your programs, or does it focus on your needs? Does it portray—in words and images—the kinds of people you are serving and your programs? Does it balance volunteer information, donor recognition, and program impact? Or does it overemphasize the social aspect of your organization and show, instead, too many pictures of people partying?

Your newsletter is one form of nonpersonal cultivation, but there are others as well. If you have a special program which is of known interest to the prospect, have the program staff person prepare a "white paper" relating your program to an article in a magazine or newspaper that focuses on a local, national, or international need that your organization is addressing through this program. A family service organization focused on their child abuse prevention program with a group of donors. An excellent article on the importance of child abuse prevention education was pulled from a major newspaper with national circulation and prestige. The article addressed the importance of this solution to a growing problem. The position paper prepared by the staff person focused entirely on what this local family service organization was doing. The clipping, with the article, was mailed to prospective funders as well as current donor-investors. The mailing to prospects included a note drawing their attention to the local agency's efforts to address a national issue about which they knew the individual or institution was concerned. It was a strong cultivation tool. For current donor-investors, the articles were mailed with a note which thanked them for helping to make such programs possible. Both notes had a high impact on the funders and prospects to which they were sent as measured by renewed gifts and notes and calls of thanks.

Cultivation also occurs unexpectedly. Favorable press coverage of an event or a program will heighten potential funder awareness of your organization and its mission. Enthused board members and other volunteers become informal advocates, often unwittingly arousing great interest among those with whom they interact socially and professionally. The largest gift from an individual (nearly one-half million dollars) to a campaign for a social service agency was made anonymously by an individual who became interested in the organization because of the enthusiasm and advocacy of one of its staff members. The donor had no prior connection to the organization but, over time, respected the commitment of the staff member.

In yet another instance, a bequest in excess of one million dollars was received by a children's services agency from a woman who had no direct experience with the organization. During her years of illness, the woman's neighbor, a volunteer for the organization, would bring her lunch from the agency's volunteer-run restaurant which operated to benefit the organization. The woman would ask her about the organization, about the children served, and about her involvement. When notification came about the provision in the will, everyone—including the neighbor—was taken by surprise. There had been no previous indication.

No deliberate cultivation took place in either of these instances. Both gifts were the spontaneous result of a relationship with an individual who was committed to an organization. These stories underscore the importance of staff and volunteers being informed and enthusiastic about the organizations they represent. We never know when our commitment—that sustained passion that people recognize and respect— will be a catalyst in converting casual interest into a gift with impact.

Most cultivation is more formal. Organizations, as part of their overall development plan, should have a component that describes its goals and objectives for cultivation. This should include a description of the activities as well as a timeline and an estimate, based on the Key Prospect List, of the number of people to involve in each activity or step. Critical to successful cultivation is a sufficient budget to support these activities. If organizations are to go beyond fund raising, they must be willing to invest in those development activities that are important—not just in fund-raising activities, which too often are urgent. Balancing what is urgent with what is important is a key factor in attaining organizational stability. Organizations unable to go beyond fund raising are often those for whom the urgent overpowers the important in terms of staff, time, and financial resources.

4. Involve

This is a powerful concept, and a powerful process. To truly involve someone means to engage them in the work and the results of the organization in such a way that they begin to feel that they are participants in a partnership. Involvement also permits a deeper exploration of the values of the potential funder, and the way in which the values of your organization can bring that individual or organization satisfaction as an investor. While some involvement begins with an initial gift, appropriately followed up by the receiving organization, most involvement of major donors develops out of the cultivation process.

Involvement differs from cultivation in the nature of the relationship. Cultivation can be a somewhat one-sided process with the organization providing information and participation opportunities and the potential funder observing and listening/learning. Involvement is a more dynamic stage of the relationship. The potential funder may become personally involved with a project, or may be enlisted to serve on a committee or task force.

A regional repertory theater has a unique way of involving its potential funders. They are invited to become part of a "Play Support Group" that forms at the beginning of preparation for each of the company's eight season productions. The Play Support Group, which includes prospective funders as well as board members who have been or will be assigned to cultivate and solicit these prospects, is present at the first reading of the play and attends subsequent readings and rehearsals. The Director shares his/her interpretation of the playwright's script with the group and invites conversation around its themes and nuances. Costume and set designers show the group their preliminary sketches as well as their evolving creations. Play Support Group members are organized, if convenient for them, to take out-of-town cast and production staff members to dinner and to look after their needs. On opening night, the Play Support Group is given special seating and recognition. As a result of their involvement, new potential funders become enthused about the theater company. Not incidentally, board members who participate in the Play Support Group have a renewed and deeper commitment to the organization

While a performing arts organization has more obvious opportunities for such involvement, other kinds of organizations can fashion creative ways to involve potential funders, and their possible solicitors, in programs that will bring them closer to the organization. In social, human and medical services, where client confidentiality is an issue, involvement with program staff in presentations and discussions can be quite engaging. An environmental organization in the San Francisco Bay Area takes potential funders and board members out on their patrol boat for excursions during which they watch for signs of oil spills or other hazards to the fragile balance of the Bay. Museums often find that involvement in docent or other classes has a high impact on a person's eventual commitment as a donor, and schools and colleges can find an abundance of ways to get potential funders involved.

Recognize involvement as a critical step, and set up systems to ensure it is a regular part of the development process. As with the other steps, board-staff partnership is a key aspect of the Involvement phase.

The Involvement phase should reveal much about the strength of the common values and interests which the potential donor shares with the organization. Involvement is a time for testing ideas with the prospect, and for handling initial questions or objections the prospective funder may raise. Encourage questions, answer objections candidly, and provide information requested by the potential funder openly and honestly. In the formation of the kind of partnerships that take organizations beyond fund raising, disclosure of information is a critical factor.

5. Evaluate

It is essential at this point to evaluate the relationship that is growing between the organization and the potential donor and to analyze the internal process. These are some of the questions that can be asked by the development committee, prospect evaluation committee, or annual or capital campaign steering committee:

- Are the right board members (or other volunteers) assigned to this prospect?
- What are this person's principal interests, concerns, enthusiasms?
- Have we provided the necessary and right information for this prospect?
- Has he/she met those individuals with whom there will be the greatest shared values?
- Are there other connections we need to build?
- Have we done adequate cultivation?
- Have we assessed capacity correctly?
- What amount do we feel would be the appropriate ask? And for what project or program?
- What is the best timing for the ask? Has that changed since our original strategy?
- Who should be included in the solicitation meeting?

The Evaluation step requires focus on the results of the first four steps in order to formulate the best strategy for the solicitation. Draft a written prospect evaluation, based on the above questions, and keep it on file so that a confidential copy can be provided to those who will be assigned as solicitors in the next step.

6. Assign

There is an old saying in fund raising: a successful solicitation occurs when the right person asks the right prospect for the right amount and the right purpose at the right time. Wishful thinking? Not necessarily. Such inspired assignments are possible if attention is given to the steps that lead up to them. The development partnership is critical in the assignment phase. Staff and volunteers work together at this phase to ensure the highest possible success by making the best possible solicitation assignment. During the cultivation phase, certain natural linkages between the prospect and individuals involved with your organization have doubtless formed. Current donors, active board members, former board members with continuing involvement in the organization, or members of the community for whom the prospect has respect and with whom the organization has a strong relationship, are all potential candidates for the assignment.

It is best to assign more than one solicitor to a prospect. Team solicitations are best. Two or three individuals who represent board and staff are highly effective at calling on one or more individuals who have been appropriately cultivated and are ready to be asked. Board members provide vital community linkage; staff members offer expertise and familiarity with program and administrative issues. Teams may also be comprised of other program or development staff or other volunteers whose linkage to the prospect or commitment to the cause would be persuasive in the solicitation. In university campaigns, students are sometimes included on the team. In one tutoring organization, parents were trained and went on corporate calls.

Regardless of whether two or three solicitors are assigned, it is still very important for one person to have the primary responsibility for coordinating the solicitation, making the appointment, and bringing the prospect to the point where the solicitation can be made. This person is the lead solicitor. Information about the assignment should be entered into the database. Preparation for the solicitation should be made with the entire solicitation team, but may be preceded by a strategy meeting with the lead solicitor and the development director. In this meeting, a solicitation plan leading to the next step should be developed.

7. Solicit

If the previous six steps have been well planned and implemented, this step will follow naturally. As relationships develop, the thought of asking for the gift becomes less troublesome. At this point in the process, the prospect should be ready and, in fact, may begin to wonder why he or she is not being asked. The details of the solicitation process are covered in the next chapter, "Inviting Investment." However, some essential points regarding all solicitations are listed here because they relate to the entire donor development process:

Gauge Your Timing Carefully

A solicitation that comes so late in the process that the prospective donor has lost interest or patience with the organization is as doomed as a solicitation that is made prematurely. As you progress through the donor development process, be confident about merging or skipping steps that may not seem necessary for a particular donor, or about extending certain steps for others who do not seem as ready. This should be a fluid and flexible process; it is intended as a description, not a prescription. If prospects start asking how they can help the organization, be prepared to move into the solicitation by offering some gift options. If, in conversations, prospects share information that would indicate their interest in making a gift at that time, act on it. The development process requires intense listening skills, a great deal of intuition, and the courage to move ahead somewhat rapidly when prospects indicate that their connection and concerns have been brought to the point of action. Many prospects will reach a point where they "self-solicit" and will be waiting for the ask.

Be Specific About What You Want

Always name the dollar amount you are seeking, and describe the results that gift will have. We talk to donors about major gifts, which are often defined by an internal development goal or benchmark. It is more appropriate to talk with potential donor-investors about impact gifts. The size of an impact gift varies, as does the size of a major gift. However, the word "impact" reminds us to focus on results—and secures in our and the donor's minds that this gift will have an impact on the organization and its programs. Be clear with the donor regarding your understanding of the purpose of the gift. If the donor wishes to restrict it to a particular program or building objective, state how the donor's intent will be met if the gift is made. Likewise, if the keenest priority in your organization is for unrestricted annual or endowment money, make the case to the donor for an unrestricted gift. Be sure that those who make unrestricted gifts are recognized as appropriately as those whose gifts are restricted to a particular building or program.

Have a Menu of Recognition Opportunities Ready for Discussion, But Be Alert to Whether or To What Extent the Donor Will Want the Gift To Be Publicly (or Privately) Recognized

When asking for an impact gift, weave the potential ways the gift can be recognized into the ask. However, exercise caution in describing these opportunities. There are individuals who prefer no recognition at all and are turned away from certain organizations because they fear they will be recognized inappropriately. Test the water. Find out if and how the person would like to be recognized if the gift is made, and build your response around those desires. The reluctance of some funders, both individual and institutional, to be recognized publicly (or even private-ly) must be respected.

Remember To Approach the Solicitation From the Shared Values Basis of Philanthropy and Development

Even though you are finally doing "fund raising," remember to embed your direct ask in the context of the larger philosophical and strategic functions of philanthropy and fund raising. This keeps the ask values-driven and mission connected, and helps solicitors keep the tin cup firmly out of the process (Chapters 1 and 2).

Relax and Enjoy the Moment

As developed in Chapter 5, "Inviting Investment," the ask should be a moment of release, not pressure. All the donor's desires and the organi-zation's opportunities should come together at this moment. The solici-tation team is the catalyst for enabling donors to act on their values, and to apply their connection, concern, and capacity to the advancement of your organization.

8. Follow-Through and Acknowledge

Whatever the result of the solicitation, there is an opportunity to fur-ther the relationship by follow-through and acknowledgment. Even if the final answer is no (tips for converting "no" or for accepting it as merely a temporary setback are in the next chapter), handwritten per-sonal notes thanking prospects for their time are a gracious gesture. There have been countless instances where a no, acknowledged kindly by the solicitor or the organization, has turned into a "yes" (and an immediate gift).

The board/volunteer/staff partnership is particularly critical here. Organizations should provide staff support to volunteers in assembling information needed for follow-through, or provide stationery and postage for the notes that are written. Follow-through is required if the answer is still pending following the solicitation: if the prospect needs more time or information, both must be provided with a clear indication of the next steps that will be implemented. The follow-through schedule for each pending solicitation should be suggested and carried out by staff working with the volunteer leadership. If financial or program information has been requested, it needs to be supplied as quickly as possible. If the prospect has indicated an interest in meeting with other funders, certain program staff, or would like to tour your facility, the request should be arranged as part of this step in the process.

There is great urgency in this step. Failure to follow through appropriately can negate the entire effort that has gone into the process to this point.

The phrase follow-through rather than follow-*up*, as mentioned previously, is deliberate. Follow-through is a continuous, seamless action. Follow-up implies a renewal of activity. Implementation of the development process requires follow-through at *every* step—even solicitation—if lasting and renewable relationships are to be built and sustained.

9. Steward

Stewardship of the gift is a venerable concept in good nonprofit management. Stewardship of the giver, fully explored in Chapter 7, is a newer concept and one that is of equal importance. In churches, "stewardship" is often the name given to the annual campaign for congregate pledges. Originally, to be a "steward" was to be a "keeper of the hall" (old English). In the context of the development process, stewardship is the organization's privileged responsibility to be watchful "keepers" of those who, through their gifts, are "keeping" the organization healthy.

Most organizations recognize the importance of accountability in the use of donated funds. But, in many organizations, there is an alarming laxness in stewardship of the donor that results in difficulty and resistance during the fund-raising process. Low annual giving renewal rates may be a symptom of poor stewardship. The results of poor stewardship are often revealed during a capital campaign feasibility study or, sometimes, after a campaign has begun. Neglected investors are not apt to reinvest. Saying thank you is not enough. Organizations must convey the continuing value and impact of the investment in order to solidify relationships.

Stewardship can be viewed as "cultivation after the fact." It affords donors the same attention and thoughtfulness as prospects. Stewardship stops the too-common practice of stuffing our donors into the donor file as soon as the gift is made. The moment at which a prospective donor-investor makes a gift, he or she begins a new relationship with the organization. We must not look upon that same moment as the end of a somewhat long, exhausting, and tedious development process. We must view it as the beginning of stewardship.

Stewardship should be based on the donor's, not the organization's, desires. While certain stewardship practices (prompt thank you letters, courteous and timely notification of upcoming events or activities of interest to the donor) are standard, we must be willing to tailor our other stewardship practices to fit the needs of the donor. For example, at one museum, a donor who had made a gift of significant impact was offered membership in the highest recognition level. He refused that recognition, saying he was already involved in too many recognition groups. Rather than immediately offering another alternative, the museum asked him what he would like to have in recognition of his very generous gift. He knew what he wanted: six hours of "consulting" time with the curator of the museum's collection in which he had the keenest interest and was, himself, a modest collector. It was arranged, and the donor's connection with the museum increased along with his knowledge.

Astonishingly, sometimes the best stewardship is no contact at all— *as long as that is what the donor wants!* One of the principal funders for a midwestern university capital campaign, when questioned in a post-campaign survey designed to assess funder satisfaction with the development practices of the university, was asked how he would describe the stewardship the university had provided. "Excellent," he said. "The best of any organization we fund." Pressed to describe what the university had done to warrant this praise, he said, "Nothing. They leave us alone." Questioned further, he revealed that this particular foundation wants neither recognition or follow-up after the formal thank you. They convey this information to those they fund and nearly all choose to ignore their request. The university, by honoring the request and "leaving them alone," was, in fact, providing the best stewardship of all: the kind the donor wanted.

The importance of strong stewardship—consistent and based on the donor's needs and preferences—cannot be overstated. It is one of the most critical factors in strong organizations. It is covered extensively in Chapter 8.

10. Renew

People like renewing their investment if they feel the gift has made an impact. Feedback that focuses on results, and proper stewardship of the gift and the giver, will ensure your organization's right to renew the gift. Those who fear going back to the same donors in the following year miss the point. You do not seek funds because you have needs, but because you meet needs. The needs you meet do not diminish; in today's social and cultural environment they only increase. If you are doing a good job as an organization and can point to results, and if you can substantiate the growing need in the community for your programs and services, then you should be able to turn with pride of achievement to your investors and invite them to increase their investment.

Renewal of donors who have made impact gifts starts the cycle over again, with all its partnership implications. You will want to requalify donors based on their recent gifts and then proceed (albeit more quickly) through the other steps leading up to the solicitation. Your donors, if treated like partners with you and your organization in meeting community needs, will want to reinvest.

SUMMARY

The nonprofit sector depends on multiple partnerships within their organizations and in the community to act on behalf of community-based organizations. Of all of these partnerships, the development partnership is the most powerful and inclusive. It involves staff and volunteers and engages, ultimately, funders as well. It is the pivotal partnership for all nonprofits, and ensures the success of donor and fund development that is based on the mission and values of the organization. The development partnership is grown and nurtured around a framework that offers ten steps in the donor and fund development process—each of which is a partnership between staff and board and only one of which requires asking for funds directly. Forging strong partnerships for the development process is an important activity for all nonprofits, one with great immediate and long-term rewards for the organization and its staff, those it involves on its board and in other volunteer capacities, and its funders.

5 Inviting Investment

Organizations are able to go beyond fund raising when they view solicitation as the opportunity to invite investment. As the culmination of the first six steps of the development process, solicitation is the activity whereby we actually ask individuals or organizations for funds. It enables those we have cultivated to act on their values by investing in our organizations. While *solicitation* may feel like a one-sided equation, with the labor and the benefit focused on the not-for-profit organization, positioning the process as *investment* balances the organization and the potential donor-investor as equal players in the transaction.

The organization has, by this point (see Chapter 4), discovered the concerns, connection, and capacity of the prospect. The potential donor-investor knows the organization and is familiar with not only its programs, but their results. The invitation to invest is a logical conclusion to this process for both the organization and the prospect.

Just as "development" is not a euphemism for fund raising, "investment" is not a euphemism for donation. Development and investment are different, stronger concepts, and they describe different, more powerful results. All investors in not-for-profit organizations are donors, but not all donors are investors. The investor relationship is not measured by the size of the gift, but by the intensity of the connection the donor and the organization feel with each other. Some major or impact gifts are given by people who do not have an investor relationship with the organization; many smaller gifts are impulsive, and may also lack the true investor motivation. In both cases, a relationship can be cultivated by the organization. The investor relationship is dynamic (Chapter 2); the donor relationship may be passive. Organizations that follow the ten steps in the development process build more than a donor base: they build investors. Investors require more time and energy from board and staff to identify, nurture, and sustain, but the long-term benefit is substantial.

DEFINING DONOR-INVESTOR

An investor, or a donor-investor, is an individual or organization whose financial commitment to a nonprofit is undergirded by a belief in their shared values and in the ability of the investor and the organization to mutually benefit each other and the community. Investment should be approached as though it will be long-term and renewable. Quick-fix fund raising does not stimulate investment. Investors in nonprofits look for two bottom lines (financial and values) but one principal return: the knowledge that their investment will have the intended results and make an impact on the organization and the community. When approached for subsequent gifts, the investor is more apt to renew because the gift has been given in the belief that the organization is capable of meeting the community's need for a particular program or service, not because of the organization's need for money. The wise investor knows that the community's need for these programs or services is apt to always be there.

BUILDING A BASE OF DONOR-INVESTORS

It is not easy to bring long-term investors into an organization. Engaging investors takes lots of work by board and staff, and requires a deep institutional commitment to create and sustain an environment in which investments will flourish. The effort required to involve potential donor-investors demands follow-through which many organizations feel they cannot provide. Driven by an urgent need for funds and by lack of understanding about the development process, organizations end up using fund raising solicitation techniques without benefit of proper strategic relationship building. They let their donors lie fallow once the gift has been made, only reactivating the contact when another gift is needed or given. The result is a disjointed, exhausting, and frustrating cycle of hand-to-mouth fund raising.

Intrinsic to the investment concept is an understanding of the difference between development and fund raising. The former is a sustained and systematic multistep process while the latter is a focused and immediate transaction. A successful development process enables organizations to invite investment through effective fund raising. There is little success in asking for initial or renewed gifts if organizations have not cultivated their prospects or been stewards to their donors. It just doesn't happen. Many capital campaigns get off to very slow starts because there is so much "remedial stewardship" required to bring donors and prospects into an understanding of the validity of the mission and the impact of organization. Time has to be spent building essential connections that have either been severed through neglect or never established. Too many organizations have to assemble the bicycle while riding it.

CHALLENGES TO IMPLEMENTING AN INVESTMENT ATTITUDE

If all organizations made an internal commitment to the value of development as an investment process, it could revolutionize fund raising and cause both our communities and our organizations to look upon the activities of our sector more favorably. This implies a massive program of educating communities and donors not only in the United States but also in Western Europe and other parts of the world where the development process is even less understood. In Eastern Europe, where existing systems of government support were completely stripped from the infrastructure, there has been a remarkable interest in and acceptance of American development practices. But, in Western Europe and the United Kingdom, there is still a tremendous need to undo old beliefs. The government, which was often sole supporter of charitable organizations, has diminished its support and will continue to shrink as both a steady funder and an influence. But the spectre and hope of government support does not fade, and there is a lingering dream that it will be restored. Nonprofit non-governmental organizations in the European Union countries know that the funding structure has changed irrevocably. The challenge is to bring communities and potential donor-investors, particularly individuals, to this understanding. While private response to capital appeals is improving, support for annual needs is still viewed as a governmental responsibility and annual support from individuals lags.

To a smaller extent, the same is true in the United States. Increasing fiscal conservatism by the government will not change substantially. The resources are just not there, even if the will or passion is. Some cities and counties in the United States are bankrupt. Nonprofits must increase the services they provide. To do so, we must change the way we do business. We must establish ourselves as excellent private sector investment opportunities for strengthening our communities at local, regional, and national levels.

If our sector is to survive and serve society, we will have to do a monumental job of educating our communities over the next several years. Some approaches may be subtle; others more direct. All must be used.

ASKING FOR INVESTMENT

How we ask for the gift is one of the most critical aspects of inviting investment. Tin cups, as discussed in Chapter 2, are out of vogue. We must turn the needs-benefit equation around, and move the giving process from one perceived too often as people doing us a favor (as we convince them to give us the money we need to fund a program, meet payroll, build a building), to one in which we promote and respect the mutual benefits that accrue to the donor, the organization, and the community in a true investment partnership. Asking requires volunteer and staff participation and diligent coaching and training. Effective solicitors are those in whom we can invest our confidence in their abilities to bring donor-investors into our organizations.

Here are some observations about masterful solicitors.

- They are always well-prepared, but never seem rehearsed.
- Excellent listeners, they remember they have two ears and one mouth and they use them in that ratio, particularly while they are engaging the prospect.
- Because they are well-prepared, they anticipate and are able to respond to unexpected objections.
- They are willing to admit they don't have an answer, and willing to get the answer from the right person.
- Firm in their own belief and support for the organization they represent, they have made their own gift before asking anyone else to invest.
- Their commitment and enthusiasm characterize the interaction and positively influence those with whom they meet.
- Focused on the purpose of their meeting, they get right to the point after a minimum of small talk.
- They become so familiar with the steps in the solicitation that the process appears seamless.

INVITING INVESTMENT: THE SOLICITATION STEPS

The solicitation steps in Exhibit 5.1 are a sequential subset of Step 7—Solicit—in the development process (Chapter 4). With practice, they will be internalized, and the process will become seamless.

1. Make the Appointment

This is often the hardest part of the solicitation. Getting the courage to pick up the telephone and call someone to make the appointment to ask for a gift—even someone you have been cultivating and with whom you have developed a good relationship—may be very difficult. The appointment can be made by the lead volunteer assigned to the prospect, or by a staff person. Or, in some cases, it may be made by a friend or business associate of the prospect who calls on behalf of the organization and the lead volunteer.

There are ways to make setting the appointment easier. If the appointment can be set while with the person at a meeting or event, it seems more natural and logical. "Ed, we'd like to get together with you for a half-hour sometime next week and tell you a little more about what you've just seen and talk about some of the ideas we have about the support you (and/or your company/foundation) might give to this project. Do you have your calendar with you, or may I call your

---

EXHIBIT 5.1 The Solicitation Steps

7.1	Make the appointment.
7.2	Plan the solicitation meeting carefully.
7.3	Coach the solicitation team.
7.4	Gather and go, meet and greet.
7.5	Engage the prospect.
7.6	Say what you came to say: state the case.
7.7	Invite the investment.
7.8	Keep the silence.
7.9	Work with the prospect's answer and close.
7.10	Follow-through.

secretary tomorrow and find out what days next week are good for you?"

If it is not possible to make the appointment while you are with the potential donor-investor, you will have to call. You want to use this kind of dialogue for that call as well. Keep your tone natural, and consistent with the rapport you have developed with the person so far. If you are working with a secretary or associate of the prospect, get his or her confidence by being very clear about what you want. Often a secretary or associate, when treated like a key player in making this important transaction happen, will make a great effort to help you get the appointment. If treated as though what you have to say would not be interesting to or understood by them, they will often see to it that the appointment does not happen or is difficult to get.

While a volunteer-initiated meeting may be easier to arrange, the staff person can call and say, "This is Zed Matthews from the Florentine Agency. I'm calling on behalf of Donna Jones, a board member of our organization who has met several times with Mr. Smith over the past several months and would now like to set up an appointment to discuss a campaign gift with him. Can you help me make a half-hour appointment for him with her and our Executive Director, or should I speak directly to him?" (Note: If there is strong resistance to a personal meeting, do not press for one. Instead, arrange a phone meeting. While not as effective as a personal meeting, it is better than angering the prospect and losing the opportunity to build a relationship.)

Settings for the Ask

Although common practice is to "do lunch" with someone, the solicitation meeting is really too confidential for a public setting and the general distractions (food, other people, milling crowds) detract from the focus this meeting must have. People are more comfortable on their own turf. Suggest that you will come to the prospect's home or office at a convenient time.

If an individual is being solicited for a personal gift, it is very important to include the spouse or partner if decisions are made jointly (and, increasingly, most are). In that case, you will want to suggest coming to the home either during the day on a weekday or weekend, or in the evening, so you can meet with both individuals. When the appointment has been set, follow up with a confirming note or letter. Be very clear about purpose, time, location, and who will be present. Reconfirm the meeting by telephone the day before.

2. Plan the Solicitation Meeting Carefully

The solicitation meeting with the prospect is the culmination of the entire development process to this point. It must be planned carefully. The development director, executive director, and/or lead solicitor (development committee chair, campaign [annual or capital] chair) should coordinate the planning meeting. The meeting should involve all those who will participate in the actual solicitation. The following materials should be ready for review: confidential prospect profile, the organization's case statement and other pertinent materials, and a written proposal if required or requested. At the planning meeting, decide what roles each person will play in the solicitation. Designate one person, preferably a board member, as the asker or lead solicitor. Otherwise the meeting will drift. Another member of the solicitation team should provide general program, administrative, development or financial expertise. There may also be a representative from a program or capital needs area in which the prospect is interested in investing.

Lay out the structure of the meeting based on the time you will have with the prospect. Allow time for (1) small talk (but not much); (2) open-ended questions that will encourage the prospect to speak at some length about his/her connection to the organization and concerns for the community need the organization is meeting; (3) presentation of the campaign objective or annual gift opportunity you want the prospect to consider; (4) the request for a specific gift for a designated or unrestricted purpose; and (5) the subsequent discussion that will certainly follow the ask. In a half hour meeting, you need to keep the conversation moving to cover all this ground. If you are able to present the campaign objective or annual gift opportunity at a separate earlier meeting, it gives you more time to discuss the terms of the ask. Also, if it is possible to arrange a longer meeting it could be worthwhile, particularly if there are two or three solicitors meeting with the prospect.

3. Coach the Solicitation Team

No matter how experienced a person may be in asking for money, a little coaching before a meeting can help raise confidence and comfort levels. The staff or board person in charge of deploying the solicitation teams for the annual or capital campaign should develop a brief outline of the solicitation process and review it with the solicitors. She should brief the team on the prospect's profile including giving history and other relevant confidential facts. She should also provide the team with an easy-to-read fact sheet on the organization's case for support: budget, mission, size of campaign, current campaign status, people served, brief history, and so on. In the actual solicitation meeting, the team may give this fact sheet to the prospect as a snapshot of the longer case statement. The fact sheet is an important resource for dealing with objections. The more facts and information with which solicitors are armed, the more adept they will be at turning objections into positive learning experiences for the prospect.

In the coaching session, encourage solicitors to role play. Most adults freeze at the thought of role playing. However, experience verifies that those who have role-played a solicitation with each other are much more confident during the actual solicitation. Call the role play a "practice" session, and be sure each solicitor has an opportunity to learn and try appropriate words and phrases, implement strategies for keeping the meeting focused, deal with objections a prospect may raise, and make a practice ask or close.

In coaching the solicitation team, impress upon them the importance of listening to the prospect and to each other. The solicitation meeting will stay balanced and focused if team members listen and support each other, picking up on an interest or concern of the prospect which may be strategic in the presentation of the ask.

4. Gather and Go, Meet and Greet

If you have an appointment for 2 P.M., you should all arrive at once. You can either all come together, or agree to meet outside or near the person's home or office at 1:50 P.M. If you have people who are chronically late, be sure they are brought by someone who is always early or on time. A ragged start to a meeting throws off timing and momentum. People drifting in have to be brought up to speed, and the carefully assigned roles each person has been asked to play are disrupted when one person does not get there at the beginning.

Even if you have made sure the prospect knows how many of you are coming, who each person is, and why they are coming, you should still introduce everyone and explain their role in the organization and why they are there. "Ed, I think you remember Alice Magpie, who serves on the board with me. Alice is the chair of the Program Committee this year and it is in large part due to her efforts that we have been able to leverage the grant from the city (and, if you have already submitted a proposal to him or told him what you want) that we would like you to consider helping us match." This removes much of the guess-work from a meeting like this. Your time is too short for people to sit there wondering who's there and why.

At the beginning of the meeting, there are two other critical things you should do. First, restate your understanding of the timeframe: "We have planned a 30 minute meeting. Is that still good for you?" If the prospect's schedule has changed, and you have more or less time for the meeting, you want to know at the outset and not 15 minutes into the solicitation when suddenly Ed announces he has to leave. Second, restate the purpose of your visit. "Ed, as you know, we're here to talk with you today about an investment—a gift, if you will—that we would like you to consider making towards the renovation of our job training facility for women transitioning out of our alcoholic treatment center."

5. Engage the Prospect

The most common mistake in solicitations is jumping right from the opening "stage setting" into the presentation of the funding opportunity. Unless you have met just recently with the individual and have already begun your discussions, it is better to engage the prospect in some conversation using open-ended questions before getting into the presentation. There are exceptions to this, of course. The most important exception is prompted by prospects. If they are impatient and just want to get to the point, then do not press forward with more open-ended questions. Get to the purpose immediately. If, however, you get signals that the conversation feels pleasant to them and they are enjoying this prelude, continue. Be gracious but brief.

Remember to use active listening skills. Listen to what the person is saying, and not saying. One of the major reasons for having two or three solicitors present at a solicitation meeting is the assistance in listening. If you are alone, it is hard to notice the dynamics of the meeting as well as listen to the words. During their downtime in the meeting, solicitors should listen and watch so their reentry into the conversation is more valuable.

Open the conversation with the prospect by referring to a common experience that relates to the organization. Here is some dialogue that might happen when a solicitation team calls on a prospect for a gift to the local community orchestra: "We were just delighted you could be at the concert last week. I appreciated your making a special effort to find me afterwards to thank us for the tickets. It was great to hear how much you enjoyed the performance. Didn't you mention that this was the first time you have heard the orchestra in a few years? (Listen and pause.) We know you're very busy, and we appreciate not only your attendance at the concert but your willingness to have lunch with our Music Director a few weeks ago. (Listen and pause.) We also enjoyed having you at our education program at Martin Luther King School last month." (Listen and pause.) At any point in a dialogue like this, the conversation can be redirected by the response of the prospect. Be a good listener.

You can then easily segue into appropriate questions that will lead logically to the ask. If you start, instead, with very personal small talk—"Say, Andrea, I saw you out on the golf course last Saturday with Donna Ranchert. I haven't seen her in years. What's she up to now?"—you not only exclude the others in your group but you also send the conversation in a direction whose course will be hard to correct. Keeping the focus on the organization, even in the small talk, links the pieces of the solicitation.

From the conversation about the orchestra, you can begin engaging Andrea more directly by asking her questions like the following; if, after the first one, she seems to be wanting to cut to the point of the meeting, do not labor with these questions. Examples of open-ended questions are:

- "I seem to remember you played the flute for a few years. How did you get started with music?"
- "Having not heard the orchestra in a few years, what changes did you notice?"
- "What types of orchestral music do you enjoy most?"
- "With the decline in cultural resources in our city, what role do you feel the orchestra should play in the ongoing debate about giving the public what it should have or giving it want it wants?"

Open-ended questions are powerful. They can stimulate answers that reveal a great deal about the person's concerns and values.

Even at the beginning of the meeting, watch for body language and other nonverbal indicators of how the meeting is going. Crossed arms and legs are often a negative sign, as is lack of eye contact. If a person is distracted—going through papers, taking phone calls, getting up and walking around—you may want to ask if this is still a good time for the meeting. Two responses are possible: the prospect will realize she needs to focus on her visitors and will eliminate or ignore distractions, or the prospect will admit that this is a bad time, and she is diverted over a business problem. In the latter case, you can make a positive impression by suggesting that you return at another time. (Be sure to make the appointment before leaving.) The prospect will be very grateful. Sometimes people stick with appointments that have been difficult to arrange because they do not want to disappoint anyone. Being intuitive to their distraction ultimately enhances the invitation to invest.

6. Say What You Came to Say: State the Case

Once small talk and engagement are safely behind you, say what you came to say. Adjust the length and detail of your presentation according to how much you have previously presented to the prospect about the project, program, or campaign. In your discussion, be clear, succinct, and on point about the project or your organization. Refer back to the shared values you have uncovered during the development process: "Ed, I recall when we first visited the job training site. You mentioned that you wished more recovering alcoholics could have an opportunity like that. You felt that it would prevent them from sliding into alcoholism again. We believe that the renovation of this job training site, which will enable us to increase our trainees by 60 each year, is one of the most directly beneficial things we can do as an organization to try to reduce the problem of alcoholism in our community. I remember those statistics you gave us about days lost on the job in your factory because of drinking—incredible! And I think you know that, in our other counseling program, we work with families to help them be more active partners in the long-term rehabilitation process. We'd like to think that we can make a difference—and, with your help, I believe we can. The grant from city redevelopment funds covers phase one of the renovation and we'd like you to consider helping us match their gift so we can do phase two and get this facility running at full capacity." Constructing a statement like that allows you to reinforce the prospect's beliefs and values, lets the prospect know you valued his advice or opinion, and smoothly introduces the invitation to invest.

If you are going to provide a written proposal, do not refer to it during the meeting. Give the prospect the written proposal at the close of the meeting, or send it later if it needs to be revised due to information or interaction that arises during the meeting. You will lose vital energy and eye contact, to say nothing of the participation of the team you have brought in for a lively conversation, if the prospect starts reading a proposal in the middle of the meeting! If you have already sent the proposal, as follow-up to a previous meeting, be sure all the members of the solicitation team, and the prospect, have read and are familiar with the proposal. Otherwise, refer only briefly to it, stay focused on the conversation, and delay discussion for a later phone call or meeting.

7. Invite the Investment

Once you get this far, you are almost there. You have introduced the idea of investment, and you must keep moving into the close. Take a breath and plunge forward. "As you know from the materials we went over at the site visit, Ed, the city's gift to us was $100,000. We've raised $25,000 from the board, one-third of whom, as you may know, are former clients of the program. That was a very heartening result for us. We'd like you to consider a gift of $25,000, and it is our plan, already well underway, to solicit the remaining $50,000 in midrange and smaller gifts from the community, plus a few corporate gifts which we hope you might be able to help us identify. I have the plans for that fundraising program with me and I can leave them with you. I'm confident that, with your gift, we will have the $100,000 for phase two by the end of the year. That means the construction can be completed by April, and we'll be able to let those on our waiting list know that job training is just around the corner. Would you be willing to consider a $25,000 gift?"

8. Keep the Silence

After extending the invitation to invest, keep silent. There is a saying in sales training: the person who talks first, loses. In these delicate negotiations in which our community and organizational success is involved, we need to keep silent while the prospect considers the request we have made. As a society, we do not seem to seek or welcome silence; we move from car radio to home stereo to mobile phone to personal stereos with earphones. Yet, at this moment in the long process of bringing the prospect to the decision point, we must respect silence.

Honor the prospect by allowing him time to think about this major request you have just made. People who have accrued the capital to be prospects for impact gifts have done so by carefully marshaling their resources and investing wisely. This is not a time for impulsive behavior. Time is never more relative than when we are waiting for the answer to an important question. Fifteen seconds seems like minutes; two minutes seem like an hour. In our haste to bring what is perhaps still an uncomfortable process to a swift end, we mistakenly rush to break the silence by saying something that will not only end the negotiation for that meeting but send a confusing signal to the prospective donor-investor such as:

- "If you need more time to think about this, I can call later this week."
- "If that amount is too much, let us know what you would consider."
- "If this doesn't sound like something you want to do, we'll understand."
- "Maybe our timing is off—perhaps you would like to wait until the community campaign is completed?"

Unfortunately, these comments are not merely a harvest from a rich imagination; they are drawn from real-life confessions.

We need to maintain faith while waiting, and not second-guess our prospects. We should not play bad tapes in our heads, ones that say the prospect is not really interested and we have made fools of ourselves. That is nonsense. The prospect is just trying to formulate a response. Be patient.

9. Work with the Prospect's Answer and Close

You will hear one of three basic answers, yes, maybe, or no.

If the answer is yes, be enthusiastic but businesslike. This is not a time to be overly cool; it is all right to show your pleasure. Your solicitation team and the donor should be feeling a level of joy over your mutual decision to solve a community problem or provide a community enhancement. Determine how the gift is going to be made and over what time period, discuss the kind of recognition that is available and what the donor desires, ask what kind of follow-through is needed from the organization (letters, reminders, etc.), and have the donor-investor sign the pledge form if the gift will be made over time. Never leave the pledge form behind when the transaction has not been closed; you give up your reason for returning and give control of the transaction to the prospect.

Avoid the impulse to "sell after the close." Also borrowed from sales training, this behavior is inspired by relief over getting the gift. Suddenly the tension is gone; you remember all the things you wanted to say. You remember reading somewhere once that you should relax and enjoy the moment. Instead of directing this newfound excitement and energy into making a gracious and timely exit, you start restating your case as part of your thank you: "Thank you so much! Your gift means we'll be able to provide job training to 60 more people each year. Do you know what that means? Blah, blah, blah. . . ." The donor-investor, who has made the commitment, does not need to hear all of this again. In all likelihood, your 30 minutes is more than up, and everyone should get back to work. Exit smiling, and be happy for the gift.

If the answer is maybe. Hide your disappointment. This is an easier response to deal with than when you first hear it. The conversation is far from over and the answer could be yes within a few minutes or days. The prospect (Ed) says, "Well, that's an intriguing proposition. You're right, I'm very interested in the project. But I think I need to be more informed about your overall financial picture, not just this campaign, before I'm ready to make a gift of this size." If you have come prepared with backup material, including budgets and financial statements, you can review them. You can also offer to arrange a meeting for him with your chief financial officer (unless you thought to bring your CFO along, too). Whatever the strategy required, keep it on track and set a time-frame to retain the momentum. Don't say, "Sure. I'll drop that information by for you tomorrow. When you have had a chance to read it, give us a call. Then we'll set something up." That is too vague. Instead, say you'll come by and go over it with him. Set a time right then. Keep the process moving. Most maybe answers convert to yes before long.

If the prospect says no. Be gracious. This can happen, even with a well-cultivated potential investor. However, by the time someone agrees to see you and has entered into a relationship with you, chances are strong that a gift of some size will eventually be made. The operative words here are "of some size" and "eventually." With people who have been treated like potential investors during their interactions with the organization, the "no" that you hear will probably be a qualified no. Usually the prospect will say why the answer is no. Sometimes, you have to ask what no means. "Naturally, we are disappointed. Would you mind saying what led you to this decision?" Avoid the word "why" when someone has said no: it puts people on the defensive.

Most often, the prospect will qualify the no for you without your asking: "No, I just couldn't do that large a gift this year." Your response should be, "What amount would you feel comfortable giving this year?" Or, "Could you make the gift over two years? We would be able to continue construction with a bridge loan if you would be willing to make the gift over that period of time." Note that no counteroffer (lower amount) was suggested. In philanthropy, it is not in good taste or judgment to enter into a series of offers and counteroffers. This is not a real estate transaction or other commercial negotiation. In nonprofit organizations, we diminish the donor-investor attitude when we put people on the defensive by asking for repeated levels of gifts which they are unable or unwilling to make. We don't ask, "How much could/can you give?" because the prospect may be very capable of making the gift we have asked for or even a larger one. Capacity to give is not the issue. We want to know what they would feel comfortable giving to this project.

Another qualification for "no" is timing. "I'd love to help, but you've come at the wrong time. Between now and the end of the year I'm just overwhelmed with financial responsibilities with the business and personally, what with two kids in college." The response is obvious: "What would be a better time for you? I am sure we could work out a schedule for financing the construction that would enable you to give your gift next year instead." When "no" is really just a postponement, be sure to follow-through in an agreed-upon time period. Gifts are sometimes lost to organizations because of failure to follow-through. Set up a manual or computer-based tickler file to ensure closure on all pending solicitations.

One way to phrase the follow-up question to a no based on timing or amount is an "if/then" response. "If you could make this gift over a period of a year, then would you consider our request for $10,000?" Often this alternative lets the prospect see a way to comfortably make a larger gift.

Sometimes, no really means no. "You folks know how much I like your organization, but, quite frankly, I just can't get excited about this project. I am concerned that we are running head-on into what the youth symphony is doing with their outreach program, and I don't think there is a big need for this additional program. I think there are enough resources already to meet this need." There are several options that help keep the door open.

- Continue talking with the prospect about ways in which the youth symphony program and yours are different.
- Do additional research and cultivation to find out if this is really the objection or whether it is deeper (the arts in general, redundancy in community programs of any kind, etc.).
- Find another program that will capture her interest and present it to her—underwriting a concert, funding the first flute chair for a year, and so on.

When you hear the absolute unequivocal no you cannot help but feel disappointed, perhaps puzzled, and certainly chagrined. "I hate to turn you folks down, but as I have listened to you and gone over your materials I have to say that this is just not our priority. We feel that programs like this are good for the community, but I don't think this is where we want to put our charitable dollars this year. It has been a tough decision, and we are sorry." You have invested a great deal of time in this potential donor-investor. You need to find out if there was anything about the cultivation or solicitation that you could have done better. You will want to keep the relationship alive. You may say, "Naturally, we are very disappointed, but we appreciate your interest in what we are doing and hope that you will want to stay informed and, to the extent possible, involved. May we call on you next year and tell you how the project is progressing?" The person who has turned you down is feeling uncomfortable at this point and will welcome this gracious exit line. Keep the prospect informed during the year, and remember to make an appointment as promised.

10. Follow-Through

Do whatever needs to be done following the meeting. Each response (yes, maybe, no) has its own set of follow-through requirements. Be sure you follow through quickly, professionally, and warmly, no matter what the response has been.

- If the answer was yes, remember that this individual or institutional donor-investor has just entered into a new or renewed relationship with you. Investors expect information, attention, and involvement.
- If the answer was maybe, follow through with required information or meetings with others until you have closed.
- If the answer was no, keep the door open if at all possible and try to find an opportunity or time that will be right for the gift.

This 10-step sequence is straightforward, and relatively easy to implement once an organization understands the entire development process. Its success increases with experience.

SHEDDING OLD ATTITUDES

The success of the 10-step process increases as fear of rejection subsides and solicitation teams put away their tin cups. Confidence is also a fundamental success factor. Turn negative phrases, which recur in our minds as we prepare for a solicitation and cause us to be tentative and ineffective, into positive statements:

- "I'm sure they won't want to give."
  "I think this is an opportunity they will really like."
- "They just made a gift—we can't ask them again so soon."
  "This giving opportunity is very exciting. While they may feel it is too soon after their last gift, let's ask anyway. It's their decision."
- "I don't think they are ready to be asked yet."
  "We've been tracking this cultivation very well, and I think they are ready to talk seriously about a commitment. Let's arrange a meeting and see how they respond to some initial ideas."
- "I'm sure they wouldn't want to come . . . they are so busy."
  "Their good friends, the Ryans, are coming to the event. Let's call and extend a personal invitation, and see if they and the Ryans would join us for cocktails before the larger reception. They could meet the conductor and some of the musicians."
- "He wouldn't have time for an appointment: I'll just write a letter."
  "Seeing him face-to-face would be a major advantage to us. I'll call him so he'll know how important this effort is to me. After all, we have been friends a long time."
- "I know I'll say the wrong thing."
  "Getting into these conversations is always hard for me. I do better when someone else is with me. Could you join me on this call?"
- "I can't possibly ask for that much."
  "I want to make sure that is the right amount. Have we done adequate research and cultivation to know we're on target? If so, I'm glad to ask. My gift was smaller, but it was a stretch for me and I can ask her to stretch also."
- "I am probably the wrong person to be asking for the gift."
  "I just want to make sure I am the right person to ask for the gift. This is a very important solicitation. If you feel I am, then I'll do it."

Undoubtedly, you have heard others say these negative things or said or thought them yourself. This focus on ourselves, and the tendency to second-guess the prospect, is a major deterrent to successful implementation of the solicitation process. Positive phrases, whether said or thought, build confidence in you and others.

We must not approach those who have the capacity to benefit our organizations with an attitude that we want something they don't want to give. Instead, we must approach them with the attitude that we have something they want—an opportunity to invest in an organization that is strengthening their community, solving problems of concern to them, and providing programs or services in which they believe.

The Donor's Perspective

We need to look at fund raising, the process of inviting investment, from the potential donor-investor's standpoint. Put yourself in the potential donor-investor's shoes. You have been cultivated over a period of months (or perhaps years) by an organization whose values and purposes are consistent with yours. You have concern, capacity, and connection with and for the mission and, increasingly, the organization. A relationship has been built through the effective application of all or most of the steps in the development process. There is synergy and involvement between you and the organization. You have attended events, been taken to lunch, met the Executive Director and been asked for your opinion on matters within your expertise. At this point, if you are an individual investor prospect—or an individual representing an organization over whose resources you have some influence—you will want to do something for this organization.

Testing the Waters

In one major campaign, the president of an educational organization met during the campaign planning phase with a long-time friend of the organization who was a previous large investor. The purpose of the meeting was only to test the concept of a particular capital campaign objective. The objective was a favorite of the president's, and his passion and enthusiasm were apparent. By the end of the meeting, both individuals were on the edge of their chairs with excitement about the potential for this particular project. The potential funder immediately offered, "I want to make this happen. How much do you need?" Those last four words, along with "How can I help?" are the words you want to hear after you have made a presentation to a potential donor-investor. They signify a true investment attitude.

In this instance, however, there was a problem. The project was so embryonic that there was no cost estimate yet. The president could not ask for an early gift. So, he did the wisest thing possible; he asked this individual to join the project planning task force. As the planning progressed and the project was defined, the organization asked for and received a substantial lead gift from him. This was a true investor partnership; the external funder teamed with the internal organization to create a project that would enhance the organization and its constituents.

Unasked Prospects

Some potential donor-investors self-identify and make a gift on their own initiative, but most wait to be asked. Fairly experienced donors, when finally asked by an organization for a gift, have often expressed their relief: ("I thought you'd never ask"). Successful asks are greatly influenced by timing. Too early or too late, and the results may be doomed or diminished. Untold gifts are "left on the table" because we let our fears, anxieties, or disorganized follow-through get in the way of the relationship between the potential or renewed donor-investor and the organization.

In a major campaign for a cultural organization, an individual who was being cultivated for the lead gift had no real relationship with the organization. The pursuit of the gift was based on the prospect's perceived desire to attain community recognition through a significant naming opportunity. After months of discussions with the individual and her family, the negotiation broke down and the potential donor withdrew. The organization's board of directors, which had been meeting more often than usual and was very involved in some exciting facilities and program planning, had been kept regularly informed of the progress of the solicitation (although the name of the prospect was appropriately kept confidential) and were promptly informed when the solicitation discussions ended. A few hours after this grim news was announced, the chair of the board received a call from one of the board members, an individual who had made a substantial gift to the organization the previous year. Although this individual was on the key prospect list, it was felt by the board development committee volunteers that his recent gift was so large they should not go back to him right away. In his phone call to the board chair, the board member asked why he had not been asked to make the leadership gift, and then proceeded to offer the lead naming gift.

The story has some fundamental points which apply to organizations of all sizes and to all investor gifts.

- The individual was already invested because of his involvement with the organization and his previous gifts. As a member of the board he was very aware of the organization's impact in the community, and very involved with the substantial and carefully crafted future plans.
- He had solid relationships with board and staff.

- Happy with the results of his previous investments, he was delighted to make another investment to ensure the success of the campaign and the future of the organization.
- Through this gift, he was ensuring the maximum possible benefit to the organization from his previous impact gift as well. With the new facility, the program he supported would have more space and prestige. The naming opportunity was very appealing to him for deeper reasons than recognition in the community. He already felt pride from the impact of his previous gifts on the institution.
- The organization had decided *not* to ask him for the leadership gift and chose, instead, someone with whom there was no relationship and for whom this was more a business transaction. They had second-guessed the objections of the person who did make the gift, instead of thinking of the leadership gift as an opportunity for him to act further on his values and deepen his investment.

How Investment Leverages Investment

Another story is pertinent. The success story of the campaign for the San Francisco Museum of Modern Art, completed in 1994, was widely reported at the time. The museum's highly committed board members and friends, determined that San Francisco should have a world-class museum for modern art, were willing to make huge commitments themselves in order to leverage gifts from others. They wanted to inspire the people of San Francisco that this was an important civic venture whose success depended not only on leadership gifts but on a broad base of community supporters. So effective was the campaign in involving the community that the number of patron ($1,000) and smaller-gift donors exceeded all expectations—most of them coming from a direct mail piece that was positioned in terms of this being an investment in the cultural future of the city (see Exhibit 5.2). The letter was a superlative example of an investor appeal, framed as an opportunity to be part of something very special. The $70 million given by the board of directors attracted widespread publicity and admiration. One of its major benefits was the leveraging of $20 million in support from others in the community. It is equally important that museum membership swelled threefold during the campaign (even though the new Museum was not yet open) and that the Museum continues to be extremely well-attended by residents and visitors. The base of midlevel donors also increased impressively.

EXHIBIT 5.2 A Direct Mail Letter Which Invites Investment

December 15, 199X

_____

_____

San Francisco, CA 94123

Dear Ms. _____,

Let me introduce you to San Francisco's newest landmark—the new SFMOMA.

It's an imaginative design of galleries, learning areas and performance spaces, integrating collections, exhibitions and educational resources with greater accessibility for everyone.

Quite frankly, when I agreed to chair the final phase of the New Museum Campaign—soliciting the Bay Area community and SFMOMA members—I was flattered to have the privilege to invite members to help complete this project.

If anybody's been waiting for this museum, it's you.

In fact, I believe your question is not whether you will help support the new museum, but how much to give.

All in the community will be given a chance to participate in the museum's completion and we're confident the response will be strong. But the reality is we must ask, and rely on, museum members like yourself for the bolder commitments.

In a few days you will receive a call from an SFMOMA representative who will be speaking with you about your participation in the New Museum Campaign.

Right now, before the call, I'm asking you to consider a pledge of $83 per quarter over three years for a total gift of $1,000, placing your name in the New Museum Grand Opening Commemorative Book.

And because this may be asking you to consider a larger gift than you may have given to SFMOMA before, I want to make some points with you, in advance of the call, about the new museum.

In addition to the distinctive Mario Botta design, planning for the new museum has involved consultation with an array of professionals with expertise ranging from museum curatorship and education, to installation and lighting design.

The impact of the new museum will be immediate and enduring:

(Continued)

EXHIBIT 5.2 *(Continued)*

- improving educational resources for all sectors of the community, opening its doors to children, adults, students, and teachers;
- attracting exciting exhibitions from the U.S. and abroad;
- increasing donations of art to a facility capable of showing and interpreting those collections and gifts;
- creating a cultural landmark of regional pride for Bay Area residents and tourists alike.

The new SFMOMA provides a rare event: a new modern art museum in America's most deserving city. There are few philanthropic activities that offer such far-reaching impact and continuing influence. It's an occasion for you to share ownership of an exhilarating new concept with a different world view than other museums, just as San Francisco is so different than other major cities.

The museum representative who calls will speak with you about the schedule of choices available for your pledge. Again, I encourage you to consider the New Museum Grand Opening Commemorative Book naming opportunity.

 - I'll add my appreciation for your faithful support and my hope that we'll add your name to the new SFMOMA.

With sincere thanks,

Steven H. Oliver

Steven H. Oliver
Chairman
New Museum Campaign Council

Inspiring Investment at all Levels

The investment attitude should frame all development and fund raising activities. While we have focused in this chapter on the face-to-face invitation to invest, other kinds of fund-raising materials and programs require a similar thrust.

Be sure direct (mass appeal) and select (personally addressed) mailings reflect the investment opportunity a gift to your organization offers. Coach phone volunteers not to use phrases like, "We're desperate. If we don't get the matching funds for this grant we will lose it." Inspire, don't discourage, potential donor-investors.

The whole development process is really an investment process. People who have been properly "developed" want to invest. The chronic fund-raising problems of many organizations can be attributed to their unwillingness to invest in the process of development. They do not put the time or resources required into the steps described in Chapter 4. These organizations find themselves exhausted year after year, trying frantically to fundraise from a donor base on which they have records (maybe) but with whom they have no relationship.

Board members in these organizations are usually able to confine their "development" activities to signing the year-end appeal, selling a few tickets for a raffle or event, and providing board approval for foundation and corporate grant proposals developed by staff. They are most often relieved that this is the extent of the demands on them. They are shy and uncomfortable about talking with people personally about giving. Routinely, they refuse to participate in phone appeals using the excuse that they themselves hate to be disturbed at dinner. There is a cartoon which shows a person answering the phone, with a spouse or friend still at the dinner table. The cartoon caption reads, "And to think, if I hadn't been home having dinner tonight I might have missed this wonderful investment opportunity." While these exact words may never be heard during a phone appeal, volunteers should not underestimate the interest and willingness of people in their communities to support their organizations.

Fear of Rejection and the Face-to-Face Ask

For many board members, even in organizations where "PS-athons" (signing letters at a group meeting) and phonathons are regular board activities, actually asking someone face-to-face for a gift fills them with paralyzing fear. Because they view the transaction from their own personal involvement in it, rather than from the perspective of the potential investor and the organization realizing mutual benefits, they submit to the most commonly expressed fear, rejection.

No one wants to be told no. Remember that the fear of rejection comes from the belief that the most common response to a request for funds will be negative. Believers in the development or investing process know that those who will turn us down have self-selected out of the process, for the most part, before the ask is made. Those with whom we seek that precious investor relationship become increasingly involved with the organization through the development process (Chapter 4). If they were not interested, they would not keep responding to requests or invitations.

Boards and staff that are fearful and reluctant about fund raising, and in a state of urgency regarding the need for their campaign to be a success, should not be faulted or criticized. Instead, we should fault the legacy of misunderstanding about the importance of the development process, about the concept of investment, and most of all, about the powerful role board members play in building a better community. When these things are understood and believed, solicitors can approach the previously daunting task of asking for money with much more confidence and comfort. The tin cup is retired.

People involved in development know they are not asking for money because their organization has needs, but because the community has needs which their organization can meet.

Pressure and Release

Positioned in this way, the solicitation steps guide a transaction in which investment in a vital community resource is requested from an individual or organization whose values, interests, capacity, concerns, and connection have been reinforced by the cultivation process. Operating in the context of the three-part model of philanthropy, development and fund raising (Chapter 1), fund raising is the activity that gives donors an opportunity to act on the things they value. It is an invitation to invest. As such, the ask itself should never be a time of pressure for the prospect. Instead, it should be a time of release.

The person being asked should know the sense of fulfillment that comes from being able to make a difference, large or small, in the lives, futures, or well-being of people in the communities served by the institutions they support. The asker should also find satisfaction in knowing that an opportunity has been offered for the donor-investor to become further involved. If the prospect declines the opportunity, the asker should not take this as rejection. Instead, he should view the transaction from the prospect's perspective. This may be the wrong time, the wrong project, the wrong amount. But, keep the door open. This person is interested and, when the conditions for investment are right, may invest.

OVERCOMING OBJECTIONS

Objections are really masked values. If potential donor-investors express concern about how money is managed in your organization, you can infer that they place value on sound money management. Other investors will focus on different areas—program, planning, board involvement. Listen carefully to those objections, and respond to them with these guideposts in mind:

- Never beat an objection. Meet it, instead. "I can understand why that would be upsetting to you." "You certainly have a right to be concerned about how your investment would be handled."
- For strong objections, use the "feel, have felt, felt" sequence: "I know exactly how you must feel. I have felt that way myself (only if you honestly have), and others have said they felt that way, too." This assures the objector that these feelings are not only accepted, but understood.
- Know that there are four kinds of objections, each requiring a slightly different response:
  - *Misunderstanding.* This is the simplest. You can respond with facts. "No, while it was true that 70 percent of our board members were parents, we now have a board which is half parents and half representatives from the community. The self-interest concern you have expressed was the reason for altering that balance."
  - *Skepticism.* This requires an outside opinion or objective evidence to dispel. "I can understand why your previous experience with scholarship funding at your university was unpleasant. Let me arrange for you to meet with one of our community college scholarship donors. She can answer your questions about the way we interact with our students and donors—and how we encourage them to get to know each other. I think you'd enjoy meeting Naomi Windust, and I'd be pleased to set that up so the two of you can meet by yourselves."
  - *Disinterest.* Often, this is *seeming* disinterest. Probing reveals that there is a strong and sometimes emotional basis for apparent disinterest. An example would be donors who have stopped giving to their local symphony. A volunteer telephones and gets a somewhat cool response, accompanied by the comment, "I really just don't care about the orchestra anymore." The caller can say, "I'm sorry to hear that. We're really excited about the things that are happening now. Have you been to the concerts recently? Are you getting our publications?" This may trigger a revealing response: "Yes, I'm getting the publications. I can't believe they fired the conductor! He was the best musical director I ever heard. I just cannot imagine what they were thinking." Having uncovered the real objection, you can determine what kind it is. It may be very serious, (he was fired) or it may be a misunderstanding (the conductor resigned).

- *Real Drawback.* This is usually a game breaker. Most often, these come up early in the development-investment process or on a phone solicitation. Seldom do people with this kind of feeling about an organization allow themselves to be drawn deeply into the investment process. With such objections, seek balance. Help them see that, although the organization has failed or offended them in some way, that there are some worthy aspects of the outcome or the organization. Parents whose children are qualified for admission but not accepted to the parents' alma mater(s) are primary examples. They are angry and disappointed. The first phone call or letter they receive after the rejection triggers a whole array of feelings and the volunteer solicitor is the recipient. First, listen. Second, restate what you just heard. "If I understand you, your son, who had a 4.0, was student-body president, editor of the yearbook and ran cross-country at the national level, was not admitted to the university." Then add "I don't blame you for being disappointed. Was your son counting on going to the university, or did he have other alternatives?" Sometimes this shift away from the injured parent to the student (who is probably by that time enjoying another university) changes the focus of the parent's feelings.
- Coach all volunteers on the potential objections they may confront, and equip them with materials that will help them respond. Several organizations have developed objection-response lists that pinpoint specific objections and provide precise responses. The danger is that the volunteer, on hearing an objection, will say "Oh, that's number seven on my list. Let me look up the answer." Volunteers must internalize and master these responses! For training purposes, such lists are vital.
- Keep CLASP in mind. This acronym summarizes critical listening skills which are helpful in handling objections and in keeping the entire solicitation on track. It was a training tool developed for the Keystone Program of the Stanford Centennial Campaign.
  Clarify if you don't understand what the person has said. If you feel you would like to have them repeat it, say so. Otherwise, you may end up building an entire case around erroneous information.
  Link by listening for interests and concerns expressed by the potential donor-investor. Link them back into a program or opportunity in which you want them to invest. "A few minutes ago you mentioned your concern about the loss of music in our schools. I'd like to tell you about one of our programs. . . ." Such statements please the prospect because they indicate you are listening. They also connect what you are about to say to something he or she already feels is important.

Acknowledge the feelings evidenced when objections, interests, and ideas are expressed during the meeting. "I know just how you feel," "That's a great idea. Let me tell you something we're doing that relates very well to that." Convince the prospect that you are genuinely interested.

Summarize at intervals to keep the meeting moving forward within the timeframe, and to signal a shift in the transaction. "This opportunity to review how our community must address the needs of the homeless, and to hear your ideas about our programs, has been very enjoyable for us. Our time is nearly up, and we'd like now to make our proposal to you regarding the financial commitment we hope you will be willing to make. . . ."

Pace involves the speed and nature of the communication. If you speak at a rate that is too fast or too slow for the person with whom you are trying to communicate, the exchange will be less effective. This is good to remember when working with older people, sight or hearing impaired people, or people whose native language and yours are not the same. The signals will be obvious to you. If you speak too quickly or too slowly, you will lose their attention, and MEGO (Mine Eyes Glazeth Over) will set in. As you get to know your prospects, gauge their pace and make any necessary adjustments to yours.

INCREASING ORGANIZATIONAL INVOLVEMENT IN THE INVITATION TO INVEST

Board members, other volunteers, donors, and program staff need to feel that they can be helpful in many stages of the development process and that asking for money directly is not the only way to bring investors into organizations.

Because the development partnership is complex and inclusive, it provides opportunities for people to become involved in numerous ways. Here are two examples.

The Reluctant Board Member

In one organization there was a long-time board member who told each new board chair that she would "do anything but fund raise." Remaining on the periphery of development, she was always a willing hand when it came to stuffing envelopes or sorting lists or being a superb hostess for visitors. And, her contribution to the success of a small campaign was impressive. First, when only 6 of the 25 board members provided lists of potential prospects for the campaign, her list was among the first to be received and was the longest and most detailed. Second, when asked to review the list with the campaign committee, she spent a great deal of time providing some rich insights to her already complete written comments. Third, as the campaign committee met with the people on her list, their praise for her as the person who had connected them to the organization and kept them in touch over the years was glowing and consistent. Fourth, she was diligent about reporting to staff any conversation she had with people on her list regarding the campaign. As the campaign evolved, several of the people she recommended were in the top tier of prospects. She was responsible for connecting this organization with many people whose gifts will have long-term impact on its development and successful fund raising. But, by her own admission, she preferred not to fundraise.

The Satisfied Donor-Investor

In another campaign, an individual in the community with tremendous capacity and concern for the mission of the organization was brought in initially through a personal relationship with the campaign consultant. He developed an immense admiration and respect for this organization as he came to know the staff and board who were involved with the campaign. On several occasions, he made it a point to say how impressed he was with the way in which the organization was managed; low profile and high productivity. It was his kind of organization. His expertise relative to the project was carefully sought by campaign leadership. His limited time was used wisely. He was kept well informed as several potential sites for a new building were evaluated. His own gift was definitely an impact gift. In spite of his other major commitments in the community, he "stretched" for this organization which had come relatively late into his giving interests. But what he did after making his own gift was very significant. He leveraged several gifts from local foundations, one of which was larger than the one requested by the organization in its proposal, and he worked creatively to secure several corporate and individual gifts.

Satisfied investors not only commit their own resources. They are also willing to become advocates for the organization. It is not unlike someone who has made a fantastic investment on Wall Street who wants to tell everyone what a good deal it is and encourage others to invest.

Inviting investment extends beyond the actual ask. The entire 10-step development process (Chapter 4) is a process of investing: time, research, and resources by the organization and its board and staff; time, interest, and concern by the prospect.

LEARNING TO LOVE THE NEW APPROACH

When the phrase investor or investment first surfaced in not-for-profit circles more than a decade ago, there were voices of resistance. There were concerns, some of which may still linger. These include:

- For some, it seems to put nonprofits on the same funding premise as businesses, thereby denying their unique position in the community. This may actually be a good comparison to make. We need to place more emphasis on "capitalizing" our sector; we need to provide the solid foundation of endowment or rotating operating reserve funds that will ensure an organization's ability to consistently meet the needs of the community even in the event its annual funding or earned income sources temporarily run dry. If people with capacity and concern would view a substantial investment in endowment or operating reserve as a way to not only strengthen the organization, but also to ensure the continuation of the program or service in the community, it would make a vast difference in our ability to consistently meet human needs. It would help stabilize our communities.
- For still others, investment implied that donor-investors would want more say in the management and image development of the organization, and the thought made some nonprofit managers uncomfortable. Managers of nonprofits should welcome community input. Organizations should actively seek wise investors who want to give their time, opinions, and ideas as well as their money. Those are all true gifts.
- For still others, it conveyed the notion that there would be some kind of monetary return or payback on the investment. This was a misunderstanding, although at least one organization reportedly tried to launch a "loan program" disguised as an investment opportunity. This thinly veiled emergency funding effort invited investors to make gifts now, which would be returned in their entirety five years later. The gifts were really no-interest loans. Although its failure to generate funds was blamed on the lack of tax benefit for the donor,

EXHIBIT 5.3 Top Ten Keys to Successful Solicitation

(As gleaned from Kay Sprinkel Grace's "Putting Away the Tin Cup"
Workshops)

10. "God gave you two ears and one mouth. Use them in that ratio when
    making an ask."
9. "We have seen the donor, and he or she is us."
8. Results, results, results!
    People helped, people helped, people helped!
    Alleviating suffering. Enhancing human potential.
    WHAT WE DO.
    WHY WE DO IT.
7. Heart to heart.
    Uncover people's VALUES through open-ended questions
    (Tell me more about . . . How did you first learn about our organiza-
    tion . . . What issues today really concern you . . .?).
6. Person to person.
    BUILD RELATIONSHIPS by being yourself. Chat a bit. Explain why you
    called. Believe in it. "Fund raising is a contact sport."
5. INVESTMENT.
    Don't think "donation." Don't think "contribution." Don't think any-
    thing that connotes a passive relationship with the organization. An
    investment is *dynamic*. Donors get a values payoff. You can "bank on
    results."
4. Agree with people.
    Whatever someone's objection, honor it. Respect it. Say you under-
    stand. But . . . try to get back to your own heart, as well as theirs. Tell
    them why, among all causes, yours is one of the most important.
    We're all in this together.
3. Make your own gift first.
    People will gauge their commitment by yours.
2. Get to the point. Make the point. ASK FOR A SPECIFIC AMOUNT.

    And . . .
    the number one key to a successful fund raising solicitation . . .
    the Nike philosophy . . .
1. JUST DO IT!

*(Prepared by Claire Axelrad, Jewish Family and Children's Services, San
Francisco, 1993.)*

another major reason was the absence of philanthropic values and principles. This was a purely financial transaction which only seemed to benefit the organization.

The true payback in the kind of investment discussed in this chapter is the satisfaction and values reinforcement derived from seeing the results of the investment at work in the community.

SUMMARY

The investment attitude has the potential to shatter the myths that keep our sector in a supplicant posture, myths that still exist in communities across the United States and around the world.

Inviting investment is the high point of the development cycle, the culmination of the six preceding steps in the development process. It requires board and staff members to act within their development partnership to ensure the most meticulous planning and implementation of the ask itself. Fund raising is a contact sport. We cannot invite investment from a distance. One organization summarized the tin cup (Chapter 2) and Investment themes (Chapter 5) in Exhibit 5.3.

The framework and the process for inviting investment are critical strategies and skills for volunteers and staff. Lasting investment only comes when the potential donor-investor has been engaged in a relationship with the organization that stimulates a desire to invest.

Capitalizing the Community's Investment: Annual Campaigns

Individual and institutional funders become involved donor-investors when they are offered regular opportunities to strengthen the organizations to which they have given. The vehicles most commonly used for building a base of donor-investors are annual and capital campaigns. All viable community-based organizations should maintain a cycle of annual fund-raising programs, and most will find themselves seeking capital funding for buildings and/or endowment at one or more times.

This chapter examines annual campaigns as they relate to the overall organizational purpose of building a base of donor-investors who will be partners with the organization in ensuring the continued delivery of programs and services. Chapter 7 presents capital campaigns in the same framework.

At the outset, a view of annual and capital campaigns as they relate to overall capitalization provides a valuable comparison.

ANNUAL AND CAPITAL CAMPAIGNS

The specific purposes for each campaign differ, but the general purpose for both is the same: to increase capitalization of an organization. Capitalization is defined as the production and retention of sufficient financial resources by a nonprofit organization to ensure its ability to withstand changes in the flow of earned or contributed revenues and keep programs and services healthy. Increased capitalization is achieved through annual campaigns which ensure an adequate cash flow to support current programs without incurring debt. Capital campaigns increase endowment and/or raise overall capacity to deliver programs through the acquisition, remodeling, or building of a new facility or the purchase of needed equipment.

Annual Campaigns involve both major and general donors to an organization in yearly opportunities to provide expendable program support. Annual does not mean once a year, it means all year-round. Fundraising activities will include mail, phone and special events. Annual campaigns ensure the visibility of the mission in the community.

Capital Campaigns for buildings, equipment, or endowment, are conducted very occasionally by most organizations. Some universities are now into a regular once-a-decade cycle of capital campaigns. In the United Kingdom and Western Europe, capital campaigns are relatively new and are being successfully conducted by educational and arts organizations, using proven but culturally adapted American development practices. Organizations in Australia and New Zealand, and in some Asian countries, are also becoming skilled capital campaigners.

Campaigns usually require increased staff, outside consultation, and an infusion of leadership. They are short-term, very intensive, and provide an excellent opportunity to increase organizational capacity overall.

The two types of campaigns differ in several ways as illustrated in Exhibit 6.1.

Capital and Annual Campaign Similarities

Both capital and annual campaigns raise vital funds and are a key way to sustain donor relationships and a sense of investment. Annual fund raising involves the donor-investor as a participant in keeping the mission visible in the community. Capital fund raising provides a rare or occasional opportunity for a donor-investor to play a major role in helping an organization build its long-term capacity, capability, and resources. Only by maintaining strong program support (annual campaigns) and building a solid foundation of endowment and facilities capacity (capital campaigns) can an organization position itself as an attractive philanthropic investment. The two functions complement each other and are also basic processes for maintaining donor-investor relationships.

EXHIBIT 6.1 The Difference Between Annual and Capital Campaigns

	Annual	Capital
Duration	On-going, all year-round	Limited time period (1–5 years)
Source of gifts	Discretionary income	Assets or estate for some; income for others
Range of gifts	Small to large	Emphasis on large in early phase; small to large in later phase
Focus	Current program support	Building, equipment, and/or endowment
Purpose	Donor acquisition, renewal, upgrade; sustain cash flow; renew mission awareness; keep relationship strong with investors.	Major capitalization of buildings, endowment, equipment; involvement of major individual and institutional funders as donor-investors

ANNUAL CAMPAIGNS

A successful annual giving program includes six principal activities:

1. *Direct (impersonal) mail* to acquire new donors;
2. *Select (personalized)* mail to renew or upgrade donors, and follow-up *phone-a-thons* in which groups of volunteers participate in an evening of calling previous or prospective donors for their gifts;
3. *Personal (handwritten or specially tailored on the word processor) mail* to make a very personal ask for a larger annual gift or set an appointment for a face-to-face call, and *personal phone calls* to follow up on personal letters or to solicit a gift directly; (the personal call to ask for a gift should be followed up by a personal letter);
4. *Face-to-face meetings* for the solicitation of larger gifts or gifts of any size from board members and other special friends of the organization;
5. *Special events* which are both *friend*-raisers (cultivation and stewardship of prospects and donors) and *fund* raisers;
6. *Foundation and corporation* annual funding.

ANNUAL CAMPAIGNS: DEVELOPMENT AS WELL AS FUND RAISING

1. Direct Mail

Direct mail, in the purest sense, is an impersonal approach using a standardized letter. It is appropriately reserved for those prospective donors with whom the organization has no current existing relationship. The purpose of the letter is the acquisition of a new donor who is then brought into a relationship with the organization. Yield from direct mail is typically small: 1.5 to 2 percent is an excellent response; .8 percent is not unusual. Such letters are mailed to "cold" or "warm" lists. These lists, which may come from the organization's own database of referred names, from an exchange with another similar organization or be rented from a mailing service, provide names of those whose philanthropic interests make them probable investors in your organization. Organizations are cautioned not to buy lists. Because the percentage of those who will give from a direct mail solicitation is increasingly smaller, it is not good practice to burden an organization's database with a list that may be 98 percent deadwood. When a list is rented, only those who give become part of the organization's database. If a list has been exchanged with another organization or purchased, it is retained as a prospect list; those who give are moved to the donor list. Periodically, evaluate these prospect lists and remove those names which have not responded for a several-year period.

The letter itself is important. Direct marketing ideas have changed, and what seems to be most effective are letters that use short sentences, a great deal of open space, crisp words that catch attention, and have a compelling ask. A simple formula for constructing a letter is: 1) touch my heart; 2) tell me what the problem is; 3) tell me what you are doing about it; and 4) tell me how I can help. An easy-to-use reply card and envelope are essential inserts, and a brochure or other information may also be included.

While the proven results of direct mailings indicate that those names on the list with at least some knowledge of or linkage to the organization or to individuals involved with the organization would be most apt to respond with a gift, there are exceptions. In one instance, a refugee resettlement organization, seeking to build a base of donors, drew on two lists. One was the address book list of the executive director, and one was a rented list from an excellent mailing house that had matched all the variable interests available in its database (refugees, Africa, church affiliation, homelessness). In a result counter to what might be predicted, the list from the mailing house had a better (5%) response than the address book list of the executive director (3%). Although this was a donor acquisition mailing it was a short list (2,000 names) and some of the letters to names on both lists were personalized by notes from the executive director.

Personalization of Mailings

One way to enhance the results of a direct mailing is to personalize it. A newly formed hospital foundation in a rapidly growing semirural area broke all records for an acquisition mailing (22% response) and received initial gifts of nearly $38,000 by using a simple technique known as a "PS-athon." More than 20 volunteers came during the course of an afternoon to write personal notes on nearly 3,000 pieces of mail. The printed letter, well constructed with a compelling message, had been signed by four prominent citizens who were already involved with the foundation. Labels had been generated using numerous lists, and each participant in the PS-athon selected labels from the lists, put them on envelopes, and then changed the "Dear Friend" greeting to "Dear (first name or more formal salutation)" by hand. A PS was added that urged the recipient to join with the signatories and the person writing the PS in this wonderful new organization that would support the hospital under construction. The response was gratifying and gave the foundation a solid base on which to build. A range of donor levels was included in the mailing, and gifts spanned those options ($25–$500). While the personalization of large mailings requires using first class or first-class pre-sort rather than bulk postage, the results justify the cost.

Following Through on Donor Acquisition

The follow-up to an initial mailing is critical. An acknowledgment letter sent 24 to 48 hours after receipt of the gift is an excellent policy to adopt. In the United States, the IRS-appropriate wording regarding any reduction in deductibility of the gift for goods or services received by the donor must be contained in that letter or in a receipt. But the acknowledgment should go further. For too long, organizations have used an internal gift threshold ($100, $500, $1,000) as a way to determine whether or not a donor is brought into a more personal relationship. At these levels, donors are offered opportunities to come to special events or receptions, or they receive a personal call or letter, in addition to the standard receipt or letter, from a board or staff member thanking them for their gift. These internal thresholds build some relationships, but they may also discourage others. Donors can be in a database for years and never receive the kind of personal outreach that could convert them into donor-investors. Many potentially large donor-investors may be hidden in the database for want of some kind of outreach that will unfold their values and their connection to the organization. An initial personal contact, after the first gift, can serve both the organization and the donor.

The Thankathon

"Thankathons"—begun a decade or more ago on college campuses—should be a mainstay in the donor development techniques of all organizations. The thankathon serves a purpose besides thanking donors: it also provides volunteers with opportunities to interact with donors in a conversation that is not driven by asking for money. This increases both the willingness and the comfort level of the volunteers. Shortly after the majority of the gifts have come in from a mailing, a thankathon can be organized. The chair or a member of the development committee is put in charge of organizing other volunteers to participate.

A thankathon uses some of the same structure as a phonathon, which many organizations use for raising money directly or for following up on mail appeals. The key ingredients of a successful thankathon are the same: willing volunteers, a location where there are adequate phones, accurate lists with phone numbers and relevant nonconfidential information including previous gifts and any volunteer involvement, and supervision by a volunteer or staff leader.

A central location for the thankathon works best: the organization's office (if there are enough telephone lines) or a real estate or stock brokerage firm office of a board member or other volunteer. Volunteers, with or without staff participation, are provided with lists of those who have made a recent gift. According to the policies of the organization, the volunteer may or may not know the size of the gift. Volunteers then call donors, using "talking tips" that have been prepared by staff or other volunteers, and thank them for their gifts. Messages can be left on answering machines. When contact is made, the response is warm. Donors are surprised and gratified, and many will ask if this is a call for more money. The answer, of course, is no. This is a call to thank them for their most recent gift. If donors are willing to chat, equip the callers with a few questions (what the donor knows about the organization, what inspired them to give, etc.) so the body of information about the donor can begin to build. More than one thankathon has been followed by additional unsolicited gifts from donors who were touched by the outreach they received. And more than one potentially large donor or estate donor has been initially identified through a thankathon.

2. Select Mail

Select Mail is used for renewing or upgrading gifts from existing donors. In donor development, renewal and upgrade are critical steps in building long-term relationships. These letters are personalized (no "Dear Friend" salutation) and indicate the amount of the previous year's gift as a basis for requesting a renewal or upgrade. The letter must be personalized through a word processing program, be accurate with all program statistics and donor information, and focus on results. Donors want to know what impact their previous gift(s) made in the community through the work of the organization: how many people were fed, how many children were served, how the reviewers welcomed the concerts, and so on. Donors also want to know the status of the need the organization is meeting: how many more seniors still need meals at home, how many more families need child care assistance, how many more schools need the performing or visual arts program. Profile a recipient or participant in the program by way of illustrating, through one example, the impact the donor's investment made on others as well. Keep the message positive, even if the problem you are solving together remains difficult. People want to invest in progress, success, and results. Whiny or depressing letters may garner some sympathy gifts, but true investments are made in those organizations that position themselves as problem-solvers and show their results. The response to letters positioned in this way is strong: donor-investors feel as though they are partners in pursuing the mission and opportunities with the organization. They feel as though their investment is working. At this level, renewal and upgrade of the gift begin to form the basis for an organization to move into a cycle that will enable them to move beyond fund raising and into true donor development and relationship-building.

For both direct and select mail, organizations may use telephone calls after the letters have been sent, if no gift has been received, as a follow-up solicitation technique. This is not a thankathon. The phone follow-up is conducted as a phonathon, and its purpose is to ask the donor for the gift that was requested in the letter to which the person has not yet responded. When the gift comes in, the follow-up to select mail is the same as for direct mail: a letter with appropriate receipt and a thank you call either through a thankathon or, in some cases, personally from a board member or staff person.

3. Personal Mail

Personalized Letters

Personalized letters generated on a word processor or written by hand from one individual to another are highly effective in solicitations. These letters may be sent to existing donors as a next-level solicitation technique, or, in some instances, may be used as the first outreach to a special prospect from someone who knows that prospect well. The power of the handwritten message cannot be underestimated: a full letter, a note on a word-processed letter, or a thank you note all spiral in their effectiveness when handwritten. A lost art, especially in this age of technology, the handwritten letter is read and valued far more than word processed letters. In the donor-investor development cycle, there is a noble place for the handwritten letter or note.

Even those who claim their handwriting excludes them from such an exercise can be persuaded that just a few sentences added on to a word processed letter can make all the difference. In one organization, the CEO writes handwritten notes at every opportunity. These notes are often saved by their recipients and clipped inside the front of their board or committee member binders. Volunteer and staff leaders should fold this idea into their array of techniques for building donor relationships. In a major university campaign, the chair of one program was a talented amateur photographer who made photo note cards for her personal use. The university regularly supplied her with lists of volunteers and donors who deserved or needed special recognition or attention. She would write a handwritten note on one of her photo notecards. During the course of the campaign, more than 200 of these photo notecards were sent to volunteers and donors. The response was very positive, and several volunteers and donors reported they had framed the mounted 4" by 6" photos from the cards. The relationship-building impact of receiving these special handwritten notes was measurable in volunteer retention and donor feedback. The recipients felt they had received unique acknowledgment.

Pre-solicitation Letters

Letters which state a solicitation is impending, but do not ask directly for the gift, are called "presolicitation" letters. No amount is suggested in this kind of letter. Instead, the letter requests that the individual read brief materials which are enclosed, and expect a telephone call from the letter writer or another individual within a prescribed period of time. An essential aspect of this type of solicitation is making the follow-up phone call within the stated time period. Many prospective and previous donors have been puzzled by failure of the writer to follow through with the stated intent to call and ask for a gift or discuss a campaign. These letters should be very personalized, and may be signed by the person who is going to call. Or, the writer may say that another volunteer will be calling.

Follow up on a gift that comes as a result of a personal letter with an appropriate letter and receipt, plus a very personal phone call. This is a delicate and important step in the relationship-building process, and must be executed in keeping with both professional and personal standards.

4. Face-to-Face Solicitation

Face-to-face solicitation of gifts is, of course, the most successful and proven way to engage or reaffirm the investor relationship, reinforce previous giving, share enthusiasm and results, and convey the sense of partnership between the organization and the donor in accomplishing the mission of the organization. There is no substitute for this type of solicitation. Every organization should strive to annually increase the number of prospective and previous donors who are solicited in this manner. This requires increasing the number of trained volunteers who are willing to and capable of participating in this kind of solicitation.

The obvious prospects and donors for face-to-face solicitation are those from whom the anticipated gift is the greatest, which includes not only individual donor-investors, but those individuals who represent corporations and foundations. The techniques for making the ask are covered in Chapter 5. It is the importance of those asks in the annual funding cycle and in relationship-building that are the focus in this chapter. The face-to-face ask, in an organization which is dedicated to developing its donor base into a solid constituency of donor-investors, will be extended beyond major donors, corporations, and foundations to include the following individuals, whether or not their gifts qualify as "major" in the organization's giving level listing:

- All board and key nonboard committee members;
- Those whose gifts represent a major commitment and investment to the organization relative to their capacity to give; and
- Those who have committed a planned (estate) gift to the organization.

Each of these individuals is a major stakeholder in the organization, and should be given the courtesy of an annual face-to-face solicitation.

Board Member Solicitations

Too many organizations solicit their board members by letter, phone call, or "group ask" at a board meeting. These same board members are then expected to go out and solicit gifts face-to-face from others, when they have not been asked themselves in the way they are expected to ask. It is small wonder so many board members are hesitant about making a personal solicitation: they have not had a model to follow based on their own ask. In organizations that understand that going beyond fund raising begins with the board, the annual solicitation of board members is the benchmark for all other major solicitations. The executive director and the board chair have a personal meeting with each board member, individually, on an annual basis. Details of this meeting are discussed in Chapter 9.

Solicitation of Non-major "Major" Donors

In every organization, there are certain donor-investors whose gifts, relative to their capacity to give, are significant. These are the individuals, often living on a fixed income, who send in $25 a month, or $5 a week, or make an annual gift which represents nearly all of their philanthropic discretionary income. Often these are individuals who are elderly, or who may have a sense of involvement with the organization based on some previous service or volunteer experience. An annual visit with them, just to thank them, update them on programs, and tell them how much their gift means to the organization, can do a great deal to build the sense of relationship that dignifies our sector.

Sometimes, the relationship will demand other extraordinary actions. In one unit of the American Cancer Society, the staff was asked by one of their long-time donors, who was widowed, had no family, and lived alone on a farm outside of town, to call him every morning just to make sure he was alive. They did. They also made frequent visits to him when they were in the area. One morning, about two years into their outreach to him, he did not answer the phone. They called the local fire department which went to the farm. They found that he had died sometime during the night. Had these staff people not carried out their promise to him, it could have been considerable time before he was found. His estate, while modest by some standards, was left entirely to the ACS local unit and had a significant impact on their programming for many years to come.

Personal Solicitation of Those Who Have Made Planned Gifts

This approach will strengthen the relationship with those who have made this long-term commitment to your organization. These people are the futurists of the organization. They have made an investment in programs and people they will never see. A planned gift is an act of faith. It is an expression of the donor's belief that the organization in which they are investing is sound, stable, and important. It is also an affirmation of the donor's belief in the importance of the need that is being met, and that the need will not go away. Donors who have made it known that their estate plans include your organization should be treated like major donors even if their annual support falls below the level the organization has targeted for special attention.

Encouragement to give annually, no matter the size of the gift, keeps the planned gift donor involved in the organization. It encourages and strengthens the relationship, and may lead to an increase in the estate gift or a more vigorous participation in annual giving programs. All planned donors should be asked for an annual gift, unless specific instructions prohibit such solicitations. A personal call on these individuals, at least yearly, is critical. Even if an annual gift is not made, the stewardship aspect of such visits is powerful.

The Board's Role in Face-to-Face Solicitations

Board members need to be very active organizers of and the primary participants in face-to-face solicitations. In the United States, where there is a higher comfort level in speaking with people directly about a contribution which reflects knowledge of the potential donor's financial capacity, face-to-face solicitations are increasingly more common and comfortable. Elsewhere, particularly in Western Europe, where there is still much privacy associated with financial capacity and philanthropy, such solicitations are infrequent. There, reliance on personal letters is strong. As the needs of Western European organizations for private funds increase with government pull-backs, solicitation patterns will have to shift. Education about philanthropy and its accomplishments will have to be coupled with an easing of taboos on discussing financial capacity so that appropriate personal solicitations can occur. Australia and New Zealand have a somewhat more open attitude about the implied understanding of an individual's wealth and capacity, but hesitations still remain about the face-to-face solicitation in which those issues could be probed. In the process of evolving donors into donor-investors, these obstacles to personal solicitation can be reduced if the organization approaches the transaction from the sensitivities of the donor rather than from the desires of the organization.

5. Special Events

Special events are both friend raisers and fund raisers. Organizations that depend on an exhausting cycle of special events to raise their annual current program support funds will never go beyond fund raising. Special events are one form of donor acquisition (along with direct mail) and they are useful as stewardship strategies. Even when an event makes a considerable amount of money, two factors must be considered carefully: (1) the *real* cost of the event, including staff time and other indirect expenses; and (2) follow-up to the event. If community members only interact with an organization at their annual spectacular Haunted House Ball and receive no other outreach or information during the year, then the relationship-building opportunity is lost or diminished. Only when the event is positioned in the annual cycle of development activities, and when careful follow-through is done, can the value of events be increased. A few planning and follow-up procedures will heighten the long-term value of a special event to an organization:

- In planning the event, use a checklist or questionnaire that assesses the true costs in time and money, the consistency of the event with the mission of the organization, the resources available (volunteers, staff and money) to allocate to this event, its position relative to the calendar of other community events, etc. (See Exhibit 6.2).
- Draw up a realistic budget and stick to it. Costs of events have a way of mushrooming unless the budget is carefully controlled.
- Have an action plan in which all tasks and assignments are carefully defined and on which there has been agreement by all those who will work on the event.
- Have program/organization description brochures at the event along with a photo display or other means (video) for presenting the purpose and activities of the organization.
- After the event, review the list of attendees and devise follow-up for each. At a minimum, conduct a thankathon in which each participant is thanked and informed about the net amount raised (if solid) and the impact it will make on the organization and the community.
- Send copies of your organization's newsletter, with an accompanying note, to all attendees. Keep them informed throughout the year about the organization's other activities.

EXHIBIT 6.2 Event Planning Form

This form is to help volunteers in planning events for the (organization). If you have an idea for a special event, please fill in this form as completely as possible, then bring it in to the office. Thanks!

I.   Description of the Event:

II.   Purpose(s) of the Event, in measurable terms:
     II.a.   Audience(s):

III.   Planned date(s) of the Event:
     _____ I (we) have checked this date with the following calendars:

IV.   Chair for the event:

V. Committees:	# Volunteers/ Hours Needed	# Staff Hours Needed
Planning/Oversight Chair:		
Underwriting/Sponsorships Chair:		
Advertising: selling ads in the printed program Chair:		
Printing/Mailing Chair:		
Publicity/Media Chair:		
Ticket Sales Chair:		
Program/Entertainment Chair:		
Finance/Budget/Records Chair:		
Food/Wine Chair:		
Logistics: Set-up, Decorations, Clean-up Chair:		

(Continued)

EXHIBIT 6.2 *(Continued)*

VI: Planning Timeline—Day and date of event: _____

Three months in advance: _____
      To do: (activity deadline date)

Two months in advance: _____
      To do:

Six weeks in advance: _____
      To do:

One month in advance: _____
      To do:

Three weeks in advance: _____
      To do:

Two weeks in advance: _____
      To do:

One week in advance: _____
      To do:

Day Before Event: _____
      To do:

DATE OF EVENT: _____
      To do:

Follow-up Activities: _____

Please mark at least two interim "bailout" dates for this event. "Bailout" dates are deadlines by which certain tasks *MUST* be accomplished in order for the event to proceed as planned. Consider changing, postponing, or cancelling the event to cut losses if these deadlines are not met.

(Continued)

EXHIBIT 6.2 *(Continued)*

VII: Planning Budget

Item	Projected/Estimated (Expense estimates based on firm bids)	Actual
Expenses:		
Facility Cost	$ _____	$ _____
Facility Prep	_____	_____
Equipment Rental	_____	_____
Stationery/Invitations	_____	_____
Printing	_____	_____
Postage	_____	_____
Photography	_____	_____
Supplies	_____	_____
Meal Cost	_____	_____
Complimentary Meals	_____	_____
Wine	_____	_____
Decorations	_____	_____
Centerpieces/Flowers	_____	_____
Door Prizes/Awards	_____	_____
Recognition Materials/Gifts	_____	_____
Security	_____	_____
Transportation	_____	_____
Insurance	_____	_____
Other	_____	_____
Contingency ___%	_____	_____
Expense Total:	$ _____	$ _____

(Continued)

EXHIBIT 6.2 *(Continued)*

Income:	Projected/Estimated	Actual
Attendance/Ticket Sales	_____ × $ _____ = $ _____	(#) _____
		$ _____
Cash Sponsorships/Contributions		
1.	$ _____	
2.	_____	
3.	_____	
4.	_____	
5.	_____	
Gross Income	$ _____	$ _____
Gross Expenses	$ _____	$ _____
NET INCOME	$ _____	$ _____
In-Kind Contributions		
1.	6.	
2.	7.	
3.	8.	
4.	9.	
5.	10.	

Don't forget:

☐ Liquor License ☐ Parking ☐ Handicapped accessibility

☐ Insurance ☐ Child Care ☐ Emergency planning

(Form developed by Lisa C. Bennett)

- Add these names to your prospective donor lists for the next acquisition mailing.
- Do a special "volunteer opportunities" insert or separate mailing the first time you mail to these individuals. Include a nonfund-raising program description brochure about the organization if it was not distributed at the event.

6. Foundations and Corporations

Foundation and corporate fund raising fits into the annual cycle to the extent these gifts are solicited annually and represent a form of modest but regular support. Large corporate and foundation gifts for capital campaign or other special purposes—like those for very large gift individual donors—do not fall into this cycle, but the relationships built during the annual outreach are those on which the success of the larger

asks will be based. Often, employee fund gifts are given annually, even if corporate gifts are not. Corporations which match gifts also deserve recognition and a sustained relationship.

Maintaining an annual relationship with corporate and foundation representatives is an essential aspect of donor development. Even in years when an organization is not funded, outreach and stewardship should be afforded to those institutional investors who have played a significant role in capitalizing the organization in the past. These relationships become resources when planning and implementing larger funding drives, or when assembling community advisory boards for general or capital campaign purposes. Funders, whether institutional or individual, must never gain the impression that their only value to you is the money they give. They must believe that their opinions and feedback are important as well. And they must know the impact of their gifts.

Regular communication to donors from the organizations they are funding should convey results: number of people fed in a hunger program, how the dropout rate among high risk students is declining, what treatment breakthroughs have been attained with a new piece of medical equipment. If donors are satisfied with the impact their gifts are making and the way in which their gifts are being managed, they will continue to support the organization. A common myth among organizations that continue to be needs-focused, rather than results-focused, is that it is not a good idea to go back to donors who have recently given substantially to the organization. A needs focus leads to apology for coming back to the donor for more money; a results focus invites the donor to reinvest in a program that is making a major difference in the community. It is the latter approach that gives renewed energy and spirit to fund raising—even in those organizations which have gone beyond fund raising and have implemented solid development practices.

Cycling Annual Fund Activities

Annual fund raising should be energizing to an organization. A carefully crafted cycle should reflect evaluation (see Chapter 11, The Power of Planning) of resources, needs, and potential market, and be timed to provide a regular influx of cash to meet current program support requirements. This requires a process in which the development staff helps set an annual fund goal that is a carefully determined figure within the larger budget. For arts organizations dependent on season or individual ticket income, or organizations which rely on regularly calendared grants from government sources, there are usually periods of diminished cash availability. One important role the annual fund plays is to ensure that periods of scarcity in earned income are countered by annual fund programs which will raise needed funds.

Organizations should develop an annual fund cycle, in which the appropriate annual fund-raising activities are planned in such a way that the cash flow from earned and contributed revenue stays balanced. Program, administrative, and development staff should all be guided by this annual calendar. Exhibit 6.3 shows a sample performing arts organization's cycle. It is a tool for managing fund raising involving volunteers, and for anticipating and responding to cash flow management needs.

Using the Annual Fund Cycle to Capitalize Community Investment

While we think of capitalization as periodic infusion of major dollars into an organization through endowment or building campaigns, the annual fund also functions as an important element in long-term capitalization. An organization whose annual fund raising is weak, even if the endowment is strong, will erode its capital holdings through annual or accumulated deficits. Several of America's symphony orchestras have failed because annual and earned income was insufficient to sustain rising costs. Endowments were invaded, and the orchestras eventually closed their doors. While several have reorganized, even the temporary demise of these important cultural resources was damaging to the community. Moreover, the donor-investors who had sustained these orchestras through their regular annual and occasional capital funding programs were reluctant to provide further capitalization to the new organizations. When they did, they placed certain restrictions regarding budget, endowment, and general management.

Annual fund raising should be guided by an understanding that key donor-investors want to protect their investments. Major individual donors to capital or endowment needs should be included in the annual fund unless they have specifically stated they only wish to participate in endowment or capital funding. Certain institutional funders, including corporations and some foundations, may also participate in annual as well as capital fund drives. As they become increasingly committed donor-investors, they will respond to requests for a variety of opportunities within the organization.

The regional research facility of a national computer company had established a donor relationship with a local children's agency. Its annual gifts were consistent but modest, and the nonprofit agency prac-

EXHIBIT 6.3 Sample Annual Giving Cycle: Performing Arts Organization

	Annual Giving	Earned Income
January	Follow-up phoning to year-end appeal	Recital
February	No new funding activity Thankathon for year-end gifts Foundation grants	Single ticket sales 3rd Concert
March	Spring mailing out 3/26	Subscription renewals begin
April	Spring mailing returns Corporate funding drive	Subscription renewals
May	Spring phone clean-up by volunteers Corporate clean-up by development committee Thankathon for spring gifts	Renewal clean-up by telemarketing firm Single ticket sales Closing Concert
June	Annual major donor campaign; board solicitations	None
July	Thankathon: no new (revenue) generating activity	7/4 Concert in Park
August	Foundation proposals researched and scheduled for fiscal year	New subscriber phone drive
September	Autumn mailing	New Subscriber phone drive Single ticket sales
October	Harvest Ball event	Single ticket sales Opening Concert
November	Phone clean-up to autumn mailing; second round of major asks Harvest Ball Thankathon	Single ticket sales 2nd Concert
December	Clean up all pending solicitations; conduct holiday thankathon with volunteer young musicians calling	Holiday concert single ticket sales

ticed good stewardship. The agency had an opportunity to purchase an important set of reading books for its therapeutic day school; however, all the funds for books and supplies had been spent for the year. The development director called the computer research facility, and talked with her contact there. He put her in touch with the employee's organization, which became interested in the project. From funds that they collected from employees for community and social activities, they made a $3,000 grant which enabled the agency to purchase the books. The following year, frustrated by not having the database on computer, the development director talked with the head of the employee's organization again, but this time about the possibility of the employees donating time to computerizing the data base. They were delighted to do this, and contributed more than 500 hours to the project. At the end of that year, the agency honored these employees with a special reception, at which time they met the teachers and saw some of the students who had benefited from their earlier gift. That relationship continues, even now, more than 15 years later.

PRESENTING MULTIPLE GIFT OPPORTUNITIES TO DONORS

When seeking multiple gifts in a single year, the approach used is critical. Donor-investors will be open to requests for multiple kinds of funding if they are always provided information about results achieved and continuing needs that must be met. Solicitations should reflect program priorities and results, not funding goals alone. Annual fund solicitation letters that begin, "This year our annual fund goal is $75,000. It is important for us to meet this goal, and your gift will help us make it! Please give generously to our annual fund with a gift of $100" miss the point. People don't invest in annual funds, they invest in organizations. The annual fund is a vehicle for investing in an organization, just as the organization is a vehicle for investing in the community.

"Annual fund" is really an internal accounting and function title for the means by which we raise current program support. It implies fund raising that is driven by the organization's fiscal year, rather than by the external needs the organization is meeting. Stanford University, following its successful Centennial Campaign in the 1980s, dropped the word "Annual" and now involves donors in *The Stanford Fund*. This name change, while seemingly subtle, is powerful. Removal of the word annual gives the fund a sense of permanence, and places it appropriately in its role as an element in the overall capitalization and stability of the university. Dropping the word annual creates a greater opportunity to focus on multiple opportunities to contribute on an ongoing basis. It also stretches donor understanding about the size and frequency of their gifts: They can give larger gifts, and/or give more often.

Potential and current funders, who have been brought into a relationship with an organization, tend to look at the organization in a somewhat holistic way. The annual fund, a capital campaign, and/or endowment fund are ways for them to give to the programs in which they believe. They see an orchestra that presents quality programming and solid educational outreach into the schools; a hospital whose emergency and care facilities are of unique service to the community; a feeding program for the elderly that gives meals and companionship; or a childcare program that enables young parents to work or attend school without worry. Those who share the values that underlie these programs invest in the *organization providing* the program. We can confuse donors by thrusting at them the internal labeling we give to the various pockets in which we place our contributed revenue or the way we categorize our donors.

While it is essential to track donor-investors according to size and frequency of gifts, it is equally essential to reserve these labels for internal use only. Consider the following example of an attempted donor relations outreach: a donor of $200, uncertain if his gift had been received, telephoned the nonprofit to talk with a staff person. After several minutes on hold, he was connected with an individual who identified herself as the person in charge of "intermediate donors." The donor was insulted and never contributed to that organization again.

ELEMENTS OF A SUCCESSFUL ANNUAL CAMPAIGN

1. *Board Leadership.* While it is assumed that all successful capital campaigns will have board and community leadership, annual campaigns often become staff-driven and staff-led. While all fund raising should be a partnership between board and staff, the visible leadership in the community should be that of the board. The building of long-term relationships, which enable organizations to go beyond fund raising, begins with board leadership of the annual fund. An annual fund

committee of board and other community members must work with staff to design and implement the process for the campaign, including review of prospect lists, affirmation of the goal, recruitment of solicitation teams, strategy development for prospects, follow-through on solicitation assignments, and successful wrap-up of the campaign.

2. *Participation of volunteer teams.* These teams include not only board members, but those from the community who have an investment in the organization (former board members, committed donors). Prospect assignments to solicitors should be done with the team's participation. A three-part goal motivates the team: a) 100 percent contact with all prospects assigned; b) 100 percent calls completed within the established timeframe for a particular funding drive; and c) a minimum dollar amount raised by each team. For example, if the autumn annual appeal drive has a goal of $100,000, and there are five teams, each team has a *minimum* goal of raising $20,000. Because the contact and completion goals are also in place, the organization is assured that everyone on the assigned lists will be contacted. Goals that focus only on a dollar goal may lead teams or individuals to decide not to call on remaining prospects once they achieve their minimum. It is important to have all three goals. Friendly competition among teams, and recognition for goal achievement, spur teams on to complete all their contacts.

3. *A Plan.* A plan for each year's annual fund raising as part of the over-all development plan is imperative. It should be based on an analysis of the previous year's process and results, establish a goal that is realistic yet a stretch, provide a gift range chart based on the goal and the known prospects for the campaign, contain strategies for acquiring prospective donors and for renewing and upgrading previous donors, set firm timelines for the various components of the annual campaign that are keyed to the earned or granted income cycle of the organization, and provide objectives that will engage and guide the volunteer and staff leaders towards a successful completion in that timeframe.

4. *A goal that is realistic but a "stretch."* Viewing the annual campaign as a means for increasing the capitalization of the organization necessitates setting annual goals which are realistic but a "stretch" for the organization's donors and volunteers. An organization needs more donors and larger gifts each year. In the budgeting process, the annual fund goal is often set without adequate consultation with the development staff. It is viewed as a "plug" figure: whatever project-

ed expenses cannot be met through earned income, endowment or a capital fund drive that may be planned or underway, are "plugged" into the annual giving goal. If this figure is too ambitious, the organization is doomed to a year of cutting expenses or readjusting the contributed income line. Just as detrimental as overstating the amount that must be generated through annual contributions is an overly-cautious approach that provides no challenging increment from year-to-year. These problems can be avoided when the development manager is included in the budgeting process and when volunteer leadership provides the incentive, inspiration, and contacts to assure staff that a more ambitious goal can be met.

5. *A carefully constructed list of prospects.* Attempting an annual campaign with a prospect and donor list that has not been refined, evaluated, expanded, or cleaned up from year-to-year creates both internal and external problems for the organization. The campaign becomes difficult to implement because the lists and assignments are flawed. Previous and prospective donors (who may receive more than one appeal, a letter addressed to a deceased spouse, or not be acknowledged for their previous giving) gain the impression that the organization's systems are in disarray. This reflects poorly on the organization as a whole. List management is a year-round task, the value of which is most apparent when implementing the annual fund-raising programs. Keeping the donor-investor base accurate is essential for a successful campaign. A computer-based donor file management system is an essential tool in maintaining accurate records and tracking donor development.

6. *Strategies that include all donors in a continuum of investment opportunities.* Very often, organizations separate "annual" and "major" campaigns, rather than viewing them as a seamless continuum which can be integrated in a very powerful way. This integration builds solid relationships, and enables the donor to feel an investment in the organization, rather than in a particular funding effort.

In planning the annual contributions campaign for an organization, all potential donor-investors should be arrayed and analyzed. Different approaches for the same donor may be taken from year-to-year, based on the previous year's gift, the donor's concerns, other investments that may have been made in the organization by the donor (e.g., a planned gift or a special gift), or the individual's particular circumstances. In one year, the donor may be asked for a gift of $5,000 to lead the annual giving program. The following year, the same donor may be asked to increase his or her gift overall, assigning a portion of it to the unrestricted fund for current program support and another portion to a particular capital need. In yet another year, that same donor may be asked to make a leadership gift to an endowment or capital campaign, and only a modest gift to the fund for current program support.

When organizations get bound in by their own internal funding compartments, they often miss great opportunities to engage donors creatively in a number of funding opportunities which reveal the range and impact of the organization.

7. *Energize the volunteers with training and "product news."* Board members are reluctant to participate in fund raising because they feel uncomfortable with the asking process (see Chapter 2). Training is a requirement for successful involvement in fund raising for current program support or for capital campaigns. Training should raise the comfort level of all board members who will make phone or face-to-face asks. It should cover the philosophy, strategy and techniques of development and fund raising, and provide practice in the ask itself. The training can be done by a qualified board member, a development staff person, or an outside consultant. To be most effective, the training should occur as close as possible to the actual time the volunteers will be using their new skills. Otherwise, the information retention is poor.

All training sessions should be guided by three goals: information, motivation, and inspiration. The inspiration comes from hearing the product news. For at least 15 minutes, but preferably a half-hour, have one or more individuals who benefit from the organization's programs and services speak to the board and other volunteers about the impact the organization has had on their lives and in the community. This is not a report from a staff person about a program. For social, medical, human services, religious, educational, and similar organizations, it is a presentation by an individual (or the individual's family, employer, coworker) that comes from the heart and is compelling in its impact on the board members who must go out and ask for funds. For arts and cultural organizations, it may be from a school teacher whose classes have benefited from the in-school programs or docent-led tours, or it could be from a performing or visual artist who speaks with passion about what it means to be a part of the nonprofit.

Information is best provided by the administrative, business, and program staff of the organization. Plan a "state of the agency/orchestra/school/hospital" talk by the CEO, followed by financial and program presentations which convey vital statistics about the organization. Board members can use this information in their advocacy and fund raising. Provide fact sheets which summarize year-end financial results, service or audience levels, and the community needs which are being met as well as those which still need to be met. An organization which provides tutoring services to children from a low-income area of the community titled its fund-raising brochure, "The American Dream Has a Waiting List," and then went on to document the problem it was addressing: "Although we were able to work with 120 children this year and achieve measurable increases in reading levels, we still have 65 children on the waiting list. We would like to eliminate that waiting list next year." This kind of information will raise confidence among board members when they present their case for support or answer tough questions.

Be sure the data are clear and well-documented. The information segment is critical: it satisfies the left-brain needs of volunteers and gives them hard data to verify the need the organization is meeting in the community. If you have a full day for training, integrate an opportunity for participants to use this information in a presentation. There are two ways to do this. One way to help board members get comfortable in presenting information about the organization is to provide opportunities for them to tell each other the organization's "story" during the training session. A proven exercise is one in which board members are assigned into teams and are asked to imagine they have been invited by a local service club to make a presentation about the organization. In their preparation, board members receive no assistance from staff. Instead, staff members and the other board teams comprise the service club audience. Teams are given thirty minutes to prepare and five minutes to present. Some teams will choose one person to be the speaker, others will present a panel including all or most of the team members. The purpose of the exercise is to provide a forgiving and honest audience which will, at the end of the presentation, give feedback on the accuracy of the information presented. It is a way for board members to internalize, through practice in using it, the information provided by administrative, business, and program staff. One statewide health services organization in the Pacific Northwest used this process as the entire focus of its annual meeting for its many volunteer advocates. The results were very positive. Board members had a higher comfort level for their advocacy, and staff had assurance that board members were telling an accurate story of their constituents.

The other way is through role playing, in which three person teams are given opportunities to practice a solicitation. Two of the members of the team plan the solicitation and call on the third person, who is the prospect. A structure for the solicitation is found in Chapter 5, "Inviting Investment." Each team member benefits from rotating through all the roles: prospect, primary solicitor, staff or board partner to the primary solicitor. The facilitator or development officer rotates from group to group, listening and providing constructive feedback on both style and accuracy of presentation.

Motivation is the third essential ingredient of a training session. People's motivation increases the more they become engaged with the organization or program, and the more they see the role they can play. The entire training session should be motivating to board members. It should be well-facilitated by an inside or outside facilitator, and have a balanced array of presentations and opportunities for small group interaction. Board members should feel motivated by the professionalism of the organization in the way the session is promoted and managed. The key to continued motivation is individualized follow-up after the session. At the end of the training session, have each board and staff member declare verbally and in writing what they will do to fulfill their development and fund-raising responsibility during the coming year. This can be done in the form of a checklist provided with the training materials, or can be done as a short narrative. Lists or statements are turned in after each person in the room states to the others what they are willing and able to do. The development director, board chair, development chair or CEO issues a thank you letter to each participant for being at the training session, and restates the commitment the individual has made. It is then up to staff and board leadership to keep the person motivated and involved.

8. *Be sure support staff and materials are ready to enhance the volunteer experience.* Whatever part of the annual cycle is being undertaken, staff—as part of the staff-board partnership—should prepare materials and provide support that is professional. Volunteer packets, containing all pertinent information required by volunteers for completing their assignments, should be prepared by staff or volunteer committee members. These materials should include, but not be limited to:

- A fact sheet about the organization and/or the campaign
- Campaign or organizational case statement
- Program and budget information
- Timeline for the annual campaign
- Tips on making successful solicitations

- Principal objections the volunteer may encounter, and the appropriate responses
- A listing of key individuals involved with the board and/or the campaign
- A listing of other volunteers, with phone numbers
- A staff list
- Pledge and/or remit cards
- Stationery and envelopes for thank you letters

Professional and support staff or the volunteer leadership team, where there is no professional development staff, are there to assist board and other volunteers in every facet of their solicitations:

- Reviewing assignments to ensure the greatest degree of knowledge regarding the prospect's capacity, concerns, and connection with the organization
- Coaching in solicitation techniques
- Setting appointments if necessary
- Accompanying board members on calls
- Assisting with follow-up including timely issuance of official thank you and receipt
- Developing appropriate stewardship strategies for each prospect

The partnership between board and staff is recognized by donors, and helps solidify the investor relationship. Having a sense of shared initiative and responsibility in the solicitation process strengthens the feeling of investment and ownership on the part of board and staff.

SUMMARY

Annual campaigns provide the income stream which is the lifeblood of the organization. These expendable funds are also a form of capitalization, as they prevent an operating deficit which can erode institutional image and stability. A strong annual giving cycle invites donor-investors to participate in numerous opportunities for funding, and keeps the mission visible in the community. Annual giving is periodically complemented by the more common form of capitalization, the capital campaign. The following chapter explores aspects of capital funds drives.

Capitalizing on the Community's Investment: Capital Campaigns

A capital campaign is the second way in which organizations capitalize on the gifts of donor-investors and keep their base of financial support strong. When conducted at intervals in organizations which implement successful annual fund raising, these two kinds of campaigns help ensure the safety of community programs provided by the nonprofit. The similarities and differences between these two kinds of campaigns are summarized in Chapter 6. The focus in this chapter is on capital campaigns as they relate to the long-term capitalization of an organization.

A capital campaign, designed to raise money for a specific purpose within a particular time frame, is an exhausting, draining, exhilarating, and tightly focused effort that challenges the stamina and human resources of even the most stable organizations. When well-conceived and executed, a capital campaign has three major results: (1) The targeted financial goal for the campaign has been met or exceeded; (2) The organization's visibility has increased in the community and among its constituencies; and (3) The overall base of donors has increased.

In previous decades, only the most established educational, cultural, and healthcare organizations—universities, independent schools, hospitals, museums, symphony orchestras—dared undertake such an ambitious effort. Now the pendulum has swung (some would say too far) and organizations large and small with a wide range of missions and readiness are launching community-wide campaigns for building programs or endowment.

THE RATIONALE FOR CAPITAL CAMPAIGNS

There are numerous factors to consider when deciding whether or not to undertake a campaign. These should be examined in a feasibility study that tests both the internal readiness (case, fund raising expertise, staff and board commitment, etc.) and the external support (potential funders and leaders, community perception of the organization, other conflicting campaigns, etc.). Before discussing how to test for a capital campaign, this section will look closely at the rationale for a campaign within the context of building donor-investor relationships that will enable an organization to go beyond fund raising.

Capital campaigns are conducted to provide buildings or equipment that cannot be funded out of earned income, annual fund raising, or capital or operating reserves. They are also undertaken to launch or increase an endowment fund. Well-reasoned campaigns grow out of careful analysis of existing resources (facilities, staffing, annual and endowment income) relative to predicted community needs. These needs are identified through market and program studies which are conducted regularly in conjunction with institutional long-range planning. Anticipation of significant growth in the demand for services, without concurrent potential for significantly increasing fees or annual fund raising revenues, requires prudent organizations to consider alternatives. The same is true when confronting the need to move from a leased or inadequate building. Alternatives exist in both instances. These options will vary depending on the organization and the circumstances, but a capital campaign is almost always among the choices.

Because they see a capital campaign as a solution to their problems, organizations are surprised to discover how complex and difficult they are to plan, organize, and implement. This is particularly true when organizations have failed to develop investor relationships with their donors. Because a capital campaign gift is truly an investment, donors give in the belief that the organization is a vital community resource whose future will be strengthened by a new building or an increased endowment fund.

Some very complex organizations, particularly major universities, conduct capital campaigns in a nearly predictable cycle every 10 to 15 years. Because of their complexity, these organizations have a broad enough menu of purposes (buildings, scholarships, professorships) to justify these cyclical efforts. For other kinds of nonprofit agencies or institutions, whose mission and programs are more single-focused, a capital campaign is a rare or very occasional occurrence. Smaller organizations often find it hard to develop the rationale, or the energy, for once-a-decade major fund raising efforts.

Ironically, seed funding for an organization—the initial capitalization—is seldom (if ever) raised through a capital campaign. Seed funding is most often obtained from a few institutional or individual donor-investors who are involved in the founding of the organization. Capital campaigns require an organization, as well as a vision.

THE NEED TO CAPITALIZE NONPROFITS

The concern about "capitalizing" our organizations is authentic. Trends in funding suggest that organizations need to build endowment, raise operating reserve funds and, under some circumstances and in some communities, own their own buildings if they are to remain vital service providers to their communities. Capitalizing organizations, providing the base of endowed and expendable funds which permit adequate programming without deficit financing, can help prevent the year-to-year funding crises of many organizations. These crises are often well-publicized and pose a threat to the community's perception of the stability of the organization and of the programs they offer. Capitalization increases donor confidence and invites greater investment.

If the organization serves a valid role in the community, and if its annual fund-raising efforts, combined with revenue from services, interest on endowment or other earned sources, do not generate funds sufficient to support current programming and create/increase an endowment, renovate or build a facility, and establish an operating reserve, then there is no alternative other than the capital campaign or a reduction in services.

ATTRACTING DONORS TO CAPITAL CAMPAIGNS

The invitation to invest, discussed in Chapter 5, can draw the donor-investor to the organization. If solid stewardship is practiced (see Chapter 8), that relationship can last through the donor's lifetime and be extended in perpetuity through a planned gift. Key to gaining long-term donor-investors is helping them understand that their gift is as much an investment in the community as it is in the particular agency or institution.

Capital campaigns provide a major opportunity for funders to assess their priorities within their communities. Competing campaigns for the arts, culture, education, health, or social services, are presented to those who are capable of making impact gifts. Experienced donors put their options in priority order, considering several factors:

1. Benefit to the community
2. Benefit to the organization
3. Benefit or recognition for themselves
4. Involvement of other funders

The order of these considerations may vary according to the motivation of the particular donor, but most donors consider these four principal issues when making capital campaign gifts.

Benefit to the Community

Community benefit is the bottom line for many people. In a campaign for a local food bank, leadership gifts were secured from several foundations, corporations, and individuals with no previous record of giving to the agency. The food bank had made a compelling case, citing the more than 300 feeding programs dependent on their resources, describing the way in which enhanced facilities and equipment would increase the amount of food they could process and distribute each year, equating their increased capacity with the importance of preventing food waste in the community, and assuring potential donors that the warehouse design was functional as well as attractive to the neighborhood. The message was very clear: an improved food bank would improve the community. Feeding programs made possible by the organization touched all ages, races, neighborhoods, and conditions: children, seniors, people with AIDS, religious and secular groups, African-American, Hispanic, women, and families. With dedicated leadership, and a few inspired donors who were willing to ask others to be investors with them, the campaign was successful in its financial goal of $5 million, increasing its community visibility among corporations and individuals, and in multiplying its donor base two-fold. (See case study, Chapter 12.)

While hunger is an obviously compelling issue in any community, many arts and culture organizations hear too often that the arts are not as urgent or important. The array of social and human problems may be so overwhelming that funding for an orchestra, ballet, museum, or opera seems somehow frivolous. There are proven strategies for engaging community support for arts and culture, and for positioning the need for the arts in society as a compelling case. Years ago, a highly regarded dance company wished to produce a new, full-length, *Cinderella*. The price tag was high: nearly $1 million. Unsure about community response to this ambitious undertaking, the ballet arranged a facilitated focus group with volunteers and potential funders. Structured questions led them into a lively discussion of the balance of arts and social services in their community. So strong was the feeling about the need to resolve chronic problems with the homeless and other civic concerns that one participant suggested that *Cinderella* could be promoted as a ballet about child abuse. This approach was discouraged, needless to say, but the message was clear: somehow, the arts had to be relevant in order to capture funding. The executive director listened thoughtfully to the entire discussion about community priorities and then offered this idea: If, in the course of solving all the human and social problems in our communities, we neglected and lost the arts, our society would be sadly diminished. His message was clear and convincing. The focus group realized that investing in this dance piece was a way of investing in the future of the community by ensuring its arts programs. They also gained a greater appreciation for the urgency of funding the arts in a society too easily overwhelmed by the compelling social and human needs it faces every day.

Benefit to the Organization

At the outset of the internal planning for a capital campaign, the focus of the board and staff planners is almost entirely on the potential benefit to the organization of undertaking such a monumental funding effort. Those closest to the organization see its needs: more space, endowment, or equipment; they want the campaign to alleviate these needs. Volunteer and professional campaign planners speak passionately about the impact of the campaign on the organization. Volunteer workers are enlisted with the campaign goals clearly stated. Case materials are drawn with these benefits featured. Donors are persuaded by volunteers and staff that the campaign will produce strong and lasting benefits.

Unfortunately, sometime after the campaign is underway, doubts among staff and volunteers begin to emerge, and even the most dedicated leaders find themselves asking if the venture is worth the effort and time. It is sometimes difficult to sustain the passion when things go slowly or badly in a campaign. Internal resources are stretched. Staff increases, although needed, may be in danger of eroding the net financial gain from the campaign. Program staff, to accompany board members and administrative staff members on calls, grow impatient with the process and the time drain. The heavy front-end investment required for a campaign (feasibility study, staffing, materials) seems to bear no dividend after the initial gifts. The surge of leadership gift funding, seductive in its enthusiasm and size, fades. The campaign "troughs," and volunteer and staff leaders begin to question whether or not there is any benefit to the organization. Concerns arise as to whether the campaign goals can be met, or whether those initial gifts will have to be returned. All of these thoughts contribute to what can be the darkest moment of the campaign, and a dangerous threat to the success of potential donor involvement. It is imperative that these concerns not be conveyed to donors, nor be allowed to sap the enthusiasm of those who must do the cultivating and asking.

Antidotes for Discouraged Campaigners

Patience is required at this point, and some reflection on other campaigns and their course. All campaigns hit a low point after the first rush to get started. Because the initial gifts are usually from those most closely associated with the organization, they may have been solicited with more comfort and ease than are later gifts. Often, a campaign will not be given the green light to move ahead until one or more of those gifts has been secured, not just promised. The euphoria which prevails at the beginning of a campaign, when the feasibility study indicates adequate support, a few key gifts have been identified or committed, leadership is excited and ready to go, and the quiet phase can hardly be kept quiet, may fade. If you expect this to happen, you will not be upended when it does.

Neither will you despair, in the plateau period of your campaign, that there is no obvious benefit to the organization and find yourself unable to convey your initial fervor to the prospective donors for whom this is a primary motivation. There is plenty of benefit to the organization. Reflect on the community need which brought you to the point of undertaking the campaign; consider the long-term impact of the investment in additional staff, publications, volunteer training, and cultivation of donors; and be confident that the outcome of a well-managed and successful campaign includes an enhanced organization as well as a delighted group of donor-investors. Stay optimistic, because this plateau will pass once enough prospects have been cultivated, enough suspects are in the pipeline, and enough donors solicited who will be willing to engage others in that in which they have invested.

Keep the features and benefits of the campaign and the organization fresh and removed from the doubts which may be felt. Maintaining optimism will attract the new donor-investors who will pull you securely off the plateau and on to the next pinnacle of achievement. Some specific techniques for alleviating midcampaign depression are:

- Secure a challenge gift from an individual, foundation or corporate donor. This will give people incentive to give within a particular time frame.
- Increase cultivation events.
- Enlist new volunteers who represent new constituencies for the campaign.
- Conduct another silent prospecting session, with new lists and some new people involved in the review process.
- Hold a board or campaign steering committee retreat. Focus on the "SOS"—Share our Success—aspects of the campaign.
- Offer a refresher training course in the solicitation process, using one or more successful solicitations, and a few unsuccessful ones, to guide the learning process.

Benefit or Recognition for Themselves

Benefit or recognition for themselves is a common and understood motivation for donors who contribute major or stretch gifts to a capital campaign. It guides the preparation and publicity of naming opportunities for buildings or endowments. An appreciation of this motivation is critical in working with prospects and donors, and this motivation or need should never be ridiculed or denigrated by staff or volunteer leadership of the campaign. There has been considerable exploration of donor motivation in recent years, including writers who have examined, in particular, individuals who give generously to the arts. The apparent need of these donors for recognition and social position as a result of their giving has been identified and, in some cases, criticized, as though it were a lesser motivation than that of someone who might give less, but be perceived as more altruistic.

The motivation of those individuals and institutions who seek recognition and/or benefit to themselves from making a major or stretch gift should be examined against the standards and values of the organization. If there is no harm to or demand on the organization, and if the gift results in the bettering of the organization and an overall benefit to the community, then it does not make sense to deride the motivation for the gift, even though such derision usually is done privately. Throughout the world, philanthropy has given individuals and organizations recognition and a sense of immortality through the naming of institutions, buildings, endowments, or other opportunities within our sector. For the peers, families, and friends of these donors, such gestures provide pride and inspiration and may ignite a similar desire to give that will also benefit the community. Museums in France, universities in the United Kingdom, hospitals in Israel, schools in China, and concert halls in the United States bear the names of or are supported by endowments from people and institutions whose vision and capacity combined to help strengthen the future and services of these organizations. Capital campaigns provide vehicles whereby donor-investors can benefit an organization and a community and be recognized appropriately for it.

Hospitals and universities are generously funded by individuals and foundations that want to ensure certain long-term benefits to the community—and educational and health programs that will benefit themselves and their families directly. Medical programs are frequently funded by those who have a family history or experience with a particular disease. Community hospitals are able to attract donors by letting them know the benefits of having a trauma unit or heart surgery center in the community: when the time comes for them to use the service, it will be there. More immediately, some private secondary schools find that current parents are highly motivated to give to campaigns which will provide facilities and programs that will directly benefit their children. One such individual, with another like-minded parent, raised nearly $800,000 in six weeks to seed the construction of a vital building on the campus of his children's school. He was impatient with the school's process for getting a campaign in place, and wanted to see the facility built while his children were still enrolled. When asked what had inspired him to do this, he remarked that it was less philanthropic than it was a strong desire for his children to have the best preparation possible for university. Without the facilities and programs which this building would create, he felt their education in a particular subject area would not be competitive with students in other schools. This individual, a very philanthropic and generous member of his community, who supports health, human services, and the arts, was very clear about his immediate motivation. The building, however, will serve generations of students long after his children have graduated.

Ours is a donor-centered universe, and those organizations that understand that aspect of the development process are much better at building donor-investor relationships that will take them beyond fund raising. Individual, as well as foundation and corporate prospects, seek to make community investments for which there is a valued return: satisfaction, benefit, recognition, and/or involvement.

Involvement of Other Funders

Funders like to know who else is giving. This consideration is becoming more widespread among prospects for capital campaigns. Perhaps because of the proliferation of capital campaigns, including a disturbing number that are unsuccessful in their dollar goals or timeframe, funders are reluctant to be the first to step forward with a gift. They do not wish to make an initial investment which will not be supported by others. This is particularly true of some foundations, which wait to see which other foundations will fund the program or project. It is also true for individuals, many of whom want to know who else is involved before they will make a gift. It is rather like the dilemma of getting your first job: you need experience, but you cannot get experience until you get a job, and you cannot get a job unless you have experience. At some point, someone—the employer for the job, the funder for the campaign—has to take a risk. Capital campaigns are the same. Organizations need advocates in the community who can convince funders to be the first.

One of the many benefits of building strong long-term donor-investor relationships with funders is their willingness to take the risk of being one of the initial investors in a capital campaign. They are also willing to go out and talk with other donors and leaders in the community. These are the individuals and institutions to which an organization should take the embryonic dream for the new building, equipment, or endowment. Share with them the excitement of the planning and the development of the case for support. Their role and importance to the success of the campaign cannot be overstated.

In one campaign for a religious organization, two long-time trustees and supporters of the organization held on for decades to an architectural and programmatic vision for the institution. In the interim, a brief, largely unsuccessful campaign for endowment intervened. But they held on to their dream until it was more widely held by new staff and board leadership. Finally, in the waning years of their lives, as the trustees created a vision and plans for the completion of the facility, they each offered a very large gift to get the campaign started. Their initial gifts inspired volunteer and institutional leadership to initiate a successful capital campaign, and were responsible for leveraging the gifts of hundreds of others. The results of this campaign, in which the vision they and others had held for so long was fulfilled, will stand over time as a tribute to them and will be used and respected as a vital community resource.

While confidentiality and other constraints may prevent an organization from revealing the exact amounts that donors have given to a campaign, most donors understand that their gifts provide leverage for raising others. When leadership gifts are secured in a campaign, discuss with the donor the way in which information about that gift can be used to inspire others. In the initial, or quiet phase of a campaign, this information is conveyed in one-on-one meetings with other potential donors. When a campaign is announced to the public, the list of donors and the size of their gifts—plus the total raised to date—is often provided. Clearance with the donor is obviously essential. However, early contributors to a campaign want others to join them and are most often very willing to not only have their gift made known, but some will participate in future solicitations themselves.

WHAT TO CONSIDER BEFORE UNDERTAKING A CAPITAL CAMPAIGN

Most organizations undertake a feasibility study before embarking on a capital campaign. Productive feasibility studies have the following qualities:

- They are conducted by an outside objective consultant, thereby ensuring the candor and confidentiality of the feedback from the community.
- They test both the internal readiness (systems, staffing, enthusiasm, board involvement) and the external feasibility (potential funders and leaders, perception of the organization, impact of programming).
- Organizations trust the results and are guided by them.
- Consultant(s) employed are one(s) in which the organization has confidence regarding skills in marketing the project, interviewing community members, analyzing the data and preparing a cogent and useful report.
- The organization works cooperatively with the consultant(s) in list preparation, interview scheduling, setting of meetings, and other mutually determined aspects of the study that are defined at the outset.
- A solid contract is developed and agreed to, including a clause permitting either the organization or the consultant to terminate the agreement if necessary.

DETERMINING WHETHER TO GO AHEAD WITH A CAMPAIGN

A good feasibility study will test an organization's:

- Visibility
- Potential for support based on a gift range chart that is reviewed with all those interviewed and on which they are asked to place themselves as a preliminary non-binding indication of their potential support
- Projected goal
- Potential for enlisting campaign leadership
- Image in the community
- Perceived capacity to fund raise
- Mission importance among other community priorities
- Credibility
- Rank among other organizations the potential donor may be thinking of supporting
- Potential for identifying potential prospects

Conducting the Study

A feasibility study should be conducted by consultants in whom the organization has confidence to be the frontline marketing advance team. These individuals will make the first impression on your potential leaders and funders. They must be fully and honestly informed about the case for support, and coached about the sensitivities or unusual importance of any of those interviewed for the study. Consultants should also be willing to show you a report format, and an executive summary (with confidential information obscured) of a previous study. References are essential. Check them out.

A study will take at least two to three months, with sometimes as long as six months if there are a great number of interviews or difficulty scheduling due to time or distance. Studies should be based on approximately 40 to 50 interviews, with some larger campaigns and institutions requiring more than 100. The cost of the study will increase with the time required: more interviews will mean a higher fee. Those selected to be interviewed should represent the constituency clusters which are important to the community and the campaign, including civic, social, financial, corporate, foundation, and opinion leaders as well as board members, current and previous donors and former board members. Organizations need to identify 20 to 30 percent more names than they intend to interview, as some will be unable or unwilling to participate. Potential participants are assured their interviews are confidential.

The feasibility study builds potential donor relations. Organizations must participate in the preparation, review, and approval of the letter and questionnaire before they are used by the consultants. Be sure, as well, that all materials look professional. Again, this may be the first contact an important potential donor has with your organization.

Getting People to Participate in the Study

A preliminary case for support, no longer than two pages, should accompany the letter of invitation to those you want to interview. This is a combined fact sheet and marketing statement. It has to have a bit of a "marketing spin" to be readable, and it may be the initial information people receive about the organization. This should be prepared by staff and consultants working together. It is, in many ways, a brief prospectus. You hope that those who read it, and are interviewed, will eventually become donor-investors at a higher level, if they are already donors, or make an initial gift. It is also essential that the letter be sent out over the signature of someone highly respected in the community. This should be a volunteer leader, community leader, or high-visibility administrative staff person from the organization.

In a study for an endowment campaign for a city-sponsored cultural center, a letter from the Mayor inviting people to participate resulted in nearly 97 percent of those invited wanting to participate. At the opposite end of the success scale, the executive director of a social service organization, impatient to get the letters out, signed the letter himself. The consultants had a very difficult time getting appointments and only 40 percent participated. Those who knew him viewed him as controversial; the majority had never heard of him or the organization.

Be sure you know who will conduct the interviews in your feasibility study. Sometimes, when screening and selecting a consultant, the person you interview is not the person who does the actual interviewing for the study. In the context of building donor relations, the person doing the interview is critical.

Working with the Results of the Feasibility Study

After the consultant has assessed the internal readiness of your organization to undertake a capital campaign and the external community interest for funding and leading your campaign, he or she will prepare a comprehensive report. Do not be satisfied with reports that say, "A majority of those interviewed felt the campaign would be successful." You should:

- Know the percentage of those who felt it would be successful.
- Be able to read comments (never attributed, as that would breach confidence) that give insights as to why or why not.
- Be provided with the number of responses to each question so you know what percentage of the sample was involved in the conclusion (on scaled and weighted questions, it is very important to know what percentage of interviewees answered as that can skew the results).

The table of gifts which will be sought in the campaign, developed prior to the study and tested as part of testing the overall goal, will show how many potential gifts have been identified at each level. This information answers the most fundamental questions: Is the lead gift there? Are there enough gifts to go ahead? For most campaigns, if the sample is valid, an indication of one-third to one-half of the needed gifts is sufficient to go ahead. Any less, and the results are doubtful. Consider the following real-life examples:

- With a $20 million endowment campaign, gifts of $8.7 million were identified in the study. It proceeded and is on course.
- With an $11 million proposed campaign, $4 million were identified in the study and there were already two significant lead gifts in place. The campaign raised over $13 million.
- In a $3.7 million campaign which raised $4.2 million, an amount slightly more than $1 million was identified. In a $500,000 campaign, nearly $300,000 was identified. The campaign went over its goal.
- In a proposed $2 million campaign, only $300,000 was identified. The campaign did not go forward.

Pegging the campaign goal against early gift indications is the standard practice. Some campaigns have also lowered their goal as a result, and they have succeeded in raising the revised amount. The gifts identified in the feasibility study are not binding in any way, and interviewees are assured of that. Consultants should test the likelihood of that gift by asking another question during the study: "Among your current philanthropic priorities, where would you place this campaign?" They are offered a choice of "high," "medium," "low"; or given a numerical scale. This can be another way of interpreting the eventual likelihood of the gift and, therefore, of the veracity of the identified funds.

The results of the feasibility study should be clear, and should be accompanied by comprehensive Findings and Recommendations. The findings will probably be tied to the questions on the questionnaire, providing an easy reference for those who must use the study to implement the campaign. The recommendations should provide detail and direction for getting ready for the campaign. This is not a campaign plan, but it is the preliminary set of guidelines the organization will have to follow. A feasibility study will have one of three basic outcomes:

- *Go ahead.* The money and leadership are there.
- *Do not go ahead unless and until certain actions are taken.* These may include steps towards internal staff readiness, or board preparedness, or may be an external task like establishing and implementing a communication and public relations program to raise organizational visibility in the community before the campaign gets underway.
- *Do not go ahead in the foreseeable future.* This disappointing outcome will be based on low public esteem for the organization, conflicting campaigns which are consuming the time and funds from the most likely prospects, no financial support indicated, deep concerns about management and/or current fund raising practices, or other critical issues.

There are organizations which have gone ahead with campaigns in spite of recommendations to implement certain measures before proceeding or not to proceed at all. Some of these campaigns have succeeded, others have failed.

The Quiet Phase of a Campaign

Campaigns are "top down" (large gifts first, closing with the small) and "inside out" (start inside the "family" with the board and reach out, over the course of the campaign, to those who have less connection with the organization). The campaign constituency is often depicted as concentric circles, with the board in the middle. Board gifts come first, whether or not they are "major" in size. Once the board is 100 percent committed to the campaign, then other gifts can be solicited from previous or potential major donors who are still strongly connected to the organization.

The quiet phase is gift, not time, determinate. Its goal is to raise 60 to 65 percent of the total campaign funds. While organizations can plot a timeline and predict that the quiet phase will take a year, or eighteen months in some very large campaigns, it is difficult to predict. In one $5.5 million campaign, the "quiet phase" took two years—but the balance of the funds were raised within six months. At the end of the quiet phase, the campaign is announced to the public. Usually, these campaigns are not a well-kept secret among those who are close to the organization. There should be no media or community announcement until the leadership gifts have been raised for at least half the total amount of the campaign and the goal has been validated or adjusted. There are organizations which, when they get into the quiet phase of the campaign, determine that the goal was either too high or too low. This is one of the main purposes of the quiet phase: it is like a second feasibility study.

Strong donor relations can be built during the quiet phase. The campaign founders are a special group of people, and should be treated with the highest respect and stewardship. Incentives by organizations to get early funders should be honored throughout the campaign and afterwards. In one extraordinary campaign, in which a performing arts center was completely funded ($70 million) by private nongovernmental sources (individuals, foundations, and corporations), the initial study for the campaign was funded by a group who were called the Founders. Their financial contributions were not as great as some that came later on, but they were the community visionaries who were willing to put up the seed money for the funding and architectural feasibility studies. As the campaign took off, and other much larger funders were involved in the actual building campaign, these individuals were forgotten. Today, their connection with the organization has been severed, and many of them no longer support the center at all. Founding funders, whether or not they turn out to be the top funders for a campaign, should be accorded the stewardship they deserve for their pivotal role in making the project possible.

Going Public: Making the Announcement

When the benchmark 60 or 65 percent of the campaign funds have been committed, and the goal validated or adjusted, the campaign can go public. It is not the purpose of this brief overview to provide details of campaign management. Dozens of books are available on running a capital campaign once the public phase is announced, but a few ideas about making that announcement are worth repeating. They are offered here in the context of helping organizations create and maintain true donor-investor relationships:

- Invite all early funders to the public announcement.
- Include annual donors and members, even if not yet solicited for the campaign, in the kick-off and announcement. Get them excited.

- Plan an event that is appropriate for the scale and purpose of the campaign and the organization so that donors do not feel their contributions are being used unwisely.
- Create a media "hook" to ensure good coverage of the kick-off linked to the importance of the need this campaign will be meeting and arrange interviews with donors.
- Engage civic dignitaries if possible and introduce them to key donors;
- Whether it is a ribbon-cutting, groundbreaking, sky-breaking (as one building project had), quiet announcement of an endowment at the organization's headquarters or any other kind of symbolic event, be sure the *beneficiaries* of the building or program are present—not just funders and dignitaries—and that the beneficiaries and the donors and dignitaries are honored.
- Keep speeches and ceremony to the minimum, but be sure to include a funder who can speak from his or her heart about why a large gift was given.
- Be sure all board members are asked to be there and are identified as board members.
- If the building is in a neighborhood, invite the neighbors and introduce them to board members and donors.
- Work with a representative community of volunteers, including one or more donors, to plan and implement the event.
- Keep the cost down by getting goods and services donated if possible and let that be known to those who attend, including funders.

Maintaining Donor Relations During the Campaign

Stewardship is covered in Chapter 8, but it is critical to remember that once a donor makes a campaign gift to your organization the relationship is just beginning. It is our tendency, once a gift we have worked on for a long period of time comes in, to put that person into the donor file, close the drawer, lock it up—and then open the prospect file for another potential donor to work with. Meanwhile, the donor languishes in the file drawer, wondering what happened to the wining and dining he or she was receiving before the gift was made.

Donors are allies in a campaign. They have already invested, so they want others to invest. They are convinced, and they can convince others. They have given and want to be recognized, and we need to afford them the recognition and stewardship they want and deserve. Often, a donor will make a repeat gift towards the end of the campaign. By placing them in situations where they are convincing others to give, they often convince themselves to give more.

Donor-investors provide the solid base on which the campaign will succeed, and future campaigns will be possible. They have capitalized the organization in which they believe, and they have a sense of ownership. We must honor that ownership, and find ways in which they can exercise their stakeholder role. We can ask them to:

- Assist with solicitations.
- Review prospect lists.
- Participate in cultivation and stewardship activities (lunches, dinners, etc.).
- Review existing materials for appropriate updating.
- If they have comfort and skills in public speaking, let them be formal advocates for the organization and the campaign at service clubs and churches or other forums.
- Serve on the campaign cabinet or steering committee.
- Serve on the board.
- Provide leadership for a segment of the campaign or the organization.
- Be a resource and reference in difficult donor negotiations in which there is skepticism or uncertainty regarding the satisfaction the pending donor will receive when the gift is made.

SUMMARY

Long-Term Capitalization

Capital and annual fund raising provide donor-investors with opportunities to ensure the long-term capitalization of the organizations they value. Well-run campaigns of both kinds serve to elevate our organizations to new levels of community service, and provide incredible opportunities to engage and involve people as long-term investors in our organizations.

Organizations that plan and implement both kinds of campaigns in the larger context of building long-term relations are able to go past the *quick fix* kind of fund raising which exhausts and discourages others. Keeping the focus on the donor-investor will ensure the kind of long term support and capitalization that will stabilize and strengthen the organization.

Stewardship: The Heart of the Development Process

No practice is more important in the development process than stewardship, the continued involvement, cultivation, and care of those who give.

Stewardship is more than a practice, it is an attitude. It is more than recognition, it is the offered opportunity to stay informed and become involved. It is an organization's philosophical commitment to the value and importance of donors as well as their gifts; a belief that each donor contributes more than money, and that gifts are a *symbol* of the donor's belief in the values, purpose, and importance of the organization. Donors who feel they are valued only for their gifts, or who feel neglected after giving a gift, quickly sour on an organization or even the nonprofit sector.

WHY PRACTICE STEWARDSHIP?

A strong stewardship program is the single greatest contributor to an organization's ability to go beyond fund raising. Donors who are drawn more deeply into a relationship with an organization through effective stewardship become its advocates and promoters. A credible theory exists that part of the donor's self comes with each gift. The philosophy of stewardship is based in large part on that theory. Organizations that dismiss the importance of stewardship endanger their potential for successful donor and fund development. Disgruntled and disappointed donors voice their complaints to others in the community, intensifying the damage and warning others not to get involved. Satisfied donors draw others in. They are worth an investment in solid stewardship practices.

All stewardship and recognition practices must be backed by an honest commitment to the philosophy of stewardship. It is a philosophy based on respect that is as detectable in its absence as it is in its presence. Increasingly, donors are experienced at giving. As they act on their array of values, they provide philanthropic support for numerous organizations. They have opportunities to experience firsthand, and to compare, the various ways in which organizations interact with their donors. In confidential interviews for feasibility or development audit studies, donors will candidly reveal what they perceive to be the level of sincerity towards donors in an organization. If the stewardship program is focused only on very large donors, then those donors with potential who are not currently large donors will become discouraged at the lack of opportunities for their involvement. If the stewardship program does not begin early enough in the giving cycle (with the initial or renewed gift) then donors with potential for larger gifts or strategic volunteer roles may be lost. If the stewardship program is sporadic, changing with turnovers in staff or volunteer leadership, these experienced donors quickly notice the absence of a philosophy about stewardship even if some recognition activities continue.

WHAT STEWARDSHIP MEANS

The concept of stewardship has expanded as organizations better understand the sequential and seamless nature of an effective development process. As the sector has evolved, the word "stewardship" has had various meanings and interpretations. Some of those survive and are used today.

Stewardship is used frequently to describe the annual congregation pledge drive in some U.S. Christian churches. This specific application of the word does not inform its general use in development and fundraising. Others use it to describe their overall management and use of donated funds. Still others, drawing on the early English definition of "steward" as "keeper of the hall," give a broader interpretation. They use it to describe the ethical management and care afforded to all resources of nonprofit institutions.

Increasingly, stewardship has come to mean the essential function by which organizations develop lasting relationships with their donor-investors. This *includes* the ethical management and care of all human and financial resources. Stewardship promotes a donor-organization relationship based on mutual respect for both the source and impact of gifts. When well-implemented, stewardship provides the basis for building programs that go beyond fund raising.

In spite of its importance, this vital function is often neglected. In their urgent need to fundraise, and their relief and joy in securing a gift, organizations forget that the real relationship begins once the gift is made. In times of tight financial controls, the budget for staff and activities with direct fund raising results is maintained, while far less measurable stewardship practices may be cut. One individual, in charge of development for a large organization, expressed his frustration over this issue in a letter to a fellow professional: "I *only wish* we had adequate resources to truly create opportunities to build lasting relationships that promote loyalty and generosity." This comment is a sad commentary on institutional funding priorities. When it comes to long-term return on investment, few efforts pay as many benefits as a well-designed and implemented stewardship program.

GIVING AND STEWARDSHIP

Stewardship is essential because of the nature of giving itself. When people give, they are acting on their values. A certain level of emotion or commitment is associated with the decision to give, even if the receiving organization is not aware of it when the gift is made. Gifts sent through the mail in response to letter appeals, or those which stem from a newspaper article or special event presentation, deserve more than just a thank you letter. Organizations must get to know the donor, find out what his or her values are, and why they were moved to make a gift.

Most organizations have had unhappy experiences with angry or disillusioned donors. The emotions connected with giving can turn from a positive sense of fulfillment and satisfaction to irritation, frustration, or disappointment. In campaign after campaign, previous donors who have been identified as top prospects reveal, when initial contact is made, that they are upset with the organization because they were not kept informed about the results of their previous gifts. No one has connected them with the scholarship recipients they have funded. They have never met any of the parents whose children benefit from the preschool program. They do not feel appreciated for what they have done and are therefore unwilling to do more. Alumni donors of universities or contributing constituencies of community-based organizations resent being contacted "only when the organization needs money." People do not get angry with an organization unless they care. It is up to the organizations in our sector to minimize the potential for negative donor interaction. Stewardship is a fundamental function in keeping the relationship both positive and vigorous.

STEWARDSHIP AND BELONGING

The act of giving is a transforming act. It transforms potential donors, and current donors with greater potential, into stakeholders. Donors become donor-investors, keenly interested in how their gifts are used and what impact they will have on the organization and the community. They want a sense of ownership and connection. Well-managed stewardship practices provide opportunities for donors to deepen their interests and values.

There is powerful evidence that one of the major motivations for giving is the need to belong. People want to belong to the success of an organization; they want to feel as though they participated in its growth. They want to share in the future of an organization in which they have invested; they want to feel as though they can form that future with their opinions and ideas, as well as their gifts. Even those who do not pursue an active role with an organization derive satisfaction from belonging to the group of donor-investors who have helped it attain its mission and goals.

Years ago, a wealthy, powerful, and reclusive board chair for a major arts organization, always impatient with the process of meetings, distractedly observed a consultant-facilitated board discussion about why people give. Standing at the back of the room, visibly removed from the interaction around the table, he seemed barely to be paying attention although he was apparently listening. After hearing all the reasons for giving which the other board members offered, he asked to add one. To everyone's surprise, he said he believed people gave because they wanted to belong. This startling comment, from a shy yet powerful donor of a million dollars a year to this organization, caused an awkward and momentary silence in the discussion because of its self-revealing intensity. It provided key insights into the motivations of this particular philanthropist who, year after year, chose to remain in a leadership role as a donor and board chair.

GETTING DONORS AND PROSPECTS INTO THE KITCHEN

The Oregon Shakespeare Festival once summarized the importance of belonging through a membership piece, "The Spirit, the Art of Belonging." Artistic Director Jerry Turner concluded an insert in the season's program by quoting Berthold Brecht. Brecht once explained that he chose one restaurant over another not because the first hadn't a delectable menu, but because the second invited him into the kitchen. In the first, he said, he was a honored customer. In the second, he was a participant. He belonged.

Stewardship is the process whereby we bring our donors into an ever-closer relationship with our organizations. It is how we get them "into the kitchen." Those donor-investors who are closest to the organization—board members and other volunteers—are particularly deserving of the very best stewardship practices. When afforded this respect and acknowledgment, they will *stay* in the kitchen.

While the concept of the "kitchen" is figurative, some organizations have translated this concept into unique and striking practices for both cultivation and stewardship. A state-funded university launched a campaign to build a new fine arts building. Fortunately, the dean's approach to fund raising and stewardship of donor-investors was innovative and attention-getting. Not only did he have a "sky breaking" instead of a groundbreaking for the new building, he created a very unusual office space during the campaign. He had selected for his office an open area of a barn-like campus building which served as an overflow space for art and drama studios. The building was one of several sadly obsolete structures that had housed the fine arts programs. The architectural plans called for the new building to unite all the fine arts programs then housed all over the campus. At one end of the room he put a restaurant-sized espresso machine and a conversation area with a sofa and comfortable chairs. At the other end of the room, he left the painted backdrop of a kitchen used by a university morning television show. The result was dynamic. Faculty, friends of the university, funders, administrative staff, prospects, and other visitors were brought "into the kitchen," literally. The setting was complementary to the dean's high level of charm and persuasion. He was delighted to mull the future with his donor-investors over coffee in the kitchen of a building which would soon be replaced by a state-of-the-art facility. He was successful in gaining a new base of donor-investors who had never supported a state-funded university, in attracting unexpected and substantial support from the university administration for some state matching funds, and in engaging the arts and entertainment community who were delighted with his innovative approach.

At a resident artists' program, housed in a building converted from an old military barracks, each room was an artist's project. The kitchen was no exception. While the work area appliances were utilitarian, designed for large-quantity cooking, an eating area connected to the kitchen had been created by the artists. Its remarkable attraction was the chairs around the eating tables. Each chair was different, a work by an artist. Those who worked in wood or other sturdy materials built their chairs; those with skills in other media decorated chairs they had acquired at antique or garage sales. No two chairs were the same: each artist had left behind a signature piece. At lectures, meals, donor gatherings, development committee meetings, and other related functions, a unique sense of interaction with the artists permeated the room. The message conveyed was immediate: this was a working center for artists whose expression and creativity was encouraged by community giving and volunteering.

While both these examples are from organizations with artistic missions and available kitchens, other organizations can also effectively bring their donors "into the kitchen" by connecting them closely and often with the people, ideas, materials, vision, and future planning for their organizations.

PUTTING PRIORITY ON STEWARDSHIP

Organizations that successfully go beyond fund raising and implement donor-focused development programs will assign budget and personnel to ensure that donors feel appreciated and informed. Because most organizations cannot assign a separate staff person to the stewardship function, it should be part of every staff person's job description and every board member's stated responsibilities.

If the resources are available, stewardship can be a separate staff position. Two major universities, on completion of recent capital campaigns for which they had added professional and support staff, appropriately trimmed the size of their development offices after their campaigns. They reduced staff across all programs, with one exception: both universities added professional and support staff to direct stewardship programs. These institutions recognized that, during the post-campaign period, they had to implement strong stewardship practices. An independent school, closing a major campaign which had attracted many large gifts, turned its attention to the stewardships of smaller gift donors. It initiated a program in which it randomly singled out donors and sent them thank you letters for their gifts (see Exhibit 8.1). This outreach program is exceptional, and should have strong results.

EXHIBIT 8.1 Sample Stewardship Letter: The Lawrenceville School

October 17, 1996

Mr. John J. Donor
77 Main Street
Pittsburgh, PA

Dear Mr.

    We recently received your gift of $50.00 for Annual Giving, a welcome contribution from a name familiar to us here. In fact, our records show you have given to Lawrenceville for 18 consecutive years, an impressive record indeed. Your gifts to Annual Giving during this time total $880.

    Annual Giving enables Lawrenceville to set itself apart from other schools by affording the Head Master and Trustees the flexibility of applying funds to the areas of greatest needs—or, indeed, of greatest opportunity. Your continuing devotion to and support of Lawrenceville through Annual Giving is much appreciated.

    With heartfelt thanks from all of us here,

                        Sincerely,

                        Charles D. Brown, Jr.
                        Director of Development

CDB/cms

The Lawrenceville School
Box 6125, Lawrenceville, New Jersey 08648, Telephone (609) 896-1208, Fax (609) 895-2148

PRINCIPLES FOR CREATING A STEWARDSHIP PROGRAM

Effective stewardship begins with the organization's philosophical commitment to the importance of the interests and needs of donor-investors, and results in long-term commitment to the organization by its donor-investors. Some basic principles guide the creation of a strong stewardship program.

1. *Begin involving donors in the stewardship program with their first gift.* The thankathon, described in Chapter 6, establishes contact after the first gift and gives all donors an opportunity to hear personally that the gift is appreciated and will be used wisely. This is a critical beginning to what can become a relationship with great value to both donor and organization. Involve new major donors who are interested and knowledgeable in the review of critical donor and community materials. Invest in a *DRAFT* stamp ($3 to $5) and use it on proposed materials. Send drafts of proposed fund-raising letters, program and development campaign brochures, or funding proposals to those connected to you and the communities to which the materials may be directed. Pride of staff authorship is not the issue here. Donor and volunteer ownership is. A few will respond with suggestions, not all of which will be appropriate or applicable. Respond to the suggestions with a phone call, explaining why you will or will not follow the recommendations. Whether or not their changes are included, they will still have a heightened sense of ownership of the organization's activities. The same strategy works for engaging people in focus or discussion groups around a proposed program or direction. Involve new key donor-investors with your board members. They will bring a refreshing perspective and may have or develop an interest in supporting the program.

2. *Alternate messages to your donors.* A trusted rule says that for every one time you ask someone for money you should contact them two other times without asking for money. It is a sound principle. Examples of non-fund-raising contacts are the thankathon, an invitation to a lecture or presentation, a no-fee tea or reception to meet a visiting or resident professional, a "white paper" prepared by staff to describe an agency program which is meeting a particular community need and which is accompanied by a note thanking the donor for his or her support, or opportunities for tours or meetings that will bring them closer to the organization's programs.

3. *Allocate budget to stewardship activities.* Make stewardship activities—donor receptions, special mementos for large gift donors, dinner or refreshments for a thankathon—an integral part of the development program. The budget for specific *fund-raising* activities is usually easier to justify than the budget for development. *Fund raising* results are usually immediate and measurable. *Development* results may not be evident for years. But development, and stewardship as a primary function, make fund raising successful. Stewardship, while difficult to measure precisely in its financial return, affects the entire bottom line: an overall increase in giving, and a growth in donor retention, will follow.

4. *Be sure the stewardship practice is appropriate to the amount of the gift and the budget and image of the organization.* Donors are uneasy when they believe that a memento or event is too expensive or inconsistent with their image of the organization (e.g., socially responsible, fiscally conservative, etc.). They wonder if their gift has been used up by the acknowledgment. In the United States, the Internal Revenue Service has enforced stringent standards regarding the reduction of the deductibility of a gift based on the goods or services received by the donor. This ruling provides a wonderful opportunity to scale back the tangible benefits afforded to donors and focus on communicating the *real* benefits: the impact of the gift on the fulfillment of the mission in the community.

5. *Determine what kind of involvement your major gift and planned gift donors, some of whom may be very busy with other organizations and their own professions, want.* They may not want to belong to a particular giving "club," preferring instead to enter into some other kind of interaction with the organization. Some larger donors wish to be left alone except when they initiate contact with the organization. People do not have to belong to a giving "club" to derive a sense of belonging. Find this out at the time the gift is made, and honor the donor's wishes throughout the relationship. Information regarding the way in which people want to be involved with an organization should be part of the database information about the donor. New volunteers or staff need that information in order to effectively continue the relationship.

6. *Coordinate stewardship and cultivation outreach, so that current donors have an opportunity to convey their enthusiasm and commitment to prospective donors.* These "bookends" on a solicitation are very similar. Each is based on the same principles of involving the individual in the most meaningful way in to uncover and reinforce values. A widely published cartoon shows a volunteer walking around a beautifully set formal dining table, putting out the placecards. She is saying, "Donor,

Non-Donor, Donor, Non-Donor. . . ." She is, of course, exactly right. Mix those who have given with those who are still thinking about it. The results will be beneficial to the individuals, and to the organization.

7. *Tie stewardship outreach to the organization's mission.* Just as effective board meetings should have a "product demonstration" to continually tie board members into the mission, so should stewardship events and mementos. While plaques and mugs and other articles serve their purpose, seek out more meaningful items when possible or appropriate. A drawing by a developmentally-disabled child, framed and given to a donor, finds a place in a Wall Street office. A model of a set for a regional repertory theater production is prominently displayed in the lobby of the sponsoring corporation. A piece of sandstone, remnant of an extraordinary building preservation project at a university, sits on the desk of an American corporate executive in London. A photograph of dancers, captured performing a production she helped fund, is displayed in the living room of a Los Angeles philanthropist. The visionary leader of an endowment campaign for a Western European art museum is honored with a national award by that country's Minister of Culture. Imagination can open new avenues for cost-saving ways to appropriately thank volunteers and donors in a way that reinforces the mission of the organization and the values of the donors.

8. *Focus on intangible, rather than tangible, benefits.* This principle supports item 7, above, and also helps curb the dangerous downside of donor recognition: donors will become complacent with current benefits and not increase their gifts. In a university campaign a number of years ago, a foundation donor challenged a particular constituency to increase its annual giving by promising to match the increase. For donors of the largest annual gifts—who received many "benefits" for their contribution, including parking privileges, events tickets, a special dinner with the President—the challenge was no incentive at all. They were not immediately moved to raise their level of giving because the "floor" ($1,000+) had become a "ceiling" for them. Not until some spirited outreach was done by development staff and faculty did the leadership of that particular donor group understand that the true benefits which accrued from their gifts were not what they received, but what they gave. They came to understand that the impact of giving more was not another parking pass or dinner, but a university even more effectively positioned to provide education to its students. This realization, a shift in thinking from donor to donor-investor, was a remarkable passage in the donor development history of that university.

9. *Maintain stewardship with long time and generous donors, even when their giving flags.* Organizations, as a rule, base their stewardship strategies on internal measures of size or frequency of gift. In most cases, this is appropriate. But board and staff should remember that a donor's circumstances may change temporarily. To abandon the relationship with a funder who may be going through a period with limited discretionary income because assets are tied up, or interest or earnings are down, could be foolish. Often, we are reluctant to engage a donor in a follow-up discussion when a gift is not given or is smaller than expected. If the funder, through stewardship, has become involved with the organization, the organization should honor the relationship that has been built and find out the circumstances which led to a reduced gift or no gift at all.

One donor, who had made increasingly higher gifts to the annual fund of a university, found himself at midlife starting a new business and putting several children through college. The volunteer assigned to this person, who had made regular contact over the years, let the university know that the person's circumstances had changed and that the previous level of giving could not be sustained. The volunteer asked the university staff person if she could continue the personal solicitation relationship in spite of the fact that the individual's gift fell below the requisite level for a personal ask. The relationship was continued on the same basis for a period of six or seven years, and gradually the donor's gifts began to increase. The donor's business was a huge success and the children graduated from college. During a major fund-raising campaign several years later, the donor who had received this continuing stewardship made a gift in excess of one million dollars to the university.

Performing or producing arts organizations may find that corporate sponsors are not able to fund them every year. In the years when they are not underwriting, they should still be honored and included in receptions and at performances because of the role they have played in building the organization and contributing to the growth of arts in the community. Continued participation will influence future decisions regarding renewed sponsorships or contributions.

When planning those to include in a stewardship event, do not forget the donor whose "stretch" gift, while perhaps modest by some standards, represents a major investment which is driven by the heart and values of that donor. They, too, should be honored.

10. *Keep all previous large gift donors informed and part of your database, even those who make what seems to be a "one time only gift," unless and*

until you hear they no longer want to hear from you. Extraordinary gifts from individuals with no previous giving history are often honored extensively at the time the gift is made, after which the donor is neglected. The problem is further exacerbated when the organization provides inadequate reporting to the donor (individual or family, foundation or corporation) about the impact of the philanthropy. At a U.S. preparatory school, a personal relationship was not sustained with a mother and her son after a scholarship was established with the proceeds of the grandfather's estate. This situation was corrected after complaints from the donors. Later, when a subsequent major campaign was underway, these two donors were not contacted because the school surmised they did not have the continuing resources to be included in the large gift campaign. After the campaign was over, the mother let a friend who was leadership volunteer in the campaign know that they were angry that they had not been approached. Because of their existing investment in the school, they felt they should have at least been offered another opportunity to give.

11. *Establish relationships between donors and program staff whenever possible.* People and institutions become investors in an organization because of a belief in or connection with the mission. Their need to belong stems not from their need to become involved with the administrative or development staff, but to become partners with those who actually provide the community service. Only then can they understand how their values are being acted on. If a funder is supportive of a learning disabilities program, make sure that he or she gets to know the director of that program. Provide opportunities for the funder to attend talks or participate in discussions about that particular program area, thereby heightening knowledge, interest, and the sense of investment. One donor-investor to a public library, who had established an endowed book fund with her family, was provided with an annual detailed report by title of how the earnings from the fund had been spent. Additionally, she was given opportunities to meet the director of that collection, to see some of the books with the family bookplate affixed, and to observe the way in which the books were being used. Personal holiday cards from the library director and letters about other collections and activities were also part of the stewardship outreach mix. The result was an increased sense of investment on the part of the donor. She and her family continue to contribute annually to the fund, often with memorial or "in honor" gifts for other family members.

IMPLEMENTING A STEWARDSHIP PROGRAM

With the above principles guiding, you can create and implement a stewardship program following these steps:

1. *If the board has never adopted a policy regarding stewardship, start by creating and approving one.* The board should have a policy which implants securely into the systems of the organization the importance of donors and stewardship. This is not a detailed plan for stewardship; rather, it is a commitment to the philosophy and practice. By ensuring that a board policy is in place, stewardship is more apt to be a steady practice, rather than an occasional spurt of activity. Once you have done this—which may require some education about stewardship from a staff, board member, or outside facilitator—then you are ready to proceed.

2. *Form a stewardship planning task force involving board members, other volunteers, a development or administrative staff member, and some donors.* Involving donors in a stewardship program planning process is particularly important. They are an excellent resource for setting up a program to maintain donor relationships because they have experience and perspective. Give them a leadership role, and let them be part of the team which presents the proposed stewardship program plan to the board. Once the task force has coalesced, work from the guidelines of the board policy to develop a plan based on the following steps.

3. *Analyze the donor base according to the way in which gifts cluster, and establish four or five preliminary (test) giving recognition levels.* While recognition is not the only aspect of stewardship, it is the most visible to the community and to current and prospective donors. If yours is a new community-based social services organization and your gifts range from (e.g.) $5 to $99; $100 to $249; $250 to $499; and a few at $500 or higher, then these levels might frame your initial donor recognition and stewardship programs. For established organizations just beginning to systematize their stewardship, the levels may be higher. Recognition levels may not start until $100 or $250, and may go up to $10,000 or $25,000. Recognition is given every year, for initial, repeated, and upgraded gifts. Establish different levels during a capital campaign that will apply to those gifts only. Some organizations also acknowledge a donor's cumulative gifts when they reach a certain total. All recognition levels should be presented to the board or development committee for review before they are made final.

4. *Assign names to the giving levels that will be easy to remember and manage. Avoid being too clever or too complex. If possible, try to keep the names linked to the mission; otherwise use generic names (e.g., Donor, Patron, Benefactor).* A dance company named its top giving level the Masterpiece Society because funds from those donors are assigned each year to the creation of a new work or the revitalization of an existing work. Within the Masterpiece Society, there are levels: Silver, Gold, and Platinum. Churches and cathedrals throughout the world have used Angels to denote their large donors, and Archangels for their very large donors. Preparatory schools and universities will name their giving levels after distinguishing landmarks: Quad, Inner Quad, Tower Society. Others will name them after leadership positions in the institution: Dean's Circle, President's Club, Director's Circle, Founder's Circle. Some choose to use the name of a specific individual (founder, benefactor, first president, a distinguished leader in the field) for one or more of their giving levels.

5. *Determine the "benefits" for each level.* In the United States, as mentioned earlier, the enforcement of tax rules is stimulating organizations to establish and maintain an array of benefits which do not significantly erode the value of the donor's gift. Because receipts must now reflect the deductible portion of the gift (total gift less the value of goods and services received), be sure the deductible portion stays as high as possible. Organizations may wish to offer donors the option of declining all but the basic benefits (e.g., newsletter, free admission tickets, etc.). Many donors are choosing that option.

The array of benefits usually increases with the size of the gift. In conveying these benefits, most organizations have a simple schedule that shows basic benefits and the increment to those basic benefits at each level. This can be shown on a chart (see Exhibit 8.2), or done in narrative form. This chart shows corporate benefits for a major art museum.

Guided by principle number 8, above, try to avoid excessive tangible benefits and focus instead on benefits which will connect the donor more firmly to the mission of the organization. Benefits for corporations tend to be more tangible than those for individual donors. The giveback provides opportunities for corporations to approach giving from both a philanthropic and a marketing perspective. A positive aspect of such a benefits array is the involvement of key executives and employees who may then become individual donors to the organization.

Opportunities to participate in programs and to get to know those responsible for program delivery are, in the long run, less costly and more memorable for donors. Organizations in all countries,

EXHIBIT 8.2 Example: Corporate Annual Fund Benefits Chart

Corporate Annual Fund Charter Corporate Partner Levels and Benefits	Asian Art Museum of San Francisco				
	Porcelain Partner	Jade Partner	Bronze Partner	Silver Partner	Gold Partner
	$2,500	$5,000	$10,000	$25,000	$50,000
For Your Company					
Ability to bring clients/ customers for private tours			◆	◆	◆
Company recognition in the membership magazine		◆	◆	◆	◆
Charter Partner designation in corporate partner brochure	◆	◆	◆	◆	◆
On-site recognition of company on donor plaque		◆	◆	◆	◆
Recognition on exhibitions and programs				◆	◆
Private use of/for company events	◆	◆	20% Discount	Rental fee waiver*	Rental fee waiver*
Use of company materials				◆	◆
For Your Employees					
Free admission	50 passes	75 passes	100 passes	125 passes	150 passes
Invitation to reception for corporate members	◆	◆	◆	◆	◆
Discount on individual Museum membership	10%	10%	10%	20%	20%
Private gallery tours		◆	◆	◆	◆
Art talks in your office			◆	◆	◆
For Your Senior Executives					
Executive memberships	4	6	8	10	15
Reciprocal membership in 13 western museums	◆	◆	◆	◆	◆
Invitations to Exhibition Openings	◆	◆	◆	◆	◆
Invitations to Corporate Partner Luncheons		◆	◆	◆	◆
Behind-the-scenes tours			◆	◆	◆

*All event costs, including Museum security, are the responsibility of the corporate donor.

whether or not there are deductibility advantages for giving or rules that govern what is deductible, should construct a benefit program that is based more on a return on values than on the give-back of merchandise or events. In regions of the United States, as well as in many parts of the world, tangible benefits may be culturally inappropriate to the donor's motivation and need for anonymity or a low profile. Intangible benefits—belonging, recognition, a sense of investment—cross cultures in their acceptance.

6. *Present the levels and benefits to the development committee or board for approval.* While the specifics of the recognition program are the most visible side of stewardship, and require approval, they should be presented in the context of the overall philosophy and strategy of the stewardship program. Recognition is a part of the stewardship process. Benefits are the tactical aspect of stewardship: the philosophy and the long-term strategy must shape and guide the recognition program. It is not enough to recognize a donor: the offer for involvement must be made as well.

7. *Create a stewardship plan which includes promotion of recognition levels in all donor outreach: mailings, telephone solicitations and thankathons, personal solicitations and corporate or foundation proposals.* Emphasize that these are recognition levels, and are designed to provide a way in which donors can become involved, if they desire, in the organization. Some individuals prefer not to be listed in donor recognition materials, and others, while not objecting to having their names listed, honestly prefer not to get involved. True stewardship, including successful recognition, is based on the needs and desires of the donor, not those of the organization.

8. *Monitor the program by tracking the relationship between stewardship and recognition practices and renewal/upgrade of gifts.* The giving behavior of those who are afforded appropriate recognition and stewardship should differ from the behavior of those who are not. Establish baseline data for new donors, and do long-term tracking of their giving. In many organizations, repeated or renewed gifts have risen significantly in the fund drive which follows a thankathon. One hospital has tracked donor retention since starting its thankathons and reports a 40 percent increase. At all gift levels, and wherever the donor is on the investment continuum, stewardship heightens the potential for retention. It has also been seen, in organizations which experience administrative scandal or financial difficulties, that those donors who have been involved and informed regarding the organization and its programmatic impact in the community are more apt to remain loyal.

9. *Review the program, benefits, and impact annually, and make adjustments based on donor feedback, donor retention, and changes in the levels at which gifts cluster.* A recognition level and stewardship program which is initiated for donors of $500 or more may find that both the floor and the ceiling need to be raised in order to provide recognition and incentive for increasingly generous donor-investors. If the emphasis to donors has been on the benefit to the program of their gifts (results), rather than the benefits afforded to them for their gifts, then a demonstration of the organization's capacity to meet greater needs with larger gifts will help raise giving levels. These levels will have to be appropriately recognized.

SUMMARY

Competition for resources in the not-for-profit sector is going to increase as traditional sources of funding shrink. Donor loyalty is a known factor in successful organizations. Maintaining that loyalty is the principal goal of stewardship, and is its most powerful result.

Stewardship is the most important practice in the development process. It secures donors for the future as it honors their impact on the present. Stewardship demonstrates to donors that their thoughts, opinions, and participation are part of an involvement process which includes their gift and much more.

Budget allocation for stewardship practices, while sometimes difficult to justify in the short term, has a significant long-term impact on overall fund-raising costs. If stewardship is effective, donor retention and giving levels rise. The acquisition of new donors is balanced with the nurturing of existing donors, which provides healthy and vital feedback as well as an eventual source of renewed or increased revenues.

Because gifts are given in response to a perceived community need by funders who share the values implicit in that need, even an initial small gift is a statement of the desire to become involved with the successful fulfillment of an organization's mission and goals. It is also a signal that a current donor-investor may be interested in becoming more involved.

Keep that idea foremost in the planning for all development, and be sure that stewardship is a key practice in your organization.

▼ 9 Maximizing Board Development and Participation

Every nonprofit organization dreams of recruiting, enlisting, and maintaining a board of trustees who will be wise decision makers, visionary planners, able advocates, generous investors, willing askers, informed partners and passionate pragmatists. Those organizations whose boards are appointed by individuals outside their immediate administrative structure also share the hope that those responsible for assembling their boards will find people who meet these criteria. Putting together such a board is not an impossible dream. Organizations can influence their own board development process and move towards this ideal when they adhere to some basic principles of board recruitment, enlistment, management, and retention.

BOARD DEVELOPMENT: THE KEY TO FUND DEVELOPMENT

Dynamic board development is the proven key to successful fund development. Recruitment matrices reflect this in their focus on people with connection, concern, capacity, and clout. Every organization wants people with influence and affluence, hence the harsh rubric, "give, get, or get off" and the three W's, wealth, work, wisdom (with an implied fourth W; wallop).

Certain community organizations seem to attract more than their share of people with these attributes, while others struggle to recruit just one. The social cachet and prestige of arts, education, and hospital boards are a natural magnet for high profile community people, but this should not preclude human and social services agencies from attracting and retaining influential people.

To build the kind of boards that dreams are made of, rebalance the recruitment equation. Traditional recruitment practices have the same flaw as traditional fund-raising practices: they position the organization's needs ahead of the community or prospective board member's needs. Just as we fund raise out of desperation until we understand fund and donor development as an investment process, we frequently recruit out of desperation until we understand that board development is also an investment process. Rebalancing the equation requires us to adopt an investor attitude, based on the mutual advancement of shared values, towards board recruitment and service. Otherwise, we approach recruitment with an apologetic attitude based in a lingering notion that no one *really* wants to serve on the board.

When coupled with careless recruitment practices that put off the nomination process until the last minute, an apologetic attitude can result in the wrong people with the wrong attitude being enlisted with the wrong message. Organizations end up with new board members whose principal qualifications are that they are friends of board members. While they may be people of goodwill and intent, they may not be the ones with the most potential for advancing the organization.

Board members who are recruited in desperation know it. Called at the last minute ("We have to get our slate of nominees in by Friday") and frequently "begged" to join the board ("I know you're busy, but please do this, even as a favor to me—we really need to get some new blood on our board"), they feel as though they are doing the organization a favor.

Unless a dramatically different story emerges at the first board meeting, or during board orientation, board members recruited in this way seldom develop a level of respect for the organization that leads to commitment. The urgency posed to them in the recruitment process is an urgency to expand the board, rather than the urgency of the community needs their board service helps meet. The damage compounds when these same individuals are assured, "There is nothing much to serving on the board. Don't worry, it won't take much of your time." If this is an honest statement, then the organization has some real problems. If it is a dishonest statement, then the organization will have trouble with the new recruits when they discover what is really expected of them. In at least one instance, a recruited board member turned down the opportunity to be formally enlisted when he was told there would be few demands on him. He said it made him feel that the organization, the board, and his involvement were not very important. When he joins a board, he expects to be put to work.

MANAGING THE BOARD DEVELOPMENT PROCESS

If you want to do a good job at board development, dissolve your nominating committee and create a committee on trustees, or a board development committee. There is an inherently flawed notion in the name "nominating" committee. It too narrowly defines the function of the committee, and implies only a very occasional need to meet, perhaps once a year with an emergency meeting now and then to fill a board vacancy. The name also implies that the committee's function is over once the nomination process has been completed; it suggests that enlistment, orientation, evaluation, and retention of board members are left to some other unnamed group or to no one at all. Reformulating the committee and its functions, you convey the importance of board development.

The board committee charged with recruitment, enlistment, and retention of the board is the most important board committee. Its competency largely determines the future of the organization.

In very small organizations, the work of the committee on trustees is sometimes given to the executive committee of the board. As a temporary measure, until more board members are recruited, this is probably the best arrangement. Combining the board development function with the fund development function, under the aegis of a development committee, is a bit more difficult. While the two assignments are highly related, they are also highly demanding. One function usually suffers. The executive committee is a better place to assign this responsibility on a temporary basis.

COMMITTEE ON TRUSTEES: RESPONSIBILITIES

A committee on trustees, or board development committee, is responsible not only for the nomination of new board members, but also for recruitment, enlistment, and retention. *Recruitment* is the process of identifying and interviewing potential board members and then cultivating them until such time as you and they are ready for them to serve. Recruitment and enlistment are not the same functions. *Enlistment* is the process of formalizing the recruitment when it is the right time for the service to begin. It involves meeting with the board recruit and reviewing job descriptions, financial and time expectations, possible committee assignments, long range plans, and the other aspects of board responsibilities. Enlistment culminates with a comprehensive board orientation. *Retention* is the maintenance of a stable, productive, and satisfied board. The factors which contribute to strong boards are complex, but dynamic participation by its members is one of the most important. Management of board development must include post-enlistment attention to board member involvement.

The committee on trustees has these responsibilities:

- Meets at least quarterly to continually identify and qualify prospective board members. These meetings are staffed by the development or executive director who serves as a resource and sounding board for names as well as in a support role.
- Motivates and requires board and staff to regularly supply the committee with names of potential board candidates.
- Organizes the board orientations.
- Invites other board members to assist with recruitment and enlistments.
- Checks in periodically with board members who have missed meetings.
- Arranges an annual meeting for the CEO and board chair with each board member.
- Develops and maintains the summary board profile and recruitment matrix.
- Performs the nominating function in a timeframe that permits the best possible recruitment.

Combining all of these board-related functions into one committee allows an integration and cohesiveness to develop that can lead to greater board member involvement and satisfaction. Those recruited, enlisted, and retained in this highly professional manner perform their roles with greater responsibility and commitment.

RECRUITMENT

The board dream team is systematically developed. Good recruitment begins with the creation of a recruitment matrix. There are two principal sources of information for the matrix: the composition of the existing board and the long range or strategic institutional plan. Existing board members are analyzed by a number of different criteria including:

- Gender
- Age range
- Race/ethnicity
- Geography (where that is important)
- Profession
- Expertise (which may or may not be the same as profession)
- Expiration date of current board term and whether it is renewable
- Willingness to ask
- Capacity to give
- Connections in the community
- Other board affiliations

You may have other criteria that are pertinent to your organization; for example, an orchestra might add "love of music" to its prerequisites.

Using the Matrix

Most organizations put this information on a chart or grid (see Exhibit 9.1). Some organizations even weight the different criteria. The format you develop should be easy for board members to read and understand. This is the primary management tool for the recruitment and enlistment process. When the matrix is completed, make a summary profile of the current board. For example:

- *Gender*—55% female, 45% male.
- *Race/Ethnicity*—65% white, 15% African-American, 15% Asian, 5% Hispanic.
- *Profession*—5 community volunteers, 4 corporate executives, 1 teacher, 3 lawyers, 1 marketing director, 1 college administrator, 3 representatives of the client base, 1 banker, 1 physician.
- *Expertise*—fund raising = 6; marketing = 2; education = 2; client services = 3; financial management = 2; personnel = 1; hospital administration = 1; legal = 3.
- *Geography*—city center = 8; suburbs = 6; rural = 4; other cities = 2.

Do this type of summary for all areas of the matrix. When completed, chart the expiration dates of the board terms. In this way, you

EXHIBIT 9.1 Sample Board Matrix

Reading the codes: Confidential

1 = gender

2 = ethnicity, race (W = white; AA = African American; AS = Asian;
H = Hispanic; N = Native American; O = other)

3 = age range: 3a, 20–30; 3b, 31–45; 3c, 46–60; 3d; 61 +

4 = expertise (p = program; o = organization; d = development including
fund raising, marketing or public relations)

5 = profession (c = corporate executive; v = community volunteer;
m = marketing or public relations; fr = fund raising; l = lawyer;
fi = financial; r = retail; e = educator; ss = social services)

6 = expiration date of term (00 = 2000); R = renewable; N = non-renewable

7 = experience with programs and mission (1, 2, or 3 with 1 = very
experienced)

8 = time available for board work (1, 2, 3 with 1 = most)

9 = committee affiliation (t = Committee on Trustees; d = Development;
m = Marketing; f = Finance; e = Executive; p = Program)

Name	1	2	3	4	5	6	7	8	9
Board A	F	W	b	O	C	00R	3	3	m
Board B	M	AA	c	P	L	99N	1	2	t,e
Board C	F	AS	c	D	FR	98N	2	3	d,m

This analysis is repeated for all board members.

When it is complete, the "profile" of expertise, ethnic/racial and
gender balance, professional distribution, and so on, is matched against
the needs of the organization as reflected in the institutional plan.
Expiration dates are tracked to ensure that individuals providing a
particular expertise are replaced as their terms expire.

Recruitment is gauged to "fill the blanks" and build strength in
required areas.

The matrix should be kept current by the committee on trustees.

can track, and not lose, vital legal, financial, or educational expertise when those members rotate off the board. Identification and recruitment of people with that same expertise should begin at least a year before the retirement of the current board member.

The next step in the analysis is to match the current board profile, changes anticipated by rotation, and the expertise which will be required by the long-range or strategic institutional plan. Base recruitment on the "gaps" revealed in this analysis, and begin designing your strategy:

Area of Need	*Who to Recruit*
Annual fund raising	Community volunteers and others willing to spearhead events, mailings, phone appeals; and do face-to-face solicitations
Enhanced marketing activity or planning	Marketing consultants or directors
Staff personnel expansion or reorganization	Labor lawyers, human resources professionals
Increased institutional visibility	Media representatives or those with media connections
Projected capital campaign	Potential large investors or people with connections to potential large investors; people who know city or county politics if a building project is planned; estate planners if an endowment campaign is planned
Facilities expansion	Contractors, environmental lawyers, architects

The committee on trustees should review the plan carefully with the CEO and the board chair, highlighting those short- and long-term goals and objectives that will guide board recruitment.

A Word of Caution: Ensuring Passionate Pragmatism

Recruiting for profession or expertise is essential, but requires some caution. The concept of passionate pragmatism (Grace 1995) suggests that a danger exists when board members are recruited solely for the professional expertise they can bring to an organization (see Chapter 3). They must be willing to get more broadly involved in the organization. They must believe in its mission and values. The recruitment criteria need to be well-defined and convincingly conveyed to the prospective board member so that all expectations are clear. Too many board members who provide only their expertise tip the board balance towards a pragmatism that can lack passion and understanding for the mission and the importance of the organization. Without passion, advocacy is often minimal.

Getting Ready to Use the Matrix in Enlistment

When the committee on trustees has completed the recruitment matrix, distribute it to the board. Obviously confidential, it should be treated with the utmost discretion. To ensure clarity, allow adequate time for discussion of the matrix, particularly around sensitive areas that may strike some board members as highly personal (age range, race/ethnicity). If these criteria are too troublesome, drop them from the matrix. However, some government and foundation funders are interested in how well the board composition reflects the community or the clients. Certain community foundations have increasingly stringent recommendations regarding racial and ethnic balance. They appropriately feel that the boards of the organizations they fund should reflect the racial and ethnic composition of the community. Other funders may have similar guidelines. A board matrix which reflects the importance of complying with certain funder guidelines may require some explanation to the board. This is particularly true if balanced board composition has been a neglected or difficult practice in the past.

Matrices may reflect other changes that need to be made in board composition. Many organizations evolve from an early and consuming need to build internal programs to a more mature need to reach out into the community for visibility and support. Board members with program expertise and representation may resist a matrix which shows few program people relative to the number of corporate vice presidents, media contacts, people with influence and affluence. This is particularly true in social and human services agencies in which the initial years of board service may have been very hands-on, and the enlistment of nonprogram people signals a shift in the board culture. Apprehension also occurs when private schools move away from a parent-majority board towards one that includes alumni and others representative of the community. Respect these protective attitudes and the concerns they reflect.

The committee on trustees may need to review the institutional plan with the board to show the guidelines used in constructing the new board matrix. It is important that people feel as comfortable as possible with change.

Use the matrix as a guide. Experience reveals that few matrices are ever fulfilled 100 percent, but their existence launches the recruitment and enlistment process in a highly professional way. Distribute a written outline of the recruitment and enlistment process, including an enlistment target (number) for the next several years, to the board. Be very clear that there are steps involved in the enlistment process (see Exhibit 9.2). You do not want an enthusiastic board member to recruit someone without the committee on trustees' knowledge or involvement. This is a particular hazard when there is some pressure to fill spaces on a diminished board or to build a new or reinvented board. Assure the board that the steps will be employed with speed, but not haste. Each decision is very important to the future of the organization and therefore must be well thought out. Most board members readily see that the process is crucial, and are willing to participate in lunches or other board candidate cultivation meetings that are organized by the committee on trustees.

With this process, as with all processes, do not become so dedicated to the steps that you miss opportunities. It is good to balance your committee on trustees between those who are dedicated to procedure and will keep the system on track, and those with a bit bolder attitude who may discover an excellent candidate at a recruitment lunch and realize that the match and the timing for enlistment is perfect. If possible, enlist committee on trustees co-chairs with these differing but balanced skills.

Getting Names into the Pipeline

From this point forward, the objective is to keep board candidate names coming into the pipeline so they can be evaluated, introduced to the organization, cultivated, and, if there is a match, asked to join the board at an appropriate time. Make the collection of potential board member names a regular part of every board meeting. Once board members are aware of the integrity of the process, they are more willing to supply names. Reach into the widest constituency possible, and involve staff, former board members, advisory board members, other volunteers, and funders in the identification process. An excellent and often-overlooked source of potential board members are donor, member, and subscriber lists. These people are already invested in the organization. The com-

EXHIBIT 9.2 Process for Board Recruitment

1. Construct a recruitment matrix based on the "gaps" that will emerge when current board members retire.
2. Ask board and staff members, and key volunteers, to submit names of people they know who will fit into one of the "gaps."
3. Compile names; review by Committee on Trustees.
4. Working with the recommending board or staff member or volunteer, arrange a time for the prospective board member to meet with the CEO and the recommending board/staff/volunteer.
5. At this meeting, focus on the mission, passion, etc., of the organization and provide information for the individual. DO NOT ENLIST at this meeting. Let the individual have some time to get to know the organization (even if it is only a week). Let the process rest; see if there is consensus about inviting this person on the board now. Perhaps this person would be better on a committee at first; or perhaps this person would be good for the future (or not the right person at all for the board).
6. If the decision is made to enlist, plan a second meeting with the prospective board member at which time the board job description will be reviewed and expectations clearly related. Remember that there are talented people out there who will see this as an opportunity to make a difference. But they need to have the story straight from the outset.
7. With the approval of the Committee on Trustees, the Board President should enlist the new board member.
8. Following enlistment, the board member will fill out the board information form, attend an orientation, receive an up-to-date trustee packet, and be assigned to a committee.
9. It is the responsibility of the Committee on Trustees to see that each board member lives up to his/her commitment.
10. On an annual basis, the Executive Director and the Board Chair (or Chair of the Committee on Trustees) should meet with each board member individually for the purpose of assessing satisfaction with board service, discussing best committee placement for the coming year, and soliciting the annual gift.
11. The Committee on Trustees should update the matrix constantly to reflect changes in board composition.
12. While nominations, after the initial effort to build the board, may not arise that often, the recruitment process should never stop. It is the goal of any mature organization to have a "stable" of recruited individuals who are just waiting to come on the board. During the waiting period, they can be involved in committees and do other volunteer service.

mittee on trustees should regularly review these lists and submit selected names to the board for silent prospecting (Chapter 4). Used more often for donor qualification, silent prospecting is also an effective tool for evaluating potential board members.

If you are having trouble building a list of potential board members, there are some alternative resources that may be available to you. In some cities in the United States, there are nonprofit support organizations that annually stage a board fair where citizens interested in serving on boards can meet and talk with representatives from organizations looking for board members. Community volunteer bureaus also maintain lists of people interested in board service. Some U.S. and multinational corporations, through their human resources departments, encourage employees to become involved with nonprofit organizations. Community foundations, the United Way, service clubs (Rotary, Soroptimists, e.g.) are also good resources.

Whatever the source of the name, be sure to employ the same evaluation procedure.

The Evaluation Process

The committee on trustees should use the following procedure for evaluating names:

- At regular meetings, review names as they are received.
- Telephone those who have submitted names to gather greater detail about the qualifications of the recommended individual.
- Refer to the recruitment matrix to see what matches exist with each proposed candidate.
- Make summary notes and place in recruitment files. Do not make any gratuitous or indiscreet comments (impending divorce, business on the brink of failure, etc.) because you never know who might see the file.
- Review summary notes at a meeting, and determine priority recruitments.
- Make assignments based on the priority list, and provide each member with guidelines for approaching and evaluating the potential candidate.
- Provide regular reports of recruitment activities to the committee on trustees, and devise strategies for enlisting appropriate candidates.

If this sounds strikingly like the development/investment process, you are right. So synergistic are these two functions, that the internalization of one enhances the other. Eventually, organizations are able to spread the investment attitude effortlessly throughout these two critical practices.

Making the Recruitment Phone Call

When the candidate is contacted by the committee member, it is important to use the right words. Your part of the conversation might go something like this: "This is Margaret Michaelson. I don't believe we've ever met, but we are mutually acquainted with Roger Suarez who, with me, is a board member at the City Youth Orchestra." (There may be some chat here about Roger. Then proceed.) "Roger (be sure you have his permission to use his name) thought you might be interested in joining our board at sometime in the future. As you know, with the decline of public funding for music in our schools, the youth orchestra has become more and more important. Those of us who serve on the board feel as though we're helping build future audiences, as well as future musicians. I realize this isn't a decision you make quickly. We don't want a yes or no now. We want to invite you to learn more about how we operate and what board member responsibilities entail. It's important for us to get to know you, too, and hear your interests and enthusiasms. Roger said he thought one of your children was once involved with the orchestra. I want to invite you to have lunch with me and Mark Nakamichi, the chair of our committee on trustees, next week. We're available Thursday or Friday. Would either of those days work for you?" During the conversation, the candidate will interject and ask questions, but your "script" should include information that focuses on the importance of the organization, the community need it is meeting, why board service is important, and what the steps are in the enlistment process.

As recruitment meetings are held, be sure reports are filed by the members of the committee or by other board members assigned to candidate meetings. The matrix begins to come alive. The same kind of tiering (Chapter 4) that is done for donor-investors can be done for board candidates. Some will be enlisted immediately and others, due to their timing or yours, will be kept informed and involved but will not be enlisted for a while. Still others will not be enlisted at all, either for their reasons or yours. Handling the latter issue is delicate, but should be addressed honestly with the person. "George, our feeling is that right now, even though we're grateful for your interest in coming on our board, your involvement as a board member for four other organizations is probably a full plate without adding us. We'd like to keep you involved, and hope that, from time to time, we can come and review marketing ideas with you. You've already been so helpful to us. We'd like to stay in touch on an ad hoc basis for now. But please let us know if you complete your service on several of the other boards, because we really enjoyed getting to know you. It's just that right now, we need someone who can give us much more time."

ENLISTMENT

A systematic recruitment process facilitates enlistment. Awkward phone calls and first meetings are out of the way. The candidate, barring unforeseen changes, is committed to serve when asked. If you have been able, over the period of a year or more, to build a stable of informed and cultivated board candidates, then bringing them onto the board is a comfortable process for them and for you. One board was so good at doing this that, by the time candidates were enlisted, they knew everyone and were somewhat informed about critical program and budget issues. It was a privilege and pleasure for board members to begin their board service with a solid basis of knowledge that would accelerate their involvement.

Materials to Use in Enlistment

At the time of the actual enlistment, the committee on trustees should meet with the candidate and review the expectations of board membership. Give the new board member a notebook containing pertinent information he or she will need:

- A list of current trustees with phone numbers, home and professional addresses, secretary and spouse or partner names, committee assignments, term expiration dates
- A calendar with all board and committee meeting dates and activities for the year
- Board member job description
- A list of the committees with their chairs and members and a brief description of their responsibilities
- A blank trustee information form to fill out before the board orientation and a list of committees to rank by preference for involvement
- An alphabetical list of staff members with their phones/extensions and their home phones and addresses (unless there are reasons for confidentiality)

- A description of the various departments in the organization, the name of the head of each department, and a list of department staff members
- Brief profiles of each member of the administrative staff and the department heads
- A copy of the bylaws and articles of incorporation
- A brief history of the organization
- Financial information including most recent audited financial statement, budget for current year, financial statements, balance sheet
- Fund-raising information including annual fund performance over a several year period, endowment management information, and other reports of development activities
- A copy of the long-range or strategic institutional plan
- A copy of the vision and mission statements if not included in the plan
- Copies of current board policies
- A list of holidays observed by the organization
- Other pertinent material

This binder cannot simply be handed to a new board member during the enlistment meeting. Show the new board member the various sections of the binder. Explain that reading the binder through is very important preparation for the board orientation (and provide the date for the orientation). Review the job description and provide a verbal rundown on board members the person has not yet met. Have the person fill out the board information form at the time of the actual enlistment, and choose his or her preferred committee assignments. The purpose of giving the entire binder at this time is so the new board member can review the material before the new board member orientation. Put a tight timeframe on the need to read the material in the binder, otherwise it will go on a shelf.

Board Orientation

Orientation is really the last step in the enlistment process. Questions always arise about when to do the orientation. The best time is as soon as possible after the enlistment. While it is best if there are three or four (or more) new board members for the orientation, do not put it off if there is only one. Just adjust the format and the players. An orientation for new trustees for an organization with a very large board was almost textbook in its planning and execution. It provides an excellent model.

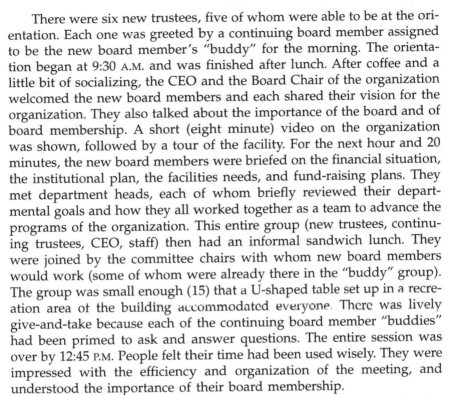

There were six new trustees, five of whom were able to be at the orientation. Each one was greeted by a continuing board member assigned to be the new board member's "buddy" for the morning. The orientation began at 9:30 A.M. and was finished after lunch. After coffee and a little bit of socializing, the CEO and the Board Chair of the organization welcomed the new board members and each shared their vision for the organization. They also talked about the importance of the board and of board membership. A short (eight minute) video on the organization was shown, followed by a tour of the facility. For the next hour and 20 minutes, the new board members were briefed on the financial situation, the institutional plan, the facilities needs, and fund-raising plans. They met department heads, each of whom briefly reviewed their departmental goals and how they all worked together as a team to advance the programs of the organization. This entire group (new trustees, continuing trustees, CEO, staff) then had an informal sandwich lunch. They were joined by the committee chairs with whom new board members would work (some of whom were already there in the "buddy" group). The group was small enough (15) that a U-shaped table set up in a recreation area of the building accommodated everyone. There was lively give-and-take because each of the continuing board member "buddies" had been primed to ask and answer questions. The entire session was over by 12:45 P.M. People felt their time had been used wisely. They were impressed with the efficiency and organization of the meeting, and understood the importance of their board membership.

The sixth new board member, out of town on business on the day of the orientation, did not miss out. As soon as she returned to town, an individual orientation was arranged. She met with the CEO and the financial officer, watched the video, toured the building and then attended a department head meeting where she was introduced and encouraged to ask questions after their regular business was finished. Afterwards, the CEO, one of the department heads, the chair of the committee on trustees and the board chair took her to lunch.

There are several positive outcomes from having continuing board members pair up with new board members and attend the orientation: (1) New board members get to know one continuing board member a little better; (2) new board members have an ear to whisper in if they have question they are reluctant to ask in front of the group or if they need clarification about someone's identity or what someone has said; and (3) continuing board members get a "booster shot" in terms of their own knowledge, enthusiasm, and commitment.

All new board members need orientation, no matter how well they may feel they already know the organization or how experienced they are at serving on other boards. It is the way in which we let them know how serious their board commitment is. If they feel they really do not have to attend, they are already showing signs of being a board member whose potential commitment may not be as deep as you had hoped.

Boards with the most stringent requirements (attendance at meetings and events, giving and asking, participation in orientation, service on committees) are often the most sought after by community-minded citizens. A county hospital formed a foundation that became the most desired community board on which to serve. The list of board requirements was very eye-opening to other local organizations that had soft-pedaled their requirements in hopes of recruiting some of the same corporate and social leaders that were eagerly signing up for this new board. There is a strong correlation between a board orientation program that sets high standards for membership and an organization that successfully builds its base of donor-investors by promoting the results of its programs. Nothing lures like success (see Exhibit 9.3 for a recipe for success).

BOARD RETENTION AND INVOLVEMENT

The responsibility for board development does not end with the enlistment. A well-recruited and properly enlisted board can still be dysfunctional if it is allowed to stagnate or ferment because its own dynamics are not evaluated regularly. Able, excited, visionary, and energetic new board members can become discouraged and inactive when confronted with veteran board members who are bored, cynical, or unenthusiastic. We turn "silk purses" into "sow's ears" when we allow board member malaise to dampen the enthusiasm of new members or prompt high turnover.

Attention to board health is important for these reasons:

- Self-perpetuating or stagnant boards eventually calcify their organizations.
- Unhappy or uninformed boards are poor advocates.
- "Revolving door" boards erode continuity in vision, planning, administration, and fund raising, and create a poor reputation in the community.
- Rebellious boards can do permanent damage to program and services.

In order to go beyond fund raising, at least one-third of the board members should place your organization as their top philanthropic priority. Another third should place your organization among their top

---

EXHIBIT 9.3 Recipe for a Successful Board Orientation

Ingredients:

A fresh bunch of enthusiastic planners
One interested board
One supportive staff
Other volunteers (to taste)
One agenda that is relevant to the short- and long-term success of the organization
Equal parts *inspiration*, *information*, and *motivation*
A mixture of training techniques and activities

Assemble the fresh bunch of enthusiastic planners, and place in an environment where it can breathe and grow. When it has grown and flowered, add it to the interested board and supportive staff. Mix thoroughly. Add other volunteers to taste, and allow whole mixture to blend. Fold in the agenda, making sure that it permeates all parts of the previous mixture. While serving, combine the equal parts of inspiration, information, and motivation with the training techniques and activities. Stir vigorously into the mixture. Serve in an atmosphere that is warm and receptive, and garnish with lavish amounts of interaction, laughter, good will, and passion derived from the vision, mission, and goals of the organization.

Will last all year. Plan to make on an annual basis, or as needed.

---

three philanthropic priorities. The remaining third will provide expertise and be less involved, but they should be recruited with the goal of moving them into the first or second group. Achieving this board composition is not an impossible goal. Such boards exist in hundreds of organizations that are now successfully creating the kinds of investor relationships with their board members and funders that will help guarantee their long-term ability to fulfill their mission.

The care and feeding of boards is the primary responsibility of the board itself, with leadership provided by the board chair and the committee on trustees working with the executive director/CEO and the development director. There are a number of factors which determine a board member's feeling of investment and belonging in the organization:

- Mutual respect—by the organization, for the organization.
- Understanding of the importance of the organization, and of the philanthropic sector.

- Value(s)—being valued, valuing the organization, sharing the organization's values and seeing them at work in the community.
- A feeling of belonging within the board and the organization.
- Belief that time spent in meetings and activities is worthwhile.
- Experiences with the board and the organization that are not only informative and worthwhile, but fun.
- A sense of the future advancement of the organization and a way to play a part in that advancement.
- Knowledge that the organization, and fellow board members, appreciate his or her gifts of time, talent, and treasure.

Periodic board self-evaluation is an excellent tool for maintaining board awareness of responsibilities and potential need for strategic change. A questionnaire can be developed by the organization and administered during the annual individual meeting among the board member, CEO and board chair (see Exhibit 9.4). For more formal instruments The National Center for Nonprofit Boards in Washington, D.C., has well-tested materials available for purchase by boards. The results of these evaluations are reviewed by the committee on trustees and used as the basis for board retreats or other planning sessions.

When management of the board is clearly assigned to a committee on trustees (or board development committee) which works with staff and board leadership, these factors become guidelines for shaping interaction and feedback. The importance of maintaining positive board dynamics is conveyed by the committee to the entire board, whose understanding of the importance of welcoming new board members and interacting positively among themselves may need refreshing. Here is where leadership steps forward. Whoever said, "It starts at the top" was right. The board chair and the CEO each have opportunities to set not only standards, but style and tone. The CEO conveys this to staff who interact with board through committees, events, volunteer work, and fund raising; the board chair conveys it to the board most obviously by his or her own behavior and participation.

There is more about board leadership in Chapters 3 and 12, but the imperative is clear. Board members with potential for being effective, once enlisted, need to be continually listened to, nurtured, and encouraged. Capable board members are not born, they are made. The lawyer with a private practice and three small children does not come to the board meeting to be bored. The banker with a heavy schedule who is also president of Rotary does not come to meetings to be misinformed. The community volunteer, who sits on other boards and sees broadly the community issues that must be met, does not come to meetings to

EXHIBIT 9.4 Board Member Questionnaire

- Have your expectations of board membership been realized?
- What changes would you suggest?
- Do you feel you're serving on the right committee(s)? Change?
- Do you feel you received adequate orientation? Change?
- Please comment on our Board Member Job Description.
- We shall all be involved in fund raising. What can the Board Development Committee do to prepare you for this?
- Are you willing to serve another term?
- Are you happy as a board member?
- Have you reviewed our long-range plan? How do you feel about the Goals and Objectives? Do they work? Which ones excite or at least interest you?
- Have you suggestions for this year's board retreat? Topics? Format?
- Are there individuals you would recommend for future board membership?

be ignored. Because board meetings are the principal place of interaction for boards, a look at what they are and what they can be is important.

BOARD OR BORED? MAKING THE MOST OF MEETINGS

Anyone who attends the board meetings of many organizations quickly realizes there are certain aspects common to all of them. The players and purposes may differ, but many of the elements are remarkably similar. Some are inevitable (treasurer's report, minutes from the previous meeting, committee reports), and others are variable (special event update, capital campaign progress report). So how can a meeting, which is fairly predictable in its agenda and course, be made into something that will play a key role in sustaining board enthusiasm? By remembering, always, that the reason most of these board members are here (or should be here) is because you have an urgent mission to fulfill in the community. Give them a "product demonstration" at each meeting so they leave having learned something new about why they are involved: testimony by a parent whose child has benefited from a learning disabilities program, enthusiastic appreciation by a student who has received a scholarship, a short video or slide presentation about environmental clean-up activities, a brief talk by a teacher who has integrated a music education program into her curriculum. These presentations can help change the institutional culture and behavior of cliquish or social boards whose motivations may be driven less by mission than by fulfilling or seeking social connections. A presentation or demonstration or video gives board members something common to see, hear, and discuss. A dance company focused its board on the funding needed for outreach to inner-city schools by having teachers and students speak at a board meeting about the impact of the current program and its potential for growth. Board members, when asked to raise money for this program, had a new level of understanding and enthusiasm which resulted in significantly more effective advocacy. A passionate advocate can present the case for programs whose sensitivity prevent the appearance of actual participants at board meetings.

The whole board meeting ritual can be very discouraging. Too often, board members do not leave feeling passionate about the mission; they leave feeling discouraged about the financial, facilities, staffing or board recruitment situation because no solutions, except raising more money or cutting an already bare-bones budget, have been offered. Urged to go out and raise money before it is too late, they can only assume a tin cup posture; the organization is desperate for funds and needs help. No matter how grim the financial situation may be—and full disclosure is essential if you are to retain board loyalty and investment—you have to turn it around in such a way that the urgency of the financial situation is because of the urgency of the community need that is being met. If it's not—if bad management is the cause of the financial problems—then that should be addressed through administrative evaluation before it gets in the way of the mission (Chapter 3).

Focus the board on the community need. Show a video. Bring in a client, or a former client. Inspire them. There is nothing more paradoxical than to see a board wade through the cash flow, hear the discouraging report on the planned special event that may have to be canceled, see photos of the deterioration of the parking lot, learn that the lease may not be renewed, and then have the valiant development director or committee chair hand out the annual fund personal solicitation assignments, asking them all to go out and be enthusiastic and excited when they invite people to invest in the organization. Does this sound like an organization in which you could ask people to invest? Is there anyone who would want to invest in it? It will be a tough sell. While each board member may intuitively understand that the organization would not have financial needs if it were not producing results, they need to be continually reconnected with why the organization exists. Otherwise, the passion will probably be missing.

Board meetings are the most visible place where we let the organization get in the way of the mission (Chapter 3). Unfortunately, some board members are so little involved in other activities with the organization that board meetings are their only exposure. Board meetings with a negative tone and poor focus may be the reason they are not more involved.

Organizations that conduct lively, mission-focused, interactive, time-sensitive, solution-oriented, and productive board meetings know how to put together meetings that inform, motivate and inspire. They provide the following:

- A good agenda, developed by the CEO and the board chair with input from the committee on trustees and from other committee and staff people, which focuses on issues as well as on reports.
- An exciting window into the organization through a "product demonstration." Not a *report* about something, but an informative, compelling firsthand presentation from someone who has benefited from the organization or who has worked with those who have benefited. This can be tied into an issue that is to be discussed.
- An established meeting timeframe which is altered only when an urgent issue demands a longer meeting (to table an urgent issue in the interest of time is not in the best interests of the organization and causes the issue to slip in priority in the minds of those asked to deal with it).
- Good attendance ensured by committee on trustee calls to those who have missed board meetings. Few things are worse than failing to reach quorum and negating the efforts of those members who are present.
- An atmosphere of trust, respect, and consideration for each other's feelings.
- A board leader who can graciously contain those board members who dominate while deliberately drawing out those who otherwise defer to their more vocal fellow members, losing their opportunity to contribute and be validated.

Board Retreats

Board retreats are a different kind of board meeting, one with great potential for elevating board commitment. When they work well, they should be called "board advances," because they have a high potential for moving the organization forward. Usually based around annual or campaign planning and evaluation, and conducted at a site away from the organization's usual meeting facility, retreats offer a unique opportunity for board members to get to know each other better while addressing issues of critical future importance. Include key administrative, development, and program staff at your board retreat to ensure clarity and continuity in fulfilling retreat plans. Small organizations in which there may be much shared responsibility between board and staff often include the entire staff at the retreat Failure to include any staff except the executive director can lead to feelings of "us versus them."

There are exceptions, of course. Some board retreats are called for the express purpose of addressing crucial staffing issues which may involve the executive director. In these cases, the retreat usually begins with an executive session where only board members are in attendance. When their business is finished, the executive director and/or other involved staff members are invited to join and to discuss the results of the board deliberations and to begin working towards implementation of changes that must be made. Needless to say, these latter kinds of retreats are tough, tense meetings. Fortunately, the vast majority of board retreats are not grim gatherings at which sensitive personnel issues are resolved. They are great opportunities for exploring issues and ideas in a more relaxed environment and for spending time getting to know each other.

Planning a Board Retreat

The first time an organization attempts to organize a board retreat there may be considerable resistance. This is especially true if board commitment is uneven and leadership is not convinced of the importance of an extended session. Convincing boards that it is vital for them to spend four hours (the minimum time for a "retreat") to three days (probably the maximum time) may be difficult. Have a solid outcomes-focused agenda to lure the committed but very busy people (see Exhibit 9.5). Your notice, sent out after the retreat idea is introduced in a regular board meeting, might announce:

"The purpose of the board retreat is to establish financial and staffing projections for the next two years so that our grant from the Benevolent Foundation will be renewed on time. To do so, we will have to undertake an evaluation of potential growth or decline in the need for program delivery, cost centers, income fluctuations, potential government funding decreases, and our other fund raising. Staff will be there to provide us with baseline data for our evaluation. At the end of the retreat, we should have the raw material for a solid proposal which will be drafted by staff, provided for our review at the November board meeting, and submitted to the Benevolent Foundation by December 31. An agenda for the meeting is attached, and the planning committee welcomes your comments and ideas about how we can make this retreat as productive as possible."

Once these outcomes have been established, and a good date and location identified, the retreat planners can get to work on the process and format of the retreat. Team building, while seldom explicitly mentioned in retreat announcements, is one of the primary reasons for having a board retreat. Otherwise, the materials for the Benevolent Foundation could probably be gathered through a series of committee meetings (finance, development, program, personnel, executive) and pieced together for the proposal. But, board commitment and cohesiveness are always enhanced in a good board retreat, and the interaction around a specific issue or project promotes team work. Specific team building activities, often urged by facilitators, may not be necessary if you have a solid and interesting agenda with lots of opportunity for small group interaction. People will team build around the work provided. An agenda which permits some down-time (but not so much that busy people will feel their time is wasted) will stimulate informal interaction not possible within the stringent time requirements of regular board meetings or even within the small group assignments at the retreat. So many times, however, the laughter which pours out of a small group session struggling with an issues-based real scenario gives the best witness to what happens when people come together with clarity and purpose. They have fun, and they accomplish much more than they would otherwise.

Ensuring a Good Board Retreat

The aspects of a good board retreat are basically the same as those for good board meetings. In addition, you will want to follow these steps and include these considerations:

1. Start planning the retreat three to four months before it is scheduled. The board retreat should be an annual calendar date. Many organizations choose the same month each year and have the retreat in place of the regular board meeting. Involve board and staff (if they are included in the retreat) on the retreat planning committee.

EXHIBIT 9.5 Board Retreat Planning Form

1. Purpose of retreat—What outcomes do you want?

2. Who to invite—Board only, board and key staff, other volunteers? Who will plan—Staff, board, combined?

3. How to market, how to fund—What will you say to Board members to get them to attend? How will you pay for the retreat?

4. What agenda—Content and format: Will it be facilitated by a professional (outsider) or handled by staff?

5. When to hold—Time of year, relationship to fiscal year and other activities?

6. Length of retreat—Half-day, full day, two day, longer?

7. Where to hold—On-site, off-site, casual or business setting?

KEEPING THE RETREAT RELEVANT: POTENTIAL TOPICS

Annual planning
Long-range planning
Mission clarification
Vision and goal setting
Program exploration and development
Capital campaign planning
Building a stronger Board (recruitment, enlistment, etc.)
Fund raising training
Management and organizational issues

(Continued)

EXHIBIT 9.5 *(Continued)*

KEEPING THE RETREAT LIVELY: A VARIETY OF TECHNIQUES

Role playing
Case studies
Problem-solving
Game simulation
Audio-visuals (overheads, videos, etc.)
Dyads, triads, small group discussions
Questionnaires
Outside facilitator or trainer
Outdoor activities
"Group memory" with easel paper

KEEPING THE RETREAT PLEASANT: ESSENTIAL LOGISTICS

Comfortable setting
Informal attire
Attractive surroundings
Time for unstructured interaction, conversation
Include an unrushed meal
Ample time for introductions, getting acquainted
"State of the Organization" remarks by Executive Director or equivalent

2. Be sure the date and place you have chosen are convenient for the majority of board and staff. Seek 100 percent attendance; be happy with 85 percent; cancel if only 70 percent sign up. Members of the committee, with the facilitator if one is being used, should visit the site to determine whether it is appropriate and has the right space and resources to support the planned activities.

3. Establish preliminary desired outcomes (results and process) at the beginning of your planning. Have the retreat as a board meeting agenda item at least three months before the anticipated time of the retreat. Brainstorm expectations and desired outcomes. Submit your tentative agenda to the board for feedback. Invite their comments and response.

4. Assess board member tolerance before committing to a very long board retreat. It is best to start with a short good retreat and gradually, over the years, extend the time as the need demands. In some years, a long retreat may not be desirable or necessary. Gauge the time to the tolerance and the need. One European organization, in

the year after its first successful distant-site two-day retreat, opted for a half-day retreat at a closer location. It was superbly attended (88 percent) and highly productive.

5. Be clear and consistent in conveying the importance of the meeting and the anticipated outcomes. Leadership must be obviously enthusiastic and committed for others to feel that way.

6. Decide early in your planning if you will use an inside or outside facilitator. Inside facilitators come without cost, but may lack the required objectivity. The advantage to an outside facilitator is professional skill and the objectivity to move the meeting along and not get tangled up in politics or difficult relationships. The principal disadvantage is cost. In some communities, local foundations will cover the cost of a facilitator if the retreat objectives are clearly tied to (e.g.) long-range planning. You will need time to apply for this funding.

7. If you choose to use an outside facilitator, be sure that he/she is available before you confirm the date. Have some backup facilitators in mind just in case.

8. Include the facilitator in your planning meetings to the extent possible. He/she needs to understand the dynamics and the issues. Provide the facilitator with a list of the outcomes you want. He or she should prepare a draft agenda which you can then revise and complete together. Do not bring a facilitator in cold to a retreat.

9. Alert the facilitator to any potentially explosive issues that could erupt in the meeting. These land mines have exploded the agenda of more than one well-planned retreat. When the facilitator is aware of the danger spots, he or she can be much more sensitive to the issues or individuals. A skillful facilitator can sometimes surface these issues within the context of a larger discussion and in such a way that they are addressed objectively. This can help neutralize the tension so the real issues can be dealt with openly.

10. Approximately two weeks to ten days before the retreat, reconfirm their attendance with all board and staff. If there is dramatic falloff in attendance, have the board chair or executive director call each board person. If that does not work, consider cancellation. If all is still on track, mail out retreat-related background materials to be read before the retreat (plans, agenda, list of participants, etc.).

11. One week before the retreat, send out a final package with directions to the site (map plus narrative directions and information regarding estimated time it will take to get there), advice about dress (casual, e.g., except for Friday dinner), information about the facility (bring your swim suit or tennis racket), final agenda/schedule (e.g., 5 P.M.

check-in; 6 P.M. registration; 6:30 P.M. opening reception), and any last-minute materials needed to enhance the agenda.

12. During the retreat, stay on time and on point to the extent possible. Even if people are having lots of fun in their small group sessions, keep the agenda moving. Be sure that people arrive on time and return from breaks promptly. Start on time regardless of who is present. If 15 minutes have been allotted for each report presentation, use a timer. It is not fair to presenters or participants to let the time get out of control. People quickly understand and appreciate a professionally-run meeting. Your board and key staff members are major investors in the organization, and a well-run productive retreat is one way to honor their investment.

13. During the meeting, troubleshoot issues that will get in the way of the agenda unless they are resolved. A two-day retreat for a social service agency was nearly derailed by the executive director's disclosure, during his opening remarks, that he had applied for government funding that would add a significant program area to the organization. The board was angry. They had not been consulted, and the program implications, while exciting, were overwhelming. Used to dealing with his visionary drive and independent behavior, they at least listened while he explained. Three hours of tense but important debate significantly altered the established agenda. However, had the issue not been addressed, none of the retreat outcomes could have been accomplished. It ended well. The board was enthused about the program, which received the government funding and is a huge success.

14. Have solid closure to the retreat. Much happens during a retreat, whether it is four hours or three days. Friendships are made. Tensions arise or are resolved. Plans are made or revised. Information is given and digested. There is time for reflection and comment. Organizations miss an opportunity to further increase the intensity of board member investment when they end their retreats in a haphazard way, when people drift out with little understanding of the next steps or the purpose of their participation. Allow enough time at the end of the retreat to do several things: a) confirm the next steps, including timeline, for any planning that has been done; b) have participants make their own individual commitments, verbally, regarding the ways they will support the plan or program and have the development or executive director make note of these commitments as they are made; c) have the facilitator give his/her closing observations; and d) close with a short "stem-winder" (inspirational talk) from a board member, staff leader, or the facilitator.

15. Follow up the retreat with a letter to each board member, thanking them for attending, summarizing the outcomes of the retreat, recounting some of the "process" moments that were fun and memorable, outlining the next steps, restating the board member's commitment, and including complete notes from the retreat. This information should also be sent to those who could not attend the retreat, with a cover letter expressing the importance of the outcomes and the way they can participate in the implementation of the decisions.

Retreats that lack thorough planning and follow-up may be viewed as isolated and time consuming experiences. This reaction erodes the investor attitude, and leads to board member unrest or disinterest.

Improving the Quality and Results of Board Solicitations

It is a given that all board members must make a financial contribution to the organizations they serve. It is no longer an option.

The size of the gift, as with any donor-investor contribution, should be appropriate to the capacity of the individual and the current demands on his or her assets or discretionary income. We know that many community funders look for 100 percent board commitment before they will entertain a proposal. That is an external motivation for having full financial support from the board. The internal reasons listed below are just as important.

- Philanthropy is not multiple choice; those who join and serve should also give.
- Board members cannot ask others to be donor-investors if they themselves are not.
- Board giving leverages gifts from others, including staff.
- There is a joy that comes from knowing that your financial support is helping achieve an important mission in the community.

We frequently employ persuasive language that includes words like "obligation" or "responsibility" when talking with board members about giving. While this may be effective with some, greater gifts are realized when board members give out of a desire to make an investment based on the excitement and satisfaction they feel over their relationship with the organization. We must grow an investor attitude, first and foremost, in our leadership.

The way in which many board gifts are solicited negates the spirit of investment. Countless organizations still solicit their board members by letter, phone or (worst of all) by announcing at a board meeting that envelopes are being distributed so they can make their board gift before they leave. While soliciting board gifts by letter or phone may possibly be excused in organizations that conduct all their fund raising that way, it also occurs in organizations that have graduated to personal solicitation of their larger investors. A problem arises when board members who have not been solicited personally are asked to meet face-to-face with others to ask for their gift. The board member who has not been solicited personally is not nearly as effective a solicitor as the board member who has.

But there are other reasons as well. The solicitation of a board member's gift is a rare annual opportunity for the CEO and the board chair to sit down one-on-one with a board member to listen as well as ask. The committee on trustees should organize a cycle of individual meetings for each board member with the executive director and the board chair (or other board leader if it is not possible for the board chair to commit to so many meetings). These can take place over a period of several months; there is no need to wait until the end of the year. At this meeting, three essential areas are covered:

1. The board member is thanked for his or her service and is asked to comment about their experience, including their concerns, complaints, and enthusiasms.
2. Future involvement is discussed, including appropriateness of current committee assignments, time or resources changes, or constraints of which the organization should be aware, and so on.
3. An annual gift is solicited, using proper solicitation techniques (see Chapter 5) and asking for a specific amount appropriate to the individual's giving history, capacity, and constraints. Gifts traditionally made at year-end can be secured several months beforehand through a pledge. If a capital campaign is starting (see Chapter 7), this is also the time to discuss the campaign and the financial contribution the organization would like the board member to consider when the campaign gets underway.

After this meeting, the board chair sends the board member a letter, recounting the meeting, summarizing the conversation, including committee preferences for the following year, and thanking the board member for his/her gift or pledge. A copy of the letter is kept in the board member's file, maintained by the committee on trustees.

This is such a simple process, and board members like it. At first, they may say that such a meeting is not necessary. They will assure you that their satisfaction is high and they will make a gift "as usual" at the end of the year. You must convince all board members to participate in an individual meeting. They will end up appreciating the time and attention. The president of the board of a children's services organization included the following summary in her report of the meetings which she and the executive director held with board members: "Overall, the meetings produce a sense of belonging, a feeling of being valued, and a willingness to continue service to the Center, both on the part of the members being interviewed and this president. Certainly the information generated is of great value in raising board performance levels and ensuring continued health and growth. This is a process that merits yearly repetition." That particular organization had approached each interview with a short list of questions with which to open the conversation (see Exhibit 9.4).

Carried out with candor and confidentiality, these interviews are an essential aspect of board management, leadership, and retention. In another benefit, board member gifts will increase in size as they feel a greater sense of belonging. And, not incidentally, their skill and comfort in asking others personally for gifts will improve dramatically. Board members are your first and closest constituents. This interview process helps ensure their leadership and support.

BOARD RETENTION AND ROTATION

Board retention becomes less difficult as board members become more invested. Turnover is kept to a minimum, and vacancies which do arise are filled with relative ease and quickness from the stable of cultivated board candidates. The board management techniques previously described help maintain board stability, and the attention to board member health can prevent the malaise and stagnation that triggers board resignations. Leadership that keeps a watchful eye for areas of potential or growing conflict among board members or between staff and board members can move deliberately to surface and calm the tension. When board development is approached systematically, there is increased board member retention and continued motivation.

Therefore, diligent attention to rotation is critical. Regardless of the dedication and financial support board members provide, they should regularly rotate off the board. Bylaws should define board terms and the rotation process. Board recruitment and enlistment procedures should convey this information to board candidates. Many boards offer renewable terms, with a final rotation off after two or three consecutive terms. Usually, bylaws provide that a former board member can be reelected after a certain period (one or two years).

An organization that was blessed with a founding board member of extraordinary knowledge and commitment still adhered to its rotation policy by naming her to the finance committee in her "year off" and keeping her very involved with fund development. Most people didn't know when she was on or off the board, and she served the organization for more than 40 years until her death at nearly 90. Alert to the end, she was a formidable presence on the board and a powerful advocate in the community.

Other organizations promote long-time or high-profile board members—particularly those whose health or professional circumstances no longer permit active board participation—to emeritus or lifetime trustee status with full voting privileges. Whatever your bylaws say, enforce them or revise them. Organizations are too often out of compliance with their own rules.

The first board matrix an organization prepares is often revealing. One organization, which had bylaw provisions calling for two consecutive three-year terms and then a year off before reelection, discovered that four of its board members had been on for ten or more years. The new committee on trustees took charge. These senior board members were thanked profusely for their service, given a lasting memento and a small party at their last board meeting, graciously rotated, and their seats made available for new board members. Three of the four are still actively involved in other ways and one of them will probably come back on the board; the fourth hadn't been to a board meeting in years.

The infusion of new ideas and new personalities on a board can do wonders for fading morale. This is particularly true in the midst of a major campaign or construction project where it seems as though the same things have been said by the same people for so long that no one hears them anymore. New voices, new questions, and new enthusiasm change the dynamics and energize the entire board. Apprehension of change is often more draining than the actuality. Even those board members who have resisted rotation find that the presence of new people and new leadership enriches their experience.

Nonrenewal of Board Members

One issue relative to rotation that is difficult for most organizations is the nonrenewal of board members who could serve another term. We end up reenlisting board members who do not attend meetings, fail to participate in committees, are reluctant to fund raise, and make a token or no gift themselves. Because this is a voluntary commitment, we are hesitant to impose standards on our board members. When a systematic program of thoughtful recruitment, enlistment and careful board management against established standards for board membership is working, this, too, recedes as an issue.

In the annual meeting with the board member, board chair, and CEO, the reasons for nonattendance or nonsupport can be raised in confidence. If there is a legitimate reason, the organization should take steps to correct the conditions or behavior responsible. Sometimes, the reasons are revealed in a board meeting or retreat. For example, the anchor person for the morning and evening news programs in a small but growing town was asked to serve on the local public schools foundation. Never present for Wednesday morning board meetings, he showed up, to everyone's surprise, for a Saturday all-day board retreat nearly a year after he had been elected. During the meeting, the facilitator had used the Harold Seymour (*Designs for Fund Raising*) profile of volunteers in which 5 percent are described as creative, 30 percent as responsible, 35 percent as responsive, and 30 percent as "inert." At the end of the meeting, board members were asked to make their commitments. Everyone was surprised when this individual said he committed to no longer "being inert." However, he said, "Can we have meetings when I can attend them?" He made the point that their reason for wanting him on the board was because of his media exposure, much of which happened five mornings and noons a week. The board meetings, always scheduled for a Wednesday morning, were impossible for him to attend. So valued was his potential, and so accepted was his earnest response, that the board meetings were changed to late afternoon and were held at the excellent meeting facility at the station.

If you must de-enlist a board member, handle the transaction carefully. You don't want angry former board members telling the community they were treated badly. Like any dismissal, this is difficult to approach. These people know they have not fulfilled their responsibilities, but they perpetually hope that they will have more time, energy or money to give. Some standard procedures can help keep the de-enlistment process objective and fair.

- Know the ways in which they have contributed work, wealth, or wisdom over the years, and thank them.
- Know the reasons why you believe they should not continue on the board, and be prepared to discuss them.

- Offer them another role within the organization on an advisory or consulting board if they want to stay involved.
- Send only your very best emissary(ies) to do the de-enlistment in person (chair of the board, committee on trustees or other appropriate board leader(s)).
- Do not delegate this task to staff. It places them in a very difficult position if, in the future, this same person is identified as a prospect for a large gift.
- Try to relax. Most often, the person to whom you are delivering the "bad news" either preempts you by resigning or is visibly relieved to be done with this obligation. Be sure to keep the door open for later involvement.
- Document the conversation for the files.

Retention and rotation cannot be left to chance. They are vital aspects of effective board development and help present a highly professional profile of your organization within the board and out in the community.

The Parking Lot As Board Room

A final word must be said about maintaining board health. Is the important business of the board taking place in the board room, or in the parking lot after the board meeting? Too many board members, unable, unwilling, or not encouraged to speak up at board meetings, speak to and confide in other board members afterwards. They stand in the hallways, or linger in the parking lot, or meet in a nearby coffee shop, sometimes for hours, dissecting issues that should have the benefit of full board discussion. While some conversation may be social, much is not. As the afternoon or evening wears on, these discussions are often continued by telephone once the board members have returned to their offices or homes. Overnight, these issues swell out of proportion, often resulting in an angry, frantic, poorly timed and badly reasoned phone call to the board chair, CEO, or chair of the committee on trustees.

Those who initiate such "rump" meetings, and who take time to make a series of phone calls to those they consider key players, clearly have some kind of interest or issue driving them. Find out what it is, and channel this energy into a constructive activity or meeting. Confront the issues, and persuade the person that the communication structure within the organization can accommodate his or her grievance, concern or idea.

Through open communication policies, in which board members are encouraged to bring even sensitive issues to board meetings or to a special meeting with the board chair, parking lot meetings of the kind just described are no longer needed. Of course, people have the right to congregate wherever they want. This is not a suggestion to start monitoring parking lot conversations. It is merely a warning based on experience; these gatherings can be the early warning signal of failing board health. The information in this chapter will help organizations create an environment in which the only meetings in the parking lot are social.

SUMMARY

Board members are an organization's major investors, regardless of the size of the gift they make. The time, effort, and advocacy they give, in addition to their gifts, have a huge impact on the overall health and community perception of the organization. When recruited and enlisted appropriately, and drawn into a working partnership that encourages them to use their expertise and energy in activities that are productive, satisfying, and fun, board members flourish, and so do the organizations they serve.

Finally, here are "5 × 5 GREAT IDEAS" for engaging and keeping your board members and other volunteers (Exhibit 9.6).

EXHIBIT 9.6 Great Ideas For Volunteer Involvement

Engage volunteers by evidencing:

Gratitude—show how you appreciate them and others

Recognition—how you fit recognition to the task, mission, and motivation

Enthusiasm—for them, and for your organization

Acknowledgment—show them time and work are valued

Time-Sensitivity—show that you make meetings worthwhile (leaders don't waste people's time)

Retain them with:

Inspiration—keep them close to the product!

Dedication—yours will lead to theirs

Energy—applied to tasks and relationships

Appropriate tasks—match their tasks to their motivation

Special thanks—be sure they are sincere, and made often

---

10 ▼ Three Levels of Board and Staff Operation

Successful organizations operate at three levels: philosophical, strategic, and tactical. While most organizations recognize these levels on an intuitive basis, few have consciously delineated or internalized the importance of each level and the way in which they intertwine to ensure a stronger and more resilient organization. This three-level approach is not meant to complicate the management of organizations. It is meant to simplify it through the understanding of the purpose and derivation of each aspect of a task and why, when these aspects are understood, the task of managing is more manageable.

In Chapter 4, the relevance of these three levels of operation to the development/investment process was explored. In this chapter, a broader application of the three-level approach will be developed.

THE IMPORTANCE OF EACH LEVEL

Organizations can more easily go beyond fund raising when they understand and implement their planning, development, fund raising, and board development at all three levels. Program management, which is not covered in this book except as it relates to attracting investors and upholding the mission of the organization, also benefits from this three-level approach. Keeping the levels in balance can considerably enhance the overall organization. When organizations get locked into a series of tactical maneuvers without benefit of philosophical mission or strategic goals, they can lose momentum, volunteers, and impact. A sense of chaos prevails, and initiatives, no matter how zealously undertaken, cannot solve problems which have been inadequately defined or considered. Without goals, there can be no true measure of impact and no meaningful evaluation. Without mission, there is no larger context from which to draw the inspiration that gives energy to the tasks.

The philosophical level—the values and community needs framework—is most often ignored. The most commonly implemented level is the tactical. Most often yearned for, but not realized, is the strategic. The interplay of these levels is essential. Without the philosophical, the strategic is difficult and the tactical can seem meaningless. Without the strategic, the philosophical is seldom acted on, and the tactical lacks direction. Without the tactical, there may be vision without implementation: strategic plans are not carried out, and the program results which validate the philosophical framework are not attained.

A look at each level is fundamental to understanding their interrelatedness.

PHILOSOPHICAL LEVEL

The most obvious manifestation of the philosophical level of organizational behavior is in the creation and implementation of a mission statement which expresses the need the nonprofit meets and the values inherent in that need. Already explored in Chapter 3, the conception, revision, and frequent review of the mission statement provide opportunities to inspire and renew board and staff. Mission is not the only philosophical concept that should guide organizations. There are more. The mission statement should be supported by other philosophical understandings, including:

1. *The importance of volunteerism as the interface between organizations and community.* This philosophical underpinning is most often reflected in the way an organization recruits and treats its volunteers (tactical) and whether or not their opinions and expertise are sought in important areas such as planning and budgeting (strategic). Some organizations welcome volunteer involvement. Others seem to resent it. The root of the behavior is in the attitude(s) of staff and board leadership regarding the value of volunteers. This is a philosophical issue.

    In the nonprofit sector, most organizations need a deep commitment to the value of volunteers. Volunteers are the vital force. They make it possible for our organizations to do what they do with fewer financial resources. They open doors in the community. Universities, whose development staffs are highly professional and entirely capable of securing major gifts, still engage volunteers in their strategic asks because they know there is no substitute for the peer-peer connection.

As a sector, volunteers so characterize our community mandate that we are sometimes referred to as the "voluntary sector." When the attitude of the CEO or program staff is condescending, or when volunteers are excluded from anything but social activities and fund raising, volunteer strength will decline. Paying lip service to volunteer involvement, and then ignoring offers of professional or personal assistance from them, severely impairs the viability of the organization.

A young and brilliant lawyer, on the board of an organization whose board chair and CEO both had difficulty delegating and involving other staff and volunteers strategically, became disinterested in the organization after his repeated offers of expert legal assistance to draft much-needed new policies and revise out-of-date bylaws were ignored. The tasks he offered to do did not get done, and the organization's image in the community remained one of an archaic and sleepy organization unable to meet the realities of late twentieth century nonprofit requirements.

Other stories are not so discouraging. In organization after organization, motivated volunteers, encouraged by staff and board leaders who sincerely value their involvement, have established donor-investor relationships on their own or leveraged community support previously thought unavailable. Empowerment, a much overused word of the 1980s, is still the goal we should have in working with volunteers.

2. *The value of the nonprofit sector, and the way in which it is changing around the world to meet dramatically altered economic, cultural and social needs.* Decades ago, when few people understood what the nonprofit sector was, those who worked in it were almost apologetic when describing their field. It was much easier for those in computers, banking, or finance to explain their careers. Lack of knowledge about the sector often led to having to explain why professional staff was paid, not volunteer. Frequently, apology accompanied the description of why fund raising was even necessary (lack of resources, inability to charge adequately for services, etc.).

Deeming the sector as "charitable" also invited an unfortunate mindset. Nonprofit organizations were viewed as *needing* "charity" rather than organizations *serving* a charitable purpose. Volunteers, including board members, were not nearly as involved at the strategic level of our organizations as they are now, and those that were tended to be women whose activities in support of these organizations were largely underappreciated by the larger community.

We have come a long way from people's perception that our sector is made up of "do-gooders" or "bandage rollers" and that professional staff people are involved in the sector because they could not succeed in the for-profit world. Intelligent, active, committed, and connected civic leaders have dispelled that image through their involvement in an ever-widening array of not-for-profit organizations. Capable staff people move comfortably to and from the voluntary and business sectors, bringing skills and perspective which enrich both. Men and women sit side-by-side at the board room table, and volunteering is no longer seen as an alternative to work: busy, contributing people work *and* volunteer.

An increasing number of companies and corporations encourage their employees to volunteer, sometimes providing paid "release time" away from the job. Many of these same companies reinforce their employees' involvement by providing financial support to those organizations for which their employees volunteer.

These are phenomenal accomplishments, most of which began in the 1980s. Understanding of the power and importance of the not-for-profit sector has swelled. In communities around the world, citizens are realizing the critical role nonprofits play in maintaining the stability of cultural, social service, human service, educational, environmental, religious, and medical services. People who work in the sector feel pride for the accomplishments and roles of the organizations they represent.

The nonprofit sector stimulated donor-investors to give over $143 billion to religion, education, arts, culture, health, human services, the environment and other community-building causes in 1995. This amount grows annually, creating services, programs and jobs. In the rest of the world, a similar pattern is emerging as sharp growth in charitable sector employment and provision of nongovernmental services brings more recognition to nonprofit organizations. Leaders of organizations, operating in this changing context, must continually inform board and staff about issues and trends in the sector, and of the overall accomplishments of philanthropy in their communities. Statistics from *Giving USA*, published annually by the American Association of Fund Raising Counsel, provide substantial information regarding the extent of support for and involvement in our philanthropy by Americans. NSFRE and

CASE have resources, as well, that are dedicated to thoughtful analysis and reporting on philanthropy. Other professional organizations, particularly those in the U.K. and continental Western Europe (EUConsult) and Australia (Fundraising Institute Australia - FIA) are beginning to collect these data. The World Fundraising Council (WFC), founded in 1985, provides information and expertise to increase effectiveness of fund-raising practices worldwide. Such baseline resources assure potential investors about the extent of support for organizations (they are not trying to do this alone!) and gives employees and volunteers of nonprofit organizations a larger context for validating their involvement.

3. *The reasons why people give to charitable organizations and the ways in which their reasons provide a mirror for organizations and communities.* Understanding an investor's motivation for giving requires a major philosophical awareness that guides both stewardship and subsequent solicitations. This varies dramatically from investor to investor and may differ even for the same donor at different times in his or her relationship with an organization.

Years of brainstorming with groups about "Why People Give" has yielded consistent answers, not only in the United States but across many countries and cultures. Although the "right" answer is "Because they are asked," that answer assumes that the person is already motivated to give. Before attributing giving to being asked, it must be linked to a motivation that will bring someone to want to make an investment when they *are* asked.

The most frequently offered motivations for why *individuals* give (corporations and foundations frequently have very different motivations for giving) are:

- Recognition
- To feel good
- Peer pressure
- To make a difference
- Guilt
- Desire to contribute to the community
- Appreciation for what the organization has done for them or others

Two of the motivations listed may seem out of place with the rest: peer pressure and guilt. Peer pressure is a reality when it comes to giving. While it may not seem a very ennobling motivation, it is why many organizations with a well-run volunteer team of askers and a regularly published donor listing do better than others. Look around you at a concert or benefit dinner, and you will see people reading the donor list. People are influenced by the giving of their peers, more than by their pressure or cajoling. Once a donor is brought in through a peer contact, it is up to the organization to build the values-based investment relationship.

Discover the philosophical connection(s) with the organization that will lead to a long-term investment relationship. Determining the donor-investor's motivation is a deeply philosophical and very important aspect of building a lasting relationship. Only when we know *why*, is it possible to attain the highest level of involvement in the *what* and the *how* of our organizations (the "what" is strategic; the "how" is tactical).

Guilt has its bright side as a motivator, and should perhaps be called something else. When describing what they mean by "guilt," brainstormers will reply that people who feel like they have so much (money) relative to others in the community (people served by non-profits), give out of feelings of guilt over their wealth and/or success. This guilt may instead be more linked to another motivation listed above, the desire to give back to the community or organizations. Generally, to persuade people to give by making them feel guilty, or by making them feel it is a moral obligation, is both difficult and risky. If they do give, they may not give in a spirit of investment, and they may not give as much. Building an investor relationship after an initial gift that is based on implied or overt reference to moral obligation can be very challenging. It requires a redefinition of the reasons for giving, and new strategies for converting the sense of pressure into a feeling of satisfaction and release.

Each of these underlying forces is a powerful motivation, and tells something very important about the potential or current investor and how to approach the cultivation and the ask. Not all people are motivated by the same philosophical instincts. In direct mail appeals, we vary our approaches to maintain the broadest possible message. Once personal relationships are established with donor-investors, we can begin listening for the motivations that will shape our strategy in developing them as investors. We see what organizational results are most interesting to them. We note which activities and events they attend. We determine what approach to stewardship is likely to be the most comfortable or satisfying for them. We realize how strongly influenced people are by the way in which the things they like and value are reflected back to them by our programs, the way we run our organizations, and the way we treat them as investors. We become their mirrors, and they are ours.

4. *The common areas of practice and vision within the larger array of similar organizations from which ideas and lessons can be drawn* (e.g., symphony orchestras, hospitals, colleges, schools, grass roots organizations). Staff and volunteers benefit from networking with other organizations in their community through professional associations or informal groups. Getting together with other professionals or volunteers who are similar service providers can result in very positive consolidation of ideas about meeting the market needs for family counseling, recreation, environment, religion, or community health clinics. Inspired by each other, members of these formal or informal associations can inform and structure policies in a community regarding service provision, often eliminating duplication of programs and raising the overall level of service in the community.

Staff and volunteers from dissimilar organizations who get together occasionally to swap ideas can also find a deeper philosophical connection: the needs of the community they are serving. In some communities, United Way or other umbrella organizations offer management assistance seminars to people from a wide range of organizations. These sessions enable participants to see their organizational similarities and differences.

An exceptional new effort is the Center for Excellence in Nonprofits in San Jose, California. Arts, education, social and human service, environmental, and religious organizations are selected for an annual cycle of workshops and meetings. The Center is largely funded by corporate, foundation, and individual contributions from the community, so enrollment fees are kept at an affordable level. Board and staff teams are sent from each organization (as many as four from each) and attend seminars on a variety of subjects that trigger very philosophical discussions about their own purpose and role in the community. In the framework of learning more about strategic planning for institutional growth, board and fund development, and fund raising, these organizations wrestle with major sector issues as they apply to their own organizations and community. This program is a model.

In other communities, organizations benefit from different types of synergy. One of the tactical areas in which this philosophical commitment to cross-organizational communication is evidenced is the development of a community-wide calendar of events. The calendar records all major events and activities planned in the community during the year, helping to avoid the discouraging situation of finding that both the hospital and the symphony have selected the same September date for their annual high-ticket gala event.

Beyond your own community there are opportunities to strengthen a sense of connection with the sector. Organizations benefit from joining and attending conferences for other organizations like themselves: a few that hold annual meetings are American Symphony Orchestra League (ASOL), Dance USA, Family Service Association, American Library Association (ALA). It is a great idea to take volunteers to these meetings. Together, staff and volunteers hear the latest trends in leadership, management, and the marketplace; they are able to reflect with others about planning, board and fund development, and fund raising; and they glimpse the common issues. Experiences like this put a comforting context around an organization's need to solve its strategic or tactical problems. Ideas which will help build strategy or inspire new activities are delivered in a setting and by presenters and facilitators that provide a much broader understanding of the issues.

5. *A general understanding of the ethics which govern the sector, and the importance of maintaining ethical practices in the organization.* Because our sector is governed by values, which are the core of its philosophical basis, we are very open to ethical scrutiny. There are some very good reasons.

- Our trustees hold the organization "in trust" for the community.
- We commit to a mission and purpose, integral to our Articles of Incorporation, that says we serve the community.
- Volunteers give their time, and join with others in giving money, to see to it that our programs are delivered.
- While it is understood that we charge for our services, we are expected to keep our fees or ticket prices affordable in order to sustain the larger educational or accessible service mission.
- We are expected, as we assume our unique role in the economy as the "third sector" (with business and government), to practice excellent financial management techniques.
- Our development staff members subscribe to the NSFRE, CASE or AHP Code of Ethics.
- We are put in a particularly respected position in our communities because we work with and provide services to (in many cases) the underserved or needy, or children or seniors, and so on.
- Our salary and overall compensation levels are expected to stay at a reasonable level relative to our financial resources, because communities want to be sure the money they give is going to help people directly, not going into overhead. But fair compensation is a professional issue of great importance. We engage in important work and must be compensated adequately.

Those of us who serve the sector understand these assumptions. They are basic to the fabric and integrity of our organizations.

People do not *expect* our organizations to be like for-profit organizations when it comes to ethical standards and practices. We have to be better. Therefore, when an organization in our sector violates community expectations through financial excesses or abuse, unethical personnel or management practices, excessive salaries or compensation, fund raising and administrative costs that consume too large a percentage of every dollar, questionable practices or outcomes in programming, or personal or professional scandal, we are much more subject to public criticism.

National investigative journalism television programs in the United States and some newspaper reporting worldwide quickly capture these stories, wherever they occur, and give them coverage. They use the example of one organization to raise questions about the entire sector. The impact of these stories is tangible. Donors become wary. All organizations are suspect. It hurts fund raising, which hurts our communities.

Sadly, there will always be violations of ethics in our sector because it is led and managed by human beings who will occasionally succumb to greed, absorbing self-interest, temptations of various kinds, and a feeling that what they do will never be found out. We have seen it all, in so few organizations over the past several years: embezzlement, outright theft, misuse of funds, phony reporting to donor-investors on the use of their funds and other unethical practices. But this handful of organizations does not represent the more than one million nonprofits in the United States or the growing number worldwide. Each organization has the responsibility to convey its own ethical standards, and those of the sector. People who are involved in your organization as board or staff need to know, from the beginning, that you have zero tolerance for unethical practices. Maintain an organizational environment where any veering away from the path is checked immediately, and where people understand the very special trust that has been placed in them by the community. It is hard to screen for potentially unethical behavior in an employment interview or in volunteer recruiting. Those who breach ethics are either quite clever or unwitting violators. Prevention, through a philosophical commitment to ethical behavior evidenced in all practices and programs of your organization, is the best strategy for avoiding ethical problems.

STRATEGIC LEVEL

The most obvious strategic activity is planning. The planning process itself is multifaceted, engaging people in a dialogue which can enhance institution-wide communications while producing a document that will guide the organization in its tactical behavior. The planning process, and its role in taking organizations beyond fund raising, is explored more fully in Chapter 11.

The pressure on most not-for-profit organizations everywhere to raise more money than ever before and to assume responsibility for additional community programs and services, causes the focus to shift to the tactical without benefit of the strategic. It is often very difficult to make the time to approach issues and opportunities in a strategic way. Because we are so focused on the urgent, we do not have time for the important. When this becomes the pattern of our activities, rather than the exception, we descend into crisis management and eventually erode external trust and internal morale. External trust diminishes when we are constantly out in the community pleading for contributions. Internal morale declines when staff and board feel as though their actions never really make a difference. One executive director of a performing arts organization, during a particularly difficult year in which the important did battle daily with the urgent and never seemed to get ahead, said he was tempted to rename his organization "Sisyphus." It is nearly impossible to effectively invite investment if the organization has an image of always being on the brink of disaster. Not only are community people reluctant to give, they are frequently reluctant to become involved. More than one valued corporate vice president, serving on the board of an organization that cannot operate strategically, has finally resigned in frustration.

Management struggles to discern the urgent from the important is analogous to the image of the ants and the elephant. While we struggle to keep the relentlessly marching ants from taking over our offices, we neglect the elephant, already inside our office, that is growing larger, eating more (of our time), and will become harder and harder to evict.

Systems liberate. People who resist strategic planning usually do not appreciate its value. They distrust the process steps required, and may even fear the product.

Sometimes opposition to planning is based in a wish not to be held accountable. Other people may see planning as an inhibitor, preventing an organization from being able to respond to changing needs. Still others see plans as too prescriptive, and dislike the control implied. Those

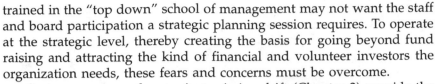
trained in the "top down" school of management may not want the staff and board participation a strategic planning session requires. To operate at the strategic level, thereby creating the basis for going beyond fund raising and attracting the kind of financial and volunteer investors the organization needs, these fears and concerns must be overcome.

Systems, as an anchor against mission drift (Chapter 3) provide the strategic stabilizer for organizations. Systems liberate because they permit organizations to operate within a clearly defined and understood framework. They standardize the routine activities of the organization, allowing more time for creative activities. Systems can be modified: one of the essential ingredients of a strategic planning process is the inclusion of methods for evaluating and changing the plan. Effective organizations reflect strategic thinking and planning in all areas of their operations. It is how they keep pace with change and retain their long-term investors.

TACTICAL LEVEL

The tactical level of operation is best summarized in the Nike Corporation's philosophy: just do it. Tactical maneuvers help ensure the following activities.

- Timely completion of fund-raising campaigns.
- Excellent follow-through for all board and committee assignments.
- Staff energy and involvement on specific and time-determinate tasks.
- Adherence to schedules for planning.
- Dedication to regular scheduling of meetings and activities.
- Excellent procedures for problem-solving.

The concern thus far in this chapter has been the difficulty staff and boards have in finding the time and support for strengthening the philosophical and strategic framework of their organizations. There is equal cause for concern regarding the tactical. Some organizations are capable of crafting an inspiring mission statement, a riveting vision, and a cogent plan, but incapable of acting on any of them. Many of the reasons for this are addressed in the chapters on boards and the development process. Organizational inertia is both caused and compounded by the inability to be tactical.

Lasting investment is only acquired when results are the focus. Investor-attractive results occur when organizations, inspired by the philosophical principles of their mission and vision and structured strategically to act on those principles, operate at the tactical level as well. Failure to act at the tactical level nullifies the philosophical and strategic footing that may have been established.

Why Organizations Have Difficulty Being Tactical

The most common reason for incapacity to act at the tactical level once a plan has been formulated is the inability to manage the implementation process. Nonprofit CEOs frequently come from a program or service background and, while they are professionally trained in the area served by the organization, they may not have had business management training. Boards, when hiring a CEO, need to provide opportunities for professionally talented and astute people to complement their existing skills with classes, courses, or seminars dealing with planning, personnel, budgets, and so on.

There may be other factors compounding the lack of management experience. Unwillingness or inability to delegate is one of the biggest blocks to accomplishing goals in organizations. Some CEOs and development directors (as well as board chairs) have not learned that the best way to take charge is to let go. They try to be in control of every department or committee, overextending their time, energy, and welcome. Staff and board morale diminish, energy and commitment flag, and people complain that nothing is achieved. Talented people, not given opportunities to grow in their volunteer or paid jobs, find other organizations where their skills can be used and their time appreciated.

Conflict is another block to implementation. Whether open and escalated or covert and simmering below the surface, the presence of conflict can deeply undermine the ability of people to function at the tactical level. Much of what passes for planning and meeting time (strategic) in some organizations is spent engaged in fomenting or quelling conflict. There is a principle that proves itself true: people have a given amount of energy. If they put it constantly into efforts to keep conflict under control and maintain balance in staff or board relationships, they do not have energy left for the task at hand.

Poor communication is another tool for snuffing activity in an organization. People who do not know what is expected of them end up not doing anything. Those who do their work, but either are criticized without constructive feedback or given no feedback at all, eventually lose motivation. Lack of clear expectations and an environment in which doors stay closed and communication is done by whisper, memo, innuendo, or confrontation will almost certainly ensure organizational inertia.

It should be easy to stay energized if the focus stays on results and does not get overly embroiled with organizational issues which are fraught with tension and mistrust. Organizations which find themselves succumbing to overanalysis of organizational problems at the cost of program delivery need to pull the mirrors down and put the windows back up. Consuming attention to internal issues shifts vital focus away from the marketplace. The organization gets in the way of the mission. The vision deteriorates.

A wise person once said that a person with vision is a visionary, but a person who shares a vision is a leader. Another truism is closely related: there is a fine line between a vision and an obsession. A vision can be shared; an obsession, most often, cannot. We become energized by what we accomplish in the community. Volunteers and staff alike feel proud of their achievements.

Ways to Become More Tactical

Success is a marvelous cure for inertia. And true success lies in staying focused on the tactical so the mission and vision are accomplished.

If an organization is languishing, unable to operate at the tactical level except when urgency drives a reaction to a need or crisis, take steps to address these issues such as:

- Convey expectations in open, facilitated meetings.
- Quell conflict in its early stages, not by mandate but by listening and facilitation.
- Encourage delegation by honoring the balance it places between authority and responsibility.
- Provide management training for CEOs and development directors new to their leadership roles (or in need of a refresher). Those who are experienced at management, members of the board and seasoned department heads, can provide coaching to others. When provided within the context of achieving shared goals, coaching is perceived not as punitive or threatening, but as a way to build teams.
- Communicate a known and respected process for problem-solving that is creative, accessible and accepted.
- Reward completed tasks appropriately, and set evaluation benchmarks when assigning a task so there is encouragement and reinforcement along the way.

- Begin staff or board meetings with a summary of the follow-up and completion achieved with previously assigned tasks. Too often, outcomes of strategies determined at lengthy and exhausting board meetings are never conveyed.
- Give feedback to staff and volunteers that encourages them to pursue even the most seemingly mundane or menial task, setting it in the context of a necessary step to achieve a larger goal or objective.

OBSTACLES TO INTEGRATING THE THREE LEVELS

The integration of these three levels of organizational operation is a challenge worth the effort. Summarized, these key obstacles throw off the balance:

1. Internal pressure of financial worries, program needs, and staffing changes which lead to impatience with anything but the task at hand: the tactical gets done, but the philosophical and strategic are put off until the crisis has passed.
2. Board or staff leadership aversion to discussion of the philosophical context of mission, fund raising, or market needs; priority is given to just "getting the job done." The philosophical is never addressed or understood and even strategic plans lack a motivating framework.
3. Lack of sufficient motivation, management skills, energy or people to implement the mission, vision, and plan at the tactical level and the absence of an environment in which such issues can be resolved effectively.
4. The inability of board and staff leadership to see why they should operate at these three levels and how they can do it.

APPLYING THE THREE-LEVEL APPROACH TO A PLANNING AREA

The long-range or strategic institutional planning process is an excellent vehicle for introducing the value of the three-level approach. Its introduction is an eye-opening and educational process. Whether the ultimate plan reflects the three levels as discrete goals and objectives, or whether the levels are integrated in the final plan, the concept should be introduced during the process.

The following is the basis for an actual plan prepared by the chair of the committee on trustees at Grace Cathedral in San Francisco. It illustrates how all three levels of activity can be incorporated into the institutional plan. It was prepared as part of a strategic task force effort to lay a critical foundation for a post-capital campaign period. Responsibility for each task lies with the committee on trustees except where stated otherwise. Dates were removed from this version as they were not pertinent to its understanding. It is used with permission of Grace Cathedral's executive committee.

Task Area: Trustee Development—The Committee on Trustees

To achieve the financial and community outreach goals of Grace Cathedral, the following general strategies for trustee (1) recruitment/enlistment, (2) education, (3) involvement, and (4) retention/rotation is proposed. Within these four strategy areas there are three levels of activity that need to be addressed: philosophical, strategic, and tactical. All three are essential for long-term board development.

I. Recruitment/Enlistment
   A. Philosophical
      1. Understand the purpose and community impact of the Cathedral and its need for a particular kind of trustee
   B. Strategic
      1. Create and maintain an accurate board matrix including term expiration dates
      2. Create, distribute to trustees, and implement a board recruitment policy; review and revise annually or as appropriate
      3. Examine bylaws of the Cathedral relative to board recruitment and tenure
         (a) Evaluate on an ongoing basis the critical long-term needs of the Cathedral and plan strategically for long-term recruitment
         (b) Develop and implement a policy/program for succession planning to ensure timely and excellent recruitment of and leadership growth for board officers
   C. Tactical
      1. Conduct bimonthly meetings of the committee on trustees
      2. Implement an ongoing process for recruitment of potential board members which involves meetings with key Cathe-

dral staff and trustees, tours of the facilities, participation in events, and so on

   3. Assign each member of the committee on trustees specific recruitment/enlistment tasks on a year-round basis

   4. Actively involve the board in potential trustee identification

   5. Create a stable of interested and qualified board candidates who meet the recruitment criteria

II. Education

  A. Philosophical

    1. Coach committee members to understand and be able to articulate the spiritual and community programs of the Cathedral to potential trustees

    2. Structure opportunities at board meetings to educate trustees regarding the spiritual and community impact of Cathedral programs and the vision of the Cathedral

  B. Strategic

    1. Annually review and revise board handbook

    2. Annually review and revise board orientation program

    3. Continually assess effectiveness of board communications (from staff to board; from committees to full board; from board to staff)

  C. Tactical

    1. Convey requirements for board membership to potential trustees during recruitment process, especially those regarding fund raising and development

    2. Conduct new board member orientation and maintain good contact with all trustees

    3. Distribute board handbook to new members and new materials to all members

    4. Keep board informed regarding issues and activities of the Cathedral

III. Involvement

  A. Philosophical

    1. At every appropriate occasion, encourage leadership to stress the commitment trustees are making to the long-term future not only of the Cathedral, but of the community through the Cathedral's work

  B. Strategic

    1. Use the board matrix to map committee structure, leadership, and membership; keep updated

    2. Keep records regarding other boards on which trustees serve to look for potential conflicts or links

C. Tactical

1. Work with Board Chair to make most appropriate committee assignments based on expertise and interest of potential, new and continuing board members

2. On a quarterly basis, monitor attendance by board members at meetings of full board and committees and do follow-up with those members whose attendance has been uneven

3. Watch for early warning signals of disenchantment with board service and address concerns in an open and timely manner

4. On an annual basis, Dean and Board Chair meet with each trustee on an individual basis to review their service, concerns, enthusiasms, constraints, and ask for their annual gift

IV. Retention/Rotation

A. Philosophical

1. Develop trustee understanding of the importance of continuity of service, but also the need to bring on new members

B. Strategic

1. Create and implement a board recognition program that will provide, at the annual meeting, opportunities for the Bishop and Dean to recognize superior service to the Cathedral

2. Develop and implement a policy regarding "de-enlistment" of board members who have little time, enthusiasm, or interest in the Cathedral

3. Create and implement an "Ambassadors" program to involve former trustees and officers in the ongoing programs of the Cathedral

C. Tactical

1. In preparation for the nomination process, Committee review, at each of its meetings, the involvement of each trustee

2. Six months prior to the expiration of board terms, Committee members contact board members to discuss renewal (if that is an option), removal (if their term is up or they should not be reenlisted), or transition to a different category of service*

* Note: at Grace Cathedral, there are three categories of Trustee: Bishop's appointees, Trustee-elected, and Congregation-elected. The first two categories go through the same recruitment/enlistment process. People sometimes shift categories to extend service.

3. Stay current on board member term expiration dates for subsequent years so smooth rotation relative to matrix representation can be achieved

When organizations sense the need to approach areas of management systemically, the three-level delineation provides an excellent template for the process. The above foundation for the committee on trustees working plan was developed within that need. As many of these steps are standardized and accepted, there may no longer be a need to break out the three levels. However, the educational impact inherent in this delineation is powerful.

SUMMARY

It is often by taking things apart that we see how they can be most effectively put together. The three level analysis and application of the philosophical, strategic, and tactical provides a framework for more effective management and leadership of nonprofit organizations.

Although some resistance is inevitable because the urgent overwhelms the important in all of our activities, pursue the analysis. It will ultimately simplify your approach.

11 The Power of Planning

To be successful in development and fund raising, organizations need a cogent institutional plan. A fund-raising and development plan is not enough. It is the institutional plan which inspires people to give. It incorporates the vision, mission, and program goals which inspire investment. The fund-raising plan guides an internal process. An institutional plan is both internal and external. It can be shared with funders and used as the motivation for giving and asking.

These are exciting but chaotic times for nonprofit organizations. While opportunities have never been greater to make a lasting impact on our communities, such efforts require systematic new paradigms for management and fund raising. Diminished government support of essential services in the United States and around the world is stretching other institutional and individual funding sources to meet growing community needs.

In this time of redefinition, organizations must give deliberate and careful consideration to the community need for their programs and services. They must organize more effectively to ensure their own continuing vitality and visibility. Donor-investors are looking for organizations in whose future they can participate. To see this future, funders need to see a plan. Both the planning process and the resulting document are critical internal tools for maintaining stability in a time of rapid change, and important external tools for attracting funders and volunteers.

In Chapter 10, the exploration of the three levels of staff and board involvement addressed some of the general principles of planning. This chapter focuses on the institutional plan and its important components, development and fund raising.

WHY ORGANIZATIONS NEED TO PLAN

It is essential to have an institutional plan if you are to invite donor-investors to become long-term supporters of your organization. Just as an investor in the for-profit sector wants to see a business plan, donor-investors need to see where an organization is going, and how their investments will be used. A smart donor-investor will need and want to see your long-range plan, understand your vision, and know how you will be implementing and evaluating your goals and objectives.

The framework for the plan must be the marketplace. Your programs exist to serve the community; and your organizational and development/fund-raising structure is in place to ensure effective program support. The community need for your services and the potential for financial and volunteer support are the two key external factors in institutional planning. Internal elements are driven by these external factors: staffing, program growth, board and volunteer expansion. Too many organizations develop plans that have no relationship to the world outside their windows. They focus on what *they* want and need, rather than on what the *community* wants and needs.

There are two basic reasons for planning:

1. To provide an internal management tool for board and staff to help them guide and assess general organizational activities, specific programs or campaigns, and financial performance; and
2. To provide an external document—usually an executive summary of the comprehensive plan—for use when meeting with potential donor-investors or when recruiting board members.

In both cases, the quality of the product is largely determined by the integrity of the process. The degree of ownership of a plan by a staff and board, established by the process used in its preparation, will determine the success of the plan. Success is measured by the commitment to implement and evaluate the plan internally, and the impact of the plan as a donor development and board recruitment tool.

Why Organizations Resist Planning

Organizations resist institutional and development planning for the following reasons:

1. There are too many urgent needs to be met and time cannot be taken for the planning process.

2. Staff leadership may be concerned about being held accountable.
3. Board leadership may be impatient with the planning process.
4. Previous plans have gathered dust on the shelf, and the organization feels it was a wasted effort.
5. The organization seems to be functioning well without one.
6. There may be a subliminal feeling by the board that the organization is so fragile that planning would be fruitless.
7. The organization does not know how to approach the task.

The following story illustrates the fallacy of the first five points above, and hints at the sixth. The seventh point inspires this chapter.

A Case History

Years ago, an educational and cultural organization with great potential for community investment nearly had to close its doors because the executive director did not believe in institutional planning. He ignored an early plan which was in place when he was hired. He squelched all board and staff attempts to revive or renew it. Because the CEO seemed visionary and was charismatic, he enjoyed some early fund-raising and programmatic successes that worked to negate any sense of urgency about formulating a new plan. The busy board, with few exceptions, did not push for a plan because it didn't want to spend time in the process. The CEO, when questioned by the new development director about the lack of a plan, expressed his belief that a plan would inhibit the organization's capacity to be flexible and responsive.

A two-year plan for development and fund raising was prepared by the development director working with the development committee. It was more tactical than strategic because there was no overarching design for the organization.

In spite of the fund-raising plan, the absence of an institutional plan made it increasingly difficult to approach funders for general program support. The board lacked reasons and results on which to base their community development and fund raising. Although the organization had been established many years before, it had a long and chaotic history of staff and board leadership problems, poor fund raising and financial management, and lackluster marketing. Much of the case for support was based on the urgent need for funds to keep the organization running rather than on the realities of the marketplace need for its services. The community interest in programming had diminished due to poor market analysis of what educational and cultural programs were needed and wanted. The CEO was superb at project funding, the funds for which were restricted and could not be used for general support.

Repeated funding crises plunged the organization into management and financial crises. Staffing cuts were made and programs were reduced. The open hours for the primary service area for members and the community were drastically cut. General fund raising dwindled, and with it the financial stability of the organization. Although the board failed to demand a plan from the executive director, neither did it set about to develop one in the absence of administrative endorsement. After several years, the board saw the problem and did not renew the CEO's contract. This move came too late: the damage had been done. The organization was shattered internally, and its image in the community was further eroded. While the absence of an institutional plan was not the only problem leading to the organization's decline, it had profound impact on its inability to recover. It also had an impact on a source of potential external funding which might have restored the organization's financial and program stability.

A potentially very large donor had been brought, through his friendship and respect for a board member, into a growing relationship with the organization. Seeing both the problems and the promise of the organization, he was ready to make a very large gift—in effect, a financial bail out—because of his passion for the mission and regard for the highly esteemed board member (who was also a major donor to the organization). Despite earnest cultivation and numerous meetings with the development director and several board members, the prospect ultimately refused to make a gift because the institution did not have a plan. As a retired president of a multinational corporation, he valued planning, even in a fast-changing world. He has since died, leaving millions to other organizations.

The organization without the plan drifted into near obscurity and failure before new visionary leadership and financial necessity combined to force a planning process that has completely repositioned it.

The lessons implicit in this case history are striking. Organizations cannot afford to ignore the necessity of a solid institutional plan. A plan is both a sternwheel and a sail, helping organizations navigate and maintain the course, and keeping them headed in the right direction.

INSTITUTIONAL AND DEVELOPMENT PLANS

Institutional and development/fund-raising plans come in several types, can be comprehensive or specific, and are produced through a variety of processes. Budgets, the financial plans for organizations, are briefly included in this overview of planning. A plan without a complete budget for the first year and budget projections for subsequent years has little value for management or fund raising, and will be insufficient for the needs of funders. [Further information on comprehensive budgeting processes can be found in other Wiley publications, Jody Blazek's *Financial Planning for Nonprofit Organizations* (1996); Jody Blazek's *Tax Planning and Compliance for Tax-Exempt Organizations, Second Edition* (1993); and Thomas A. McLaughlin's *Street Smart Financial Basics for Nonprofit Managers* (1995).]

The discussion which follows applies to the preparation of institutional plans, a key part of which must be development and fund raising.

Types of Plans:

- *Long Range*—Vision and goals span three to five years; specific, measurable objectives may be limited to one to two years; others are included but are less precise or an annual continuation of the same objective. A five-year long-range plan should have a "rolling base." The plan should be updated annually, the year just completed evaluated and retired from the plan, and a new fifth year added. A five-year plan should never expire.
- *Strategic*—An annual plan; goals may be long-term, but they are a framework for a tightly focused set of objectives encompassing the strategy of the organization. An annual strategic plan may be part of the Long Range Plan.
- *Specific*—For a specific department or activity (e.g., annual fund, membership, board development, capital campaign, special event).

Scope of Plans:

- *Institutional*—The plan covers the entire organization, and is shaped by the institutional vision. It is inclusive of all administrative and program departments and is supported by the organization's budget.
- *Departmental*—Within the institutional plan, there are discrete plans for each administrative and service area which guide their specific activities. Accompanying budgets are limited to the scope of that plan.
- *Financial*—All plans must have a budget component. Although it is difficult to project precise budget figures beyond one year, educated guesses for the five-year period of a long-range plan provide essential baseline information and benchmarks for evaluation. Program

budgets are recommended. In this format, the line item budget (staffing, benefits, other expenses) is further broken out by assignment of expenses to each department or project. This delineation makes funding proposal preparation easier because assignment of costs and sources of revenue for each program have already been determined.

Zero-based budgeting, also recommended at least every two years, is a further aid to overall positioning as an attractive investment. While sometimes perceived as a threat by departments within an organization, the process of taking the budget (and, hence, the program) to zero, looking at the market need, assessing programs, and then budgeting revenue and costs, is far more accurate than preparing a simple incremental budget in which, for example, a five percent increase in revenue and expenses is allocated across the budget. This process of zero-based pruning within an organization stimulates growth and keeps the organization focused on the marketplace needs it is meeting. The budgeting process is developed in more detail later in the chapter.

Types of Planning Processes

- *Top Down*—Principal energy and control of the process is provided by the CEO and other administrators, working with a few key board members. They develop the plan and the budget, and then present them to the rest of the staff and the board for review and approval. The entire process can be done within several weeks if intensive time can be allocated. The CEO may work alone on the plan and budget and then involve others to review and react to the preliminary draft. Some CEOs take a few of their key people away for a weekend to hammer out a budget and plan for the following year. In very small organizations, this latter process can be inclusive of all staff as well as board leadership.
- *Participatory*—Wide participation is sought through a process in which staff and board engage in a several-month process of performance analysis, needs assessment, market evaluation, resources requirements, and position appraisal before coming together as a complete or representative group in a retreat or other setting. The overall plan and budget is developed from this basic information, usually by a smaller task force. When completed in draft form, the material is presented at board and staff meetings for review and revision. The process takes several months for annual revision: the first time such a process is done, it may take as long as a year to complete.

Ownership of the plan is essential for implementation, and can result from either procedure. It is more apt to result with the second. However, if the outcomes of the first process are widely shared, and feedback is honestly sought and respected, the result can be nearly the same.

There are variations and compromises to both of these processes. The method selected is dependent on the tradition, organizational culture, time constraints, attitude about planning, external urgency to develop a plan (e.g., a potential funder has demanded one), and knowledge of the process.

Time required for the process and the resulting document will vary according to the process used. Some organizations devote nearly a year every three to five years to do a very thorough zero-based process. This is a sound approach. However, if the plan is kept current on a rolling base, with evaluation and revision done annually to retire the previous year and add a new year, even the zero-based process will probably not require more than a few months. By looking annually at shifts in the marketplace and changes in internal resources and circumstances, the plan maintains its relevance and vitality.

Gaining Support for the Planning Process

Planning for the kind of changes nonprofits are anticipating is very challenging. Funding resources are uncertain. The environment for development and fund raising may fluctuate. The position of an organization may change in the community as other similar service organizations thrive or wither. An organization's capacity to fulfill its mission may be dramatically diminished by the loss of a single funding source.

Yet, organizations must plan. Some believe it is pointless to plan in a time of rapid change because circumstances shift dramatically and quickly. Plans, when developed through a participatory process and structured to accommodate change, are fluid, dynamic, and organic. A plan is meant to be evaluated, altered, modified. A plan's validity is in large part determined by the way in which it is used, challenged, and revised.

Involving Board and Staff in Planning

To engage your board and staff in planning, be sensitive to the objections they may have. They are usually drawn from experience at other organizations or from what they have heard from others about plans and planning. Use the process that is most appropriate for your organization's size, resources, and commitment to the process. The first plan developed by an organization may be done by the Executive Director with very little assistance, or with a full participation procedure. To emphasize the importance of the plan, be positive about the impact it will have on internal management and external support and understanding. Most importantly, once the plan is developed, use it. We add fuel to the fire of those who scorn plans when, after considerable effort by one, five, or fifteen people, the plan is relegated to the shelf, never to be looked at again until it is time to revise it for the following year.

Developing a Plan That Will Work

The planning process begins with evaluation of existing plans and budgets and a thorough analysis of the current position and resources of your organization. It also requires a sharp analysis of the marketplace: demand for your services, changes that will have an impact on that demand, and opportunities to which you can respond.

It engages key volunteers and staff, and is strengthened by their involvement in review and response sessions or meeting. The goal of the process is to attain ownership for the plan by the broadest possible constituency. The degree to which ownership of the plan is secured is the degree to which commitment to the plan will be gained. Ownership is intensified when the structure of the plan is well-presented at the outset of the process, and outcomes and purpose are clear.

The essential ingredients of a plan are:

- Vision
- Mission
- Goals
- Objectives
- Action steps for each objective

These components are often confusing, and definitions of each may vary.

There is a difference between mission and vision, and a difference between goals and objectives. Action steps are usually not confused with any other part of the plan, and are frequently incorporated into a quarterly timeline produced on a computer program.

From experience with many plans and many planning exercises, the following are workable and appropriate definitions for not-for-profit planning:

1. *Vision.* Vision describes the organization and its potential impact in the future. That time may be five or ten years hence. A vision is guided by dreams, not constraints. It is what an organization hopes will happen if its dreams are realized.

    Jane Lathrop Stanford, who, with her husband, Leland, founded Stanford University in California in memory of their son, had an extremely long-term vision for the university that looked beyond the financial hardship and regionalism of the early years: "I could see a hundred years ahead, when all the present trials were forgotten. . . . The children's children's children coming here from the east, the west, the north, and the south." She was right. Her inspiring vision has guided the university and was a centerpiece in literature celebrating the university's 100th Anniversary.

    Steve Jobs, cofounder of Apple Computer, had a vision to "reinvent the future." He did.

    A vision may change with time and circumstances. It is a little noticed fact that the word revision—which is used casually to describe the process for altering or updating plans or policy documents—is *revision*, which implies that a new vision may be required.

    Vision inspires and directs fund raising and development. It is the force that will result in the long-term engagement of donor-investors.

2. *Mission.* Mission has two elements: the philosophical expression of the values-based need the organization is meeting in the community (why the organization exists) and a *brief* summary of what the organization is doing to meet that need. The first element is critical for expressing why the organization exists and the vital values to which donor-investors will respond; the second is important as a succinct statement of what the organization is doing to meet the community need. The mission is seldom revised, and it should not go into great detail. Chapter 3 looks more closely at mission and provides two examples.

3. *Goals.* Goals summarize the principal program, development, administrative, or other major accomplishments the organization hopes to achieve in order to realize its vision and fulfill its mission. Goals descend from and are validated by the vision. They are very general, not quantified, can be short- or long-term, and are evaluated annually. Most often, the majority of plan goals carry over for several years with only modest revision. A typical goal for an organization providing meals to the elderly might be: "To provide education and training in proper nutrition to clients receiving in-home meals."

4. *Objectives.* Objectives support the goals and provide more details. They are SMART. This acronym stands for the following:

Specific—Pertaining to a certain task or program.

Measurable—Unlike goals, which are general, objectives need to be quantifiable (completion date, outcomes, person(s) responsible).

Attainable—Doable within existing constraints and using available human and financial resources.

Results-Oriented—Focused on short-term activities to attain the longer term goals.

Time-Determinate—They include a date by which the task must be completed (or revised).

Objectives should also answer the question: Who will do what by when? An *objective* for the previously stated goal for the elderly would be: "By (month), (year), educational staff to develop a 30-minute nutrition education program, using audio-visual materials and lecture format, for pilot delivery at the Washington Street Senior Center site."

5. *Action Steps.* Action steps outline what needs to be done so the 30-minute audio-visual and lecture program will be ready by September. This can be set up as a spreadsheet of tasks and timelines on the computer, or by using special timeline program software available through commercial software outlets. It can also be laid out in a simple word processed timeline that states task, person(s) responsible, date due, and allows for comments. (See Exhibit 11.1). With any format selected, it is important for all people concerned with achieving the objective to know the tasks of the others involved, and the dates against which they should work to keep the project on schedule. Action plans should be reproduced, when they are completed, and distributed to each person whose name appears on the plan. It is helpful to highlight the name of each person to whom the plan is being distributed, so each participant can easily see where he or she fits into the total project.

PREPLANNING ANALYSIS

The long-term validity of the planning process and the resulting institutional or development plan will be in large part determined by the comprehensiveness of the preplanning analysis. Just as zero-based budgeting offers organizations opportunities to rethink cost allocations and income from programs and services, there is great value to analysis of the overall organization.

EXHIBIT 11.1 Action Plan

ACTION PLAN

Date_____ Project _____

Page_____

Task or Responsibility	Responsible Person(s)	Date Due	Date Done	Comments

The questions in Exhibit 11.2 may be reviewed as part of the planning meeting described below, or they may be approached on a very thorough basis by assigning task forces of board and staff to prepare an analysis for presentation at the first planning meeting. They apply equally well to general institutional and development/fund raising planning.

Results of the analysis in Exhibit 11.2, if conducted prior to the planning session, may be written and distributed to those who have a stake in the planning process and the eventual enactment of the plan. The analysis then forms the basis for the planning session. If analysis prior to the planning session is not possible, these questions can be discussed in small groups during the session itself. Each small group reports its findings. The findings then become a source of guidance and evaluation for goal and objective setting. A planning task force, often appointed at the end of a planning session to take the material from the session and craft it into a first-draft plan, also benefits from revisiting these questions as they pull the plan into shape.

EXHIBIT 11.2 Preplanning Analysis—Questions and Considerations

1. Position Analysis
    Evaluate the effectiveness of the current organization. Issues to be considered:
    — What are the most effective programs and activities?
    — Is there any evidence this effectiveness is changing?
    — Do we focus on the areas of most current community need and program potential?
    — What are our major strengths? Weaknesses?
    — How well are we using all of our current resources, especially board, other volunteers, staff?
    — What is our most limiting constraint?
    — How is our overall performance compared to other similar nonprofits?
    — How are we positioned relative to other not-for-profits?
    — Are we well-organized and staffed to accomplish our job?
    — Do we adequately involve new volunteers?
2. Marketplace Analysis
    Identify the significant changes we can anticipate in the marketplace, and assess their potential impact on the organization. Issues to be considered:
    — How will our client (or audience) base change in size during the next few years?
    — How will demographics affect our client (or audience) composition?
    — How might the trends and changes in the economy affect our efforts?
    — Are political and social attitudes likely to require modification in our approaches?
    — What new opportunities can we identify?
    — What can we learn from other similar organizations? How can we work more effectively with them?
    — Can we anticipate changes in our major sources of clients/audience?
    — Are there major changes anticipated in sources of earned or contributed revenue?
3. Organizational Development
    Evaluate the adequacy of current activities within the anticipated environment. Assess the need to develop new activities, services and programs. Issues to be considered.
    — What is the current growth rate of our constituency, and is this rate likely to remain constant? (Note: Constituency includes all those who are currently involved, or have a potential for involvement, as volunteers, participants, donors, clients, etc.)
    — How can we achieve greater participation by our constituents in programs and activities?

(Continued)

EXHIBIT 11.2 *(Continued)*

— What should be done to ensure maximum long-term commitment from present constituents?
— Do we have a well-managed contact process for new constituents?
— Are there better ways to identify and approach constituents than we have been using?
— What are we doing to overcome the weaknesses identified previously?
— What information is needed to help assess the potential of new programs?
— Do we need to test certain program elements before full implementation?
— What new systems for coordination and communication are required by these new programs?
4. Distribution of Resources
Describe the resources (staff, volunteers, funds) required to develop and implement the existing and anticipated programs and activities. Issues to be considered:
— What existing resources are underutilized? Are we using board members effectively and in the area(s) of their expertise that will lead to fulfilling involvement for them?
— Do we have any excess resources? (e.g., more volunteers in a certain program than are currently required, funding restricted or assigned to an area that is overfunded)
— What resource trade-offs can be made to increase and strengthen program and volunteer and staff involvement and satisfaction?
— How should the organization be changed, if at all? What new and different strategies are required to most appropriately manage our resources?
— Do we need some new skills and expertise? Is our board structured to help us meet our long-term goals?
— Can we form specific task forces to address special projects?
— Are our resource requirements comparable to those of other similar organizations?

PUTTING THE INGREDIENTS TOGETHER: THE TRI-POD INSTITUTIONAL PLANNING PROCESS

The following is a well-honed process, used successfully with countless organizations. It takes its name from its three (TRI) elements which are

Program, **Organization**, and **Development**. All not-for-profit organizational goals and objectives fall under one of these headings:

- *Program* includes all programs and the facilities used or needed for those programs;
- *Organization* includes all goals relating to staff and board development; and
- *Development* includes development, fund raising, public relations, and marketing.

Each of these plan components requires goals, objectives, and action plans. All three components will be driven by the vision and mission of the organization. The process begins with an exercise or discussion which generates or validates the vision, and goals are drawn from that vision. The process ensures the creation of a cogent development plan within a larger institutional plan.

The Planning Meeting

The process can include a meeting of all board and all staff for a small organization; or a board planning committee and key leadership staff for very large organizations. For example, a library involved all development staff and department heads. A small community-based organization included not only board and staff, but also clients, auxiliary volunteers, and former board members. At an independent school, faculty, administration, and board were involved. If one of these configurations is not possible for your organization, modify the array of participants to suit your needs and resources.

Resources permitting, an experienced outside facilitator is brought in to guide the planning day. This provides an objective approach which enables organizations to more easily get through difficult or controversial planning areas. This individual may also work with the organization throughout the entire planning process.

Timing of the Meeting

The planning meeting must be timed to serve the optimum role in the planning process. Several options are suggested:

1. To initiate the planning process with an organization, particularly if the board and/or staff are new to planning. The meeting is then fol-

lowed by assignment of task forces to work on the analysis questions and/or refine goals and objectives based on the visioning and goal-generating work completed at the meeting.

2. To provide an opportunity for some group process at a point in the overall process at which internal and market analyses (see above questions) have been completed. Following the meeting, refinement of the plan is completed based on the vision and goals.

3. For some organizations, whose culture or urgency do not permit a lengthy process, the planning day may be the only opportunity for consideration of the plan itself. Responsibility to prepare the plan is given to the executive director, to the process facilitator, or other designated individual. When completed, usually on a very short timeline, the plan is presented to the board in draft form for review and approval.

Generating a Vision That Inspires Institutional and Development Planning

All planning must begin with a shared vision. Getting people to discuss vision is not easy. This is particularly true of board and staff members who are very busy, quite task-oriented, and perhaps more focused on the tactical level of operation. Because this is a philosophical exercise with strategic implications, some creative work with potentially resistant groups usually overcomes the hurdle and gets them thinking about vision. Organizations that are developing or revising their plans must express or revisit the vision. Asking groups who have been consumed with the day-to-day operations of an organization to suddenly think about a time five or more years hence may require an innovative approach. One of the easiest ways to do this is an exercise that takes about an hour and a half and is fun and productive for everyone. Never has this experience failed to engage even the most skeptical participant.

Participants are provided with a simple scenario. They are asked to work in small groups, and to imagine it is the same day and month, but five (or longer) years later. The local newspaper (or a national or international newspaper or professional journal) has just published an article about the accomplishments of the organization, providing details about community impact, outstanding results, principal accomplishments during the time between the present and the future date chosen, information about board involvement, staff leadership, and so on. As Exhibit 11.3 illustrates the instructions, can be open-ended or prescriptive. If too prescriptive, imaginations can be stifled. If too open-ended, some par-

EXHIBIT 11.3 Visioning Exercise—Instructions

THE INSTITUTIONAL VISION

A vision statement summarizes the future that you imagine is possible if your organization achieves its goals. A vision needs to be present and shared if the organization is to move to the next level.

The vision must be shared to be effective. A person with vision is a visionary; one who can share the vision is a leader. Sharing the vision is a daily commitment you make to yourself, your volunteers, and your staff. The vision, like an organization's mission, can inspire and motivate those who work on your behalf. It is also very important in drawing people into a closer relationship with you. People will want to be part of your future. Its focus is on the institution and what it hopes to accomplish.

This example from Stanford University was written by Jane Stanford in 1904 when she, and the University, were facing financial ruin. It was used extensively in the materials celebrating the Centennial of the University.

"I could see a hundred years ahead, when all the present trials were forgotten . . . The children's children's children, coming here from the East, the West, the North and the South."

ENVISIONING THE FUTURE

It is 24 February, 2002. Today's edition of the *New York Times* has an article about (name of organization) and its accomplishments over the past five years. The article begins on page one of the *Lively Arts* section, and continues to a second page complete with photographs and sidebar features.

What is the headline? What is the major story the article covers?

What are the accomplishments the story reports? What photographs will be included?

What will the article say about (organization's) impact? Importance? Artistic accomplishments? Programming emphasis? Its governance? Financial condition? Staff? Community awareness and involvement? Fund-raising activities and accomplishments? National recognition?

What will be newsworthy about (the organization's) growth, importance or activities?

(Continued)

EXHIBIT 11.3 (*Continued*)

What kind of recognition will (organization) have received from its communities? What new constituencies will have become involved with (organization)?

These questions are just the beginning for your small group discussions and are advisory only . . . be imaginative, creative, innovative—and stay focused!

Logistics

You will have 45 minutes to prepare your presentation. You should have ready, in that time, a headline, lead for your story, and bullet points covering the principal ideas in the story and the sidebars (features). To ensure accomplishment of your task in the time allotted, be sure to:

1. Appoint a facilitator
2. Appoint a recorder
3. Find a reliable timekeeper

At the end of 45 minutes, each group will have 5 minutes to present its story. . . .

Enjoy!

---

ticipants do not know how to get started. Adapt the model to suit the temper and talents of the participants.

The small groups may be random or designed. One helpful configuration is to have at least one staff member in each group to provide program information for the board. You may also want to provide the groups with certain facts about the organization. The groups can brainstorm from their existing base of knowledge.

Each small group is provided with at least three sheets of easel paper and two colors of pens. Each group chooses a facilitator, who may also be the recorder or may appoint a recorder. The groups are instructed to be creative, to work together as a team, and to bring back to the larger group, after about an hour's brainstorming, their "newspaper article." Invariably, some of the stories will verge on fantasy, and others will lean to the mundane. Some will be illustrated, although not always with publishable art. With all, however, there will be recurring accomplishments, issues, market observations, and headlines. The exercise never fails to involve all participants in developing strong future scenarios for the organization which then become the basis for development and fund-raising plans.

Critical Outcomes

Each group presents its vision. Invariably, the common threads among the stories are so remarkable that the organization begins to see the shared dream even though it may have been neither expressed nor voiced in a long while. After each group has presented its story, the facilitator reviews them all for the recurring visionary ideas. The fantasies are enjoyed and set aside while the solidly applicable recurring themes and ideas are charted by the facilitator.

The strongest outcome is the implied vision for development and fund raising. With few exceptions, all program vision will require additional or expanded funding.

From these small sessions, the vision grows. This process does not create a "vision statement." Instead, it provides essential baseline information from which program, organization, and development goals will be derived. If your organization desires a vision statement, wait until the end of the planning process and have the CEO crystallize the dreams and the realities into an inviting statement. It will have more validity than trying to generate one through "group think."

Starting the Plan

Having generated the basis for goals in the visioning process, it may also be essential to look at the mission statement. While it is risky to start the planning session by *revising* the mission statement, an affirmation of the statement helps guide the planning process. If participants feel there is need for extensive revisions, identify the areas in question and assign a task force to work with the mission and come back to a future board or planning meeting with some draft statements. Entire planning sessions have been derailed by lengthy arguments over the validity, syntax, and meaning of the mission statement. At some point, the mission statement should be reviewed and related to the vision ideas that have emerged.

Outline the three planning categories—Program, Organization, and Development—to the group at the close of the visioning exercise (or at a subsequent session if the visioning is done separately from the plan). Working from the vision ideas, the facilitator asks the group to identify the principal areas of the organization present in the vision (Program, Organization, and/or Development). Usually, these break out fairly evenly. Much of the development and fund-raising vision is implied in the larger visions (new headquarters, scholarship programs, endowment strength); the program vision is easily identifiable; and the board and staff organization component may be either implied or stated directly.

Translating the Vision into Development and Fund-Raising Goals

The next step in the exercise moves the vision into more concrete statements. Depending on the time constraints and number of people involved, examination of possible goals for each of these areas can be done as a full group or in small groups. Or, you may wish to focus only on development and fund raising.

Using the vision ideas as a base, but expanding on that material to include other potential areas for growth or accomplishment, generate possible goals. The purpose of this exercise is to generate as many goals as possible or practical. Prioritization and reduction comes later. If the three areas (Program, Organization, and Development) are discussed, and assigned to three separate groups, much overlapping occurs. When these are combined or assigned to one area, the final number of potential goals is reduced. One instruction is essential: participants should not get tangled up in trying to phrase the goals perfectly. Plan writing comes later. What is more important is to get the ideas down on paper.

The facilitator records the goals if the group works as a whole, but if small groups are formed each group is responsible for recording its proposed goals. These are then presented to the entire group. Overlaps are noted and combined (e.g., both Program and Development may call for the creation of a marketing plan). When the array of possible goals has been combined, discussed, and is ready for prioritization, there is a relatively simple process to use. Each person is given five "votes" (more or less, depending on the number of potential goals listed (more goals = more votes). The fastest way to have people vote is to give each person the correct number of colored adhesive dots. They vote for the goals they feel are the most important by putting their dots next to the number of the goal. When they are out of dots, they have used all their votes. If you don't have dots, or don't like the dot process, you can supply each person with a marking pen and they can vote in the same fashion but by making a mark next to the goal. Voting can be limited to one dot per goal. A variation on the process permits people to use all their dots on one goal if they want, or apportion them in the way that reflects their priorities for the plan.

When the voting is finished, the votes are counted and goals are put in priority order. Keep the goals in their planning area (e.g., Program, Organization, Development) so the balance in the number of goals can be assessed. If one area seems short—or if an important goal has been knocked to a lower order—discuss adding others or raising one or more in priority. Many organizations try to limit themselves in their goals, thereby keeping the plan not only manageable but the objectives, which will grow out of the goals, attainable.

Building Objectives from Goals

The agreed-upon and prioritized goals need objectives to come to life. If goals are the *what*, objectives are the *how*. The language for objectives in strong institutional and development plans can be complex, and there is no need for the whole group to be constrained by proper phrasing. Instead, use the SMART and "Who will do what by when" frameworks and have people generate a list of the things that need to be done to reach the goal. Participants can work together as a whole, or in small groups. The same groupings should be used for the objectives as was used for the goals.

When these lists of activities or objectives have been generated, they are also reviewed by the whole group. They may be prioritized using the same method employed for the goal prioritization. Or, the group may decide they have done enough and that the remainder of the exercise can be handled by a smaller task force.

Aligning the Budget and Planning Processes

It is difficult and unwise to separate the budgeting and planning processes. The kind of analysis and process that generates a strong plan also inspires a healthy budgeting process. Too often, budgets are created at the last minute by the CEO with little buy-in from program or administrative staff. Budgets prepared in this way are often viewed as a threat or constraint, rather than as a vital management tool. Budgets which are developed concurrently with an extensive planning process or with an annual plan review and update are seen as requisite companions to the fulfillment of the plan. At a minimum, if not done within a larger institutional planning process, the budget analysis, preparation, and approval sequence should take three to four months, involve both board and staff, and have sufficient opportunities for review and adjustment. Boards and staffs resent budgets that are pushed through against a deadline without time for adequate preparation and review.

A declining, but unfortunately still occurring problem regarding budgeting in the not-for-profit sector, is the failure to involve the development and fund-raising staff sufficiently in the process. When this happens, development offices are informed, after the budget is completed, about how much money they must raise in order to meet the budget. In one instance, the development director for the local branch of a national organization was informed, after the budget was approved, about how much she should raise that year. The figure represented a 20 percent increase over the previous year. In addition, she was also told that certain major donors on whom she counted for substantial support would not be available to her for solicitation because they were being reserved for a national endowment campaign. Frustrated, and feeling out of the management communication loop, she battled for months for an adjustment on her goal or leniency on the policy relative to the major donors. Both efforts failed, and she resigned.

Involvement of Development Staff in Budget Planning

The realistic assessment of the capacity to fundraise, as part of a deliberate development effort, must play a critical part in the budgeting process. Staff and board volunteers must engage the development director and others responsible for fund raising in the overall analysis for budgeting and planning. The fund-raising and development effort must be driven by and responsive to the excitement and vitality of the program vision and goals.

The premise and importance of going beyond fund raising is lodged solidly in the planning process: the development office must stretch, innovate, and work tirelessly to see to it that the marketplace needs are met by the planned programming. However, to place unrealistic demands on an office or an individual is to set an organization up for failure. This is why involvement of development staff in the planning and budgeting process is required. One development director burned herself out, and ended up leaving the not-for-profit field for more than a year, when she nearly single-handedly had to mobilize herself, her staff, and the few board members willing to fund raise, to increase their fund raising 73 percent over the previous year. This daunting goal was handed to her by the budget committee, and included not only funds for current program support but also over $300,000 in funds for deficit reduction. At no time was she asked whether the staff and volunteer resources could take on this challenge. New to the job, she was determined to meet the goal. She did, but at high personal cost.

Setting Up a Successful Budgeting Process

The best budgeting processes are those that provide broad involvement of staff and volunteers and ample time for program, resources, and marketplace analysis. The preplanning analysis questions which apply to the larger planning issues may be effectively applied to budgeting as well.

Approaches to Budget Preparation

1. *Zero-Based Budgeting.* The most thorough process is zero-based budgeting. This is a process in which the entire budget is rebuilt periodically to reflect a deep analysis of the marketplace needs and the organization's existing and potential resources to meet those needs. It assumes that no funding is assigned to programs or services in the organization. The budget is a blank slate. Program directors and staff are required to look exactingly at their costs, needs, and impact, and make budget requests based not only on past practices, but on future marketplace requirements.

   Program staffs may respond defensively the first time the process is introduced: it is helpful to have outside consultation to ensure support and understanding of the process. One organization successfully implemented a zero-based process, after initial resistance, by bringing in a volunteer team from the business school at a local university. This volunteer team worked capably and correctly with the program staff to assure them that this process had the same benefit as proper pruning of trees or roses: building on the same rootstock, the resulting growth would be healthier and fuller than ever before. The process was a success, and has been repeated since with great acceptance.

   When the extensive analysis has been completed for each program, meetings are held to compare, combine, and adjust the needs from the various departments and programs. Then, based on earned and contributed revenue projections, the budget begins to evolve. Revenue and expenses are thoughtfully assessed and assigned to program and administrative areas which have been solidly evaluated through the planning process.

   The resulting budget is owned, accurate, and an effective companion to the long-range or strategic plan. This process does not have to be repeated in its entirety every year: every other year is usually sufficient provided there is modest yet careful annual evaluation. This approach to budgeting is far preferable to the approach too often taken by organizations in which an increment (or decrease) is uniformly applied across the budget to reflect an increase, or decline, in available or anticipated funding. To require all programs to reduce expenditures by five percent, for example, may be punitive to programs which need to grow to serve clients or audiences. Zero-based budgeting, in conjunction with a planning or plan evaluation process, helps ensure that the organization will allocate its resources in the area where the market need is greatest. Although zero-based budgeting may seem initially to be a threat, it is most often respected as a more fair approach in the long run.

2. *Program Budgeting.* A companion to zero-based budgeting in its effectiveness in assigning costs is program budgeting. A line item expense budget is the framework for program budgeting. However, rather than having a lump sum line for salary, benefits, printing, fund raising, and so on, each of those expenses is broken out by program and distributed across the various cost centers of the organization. Thus (see Exhibit 11.4), a children's services agency assigns its various expense lines into (e.g.) child psychiatry, social work, occupational therapy, speech and language therapy, and so on. The resulting budget, which has been approached from a zero-based or modified zero-based process, clearly assigns costs to the appropriate program. This benefits the organization in two ways: (1) it is a more effective management tool for monitoring expenses and (2) it is easier to prepare proposals and other program-related information for funders, staff, and volunteers. Program budgeting permits certain administrative costs to be assigned to program areas, enabling the organization to approach willing funders with proposals that include a certain amount of essential support costs for a particular program.

The budget process integrates with the planning process. Both should be fluid, accessible, and participatory. The resulting budget should fit into and support the plan, and be an excellent financial translation of the plan. It should be a budget that supports and includes funding for development, not just fund raising.

Getting the Plan Done

Long-range planning committees are ad hoc committees appointed by the board chair for the purpose of fulfilling a time-determinate task and/or for continued monitoring of the plan. An organization may choose to dissolve the long-range planning committee after the completion of the plan, and assign the monitoring function to the executive or finance committee. Continual evaluation is essential to the vitality and usefulness of the plan, so be sure there is some existing or specially appointed group within the organization that accepts that responsibility.

EXHIBIT 11.4 Example of Program Budget Expenses

	Administration and/or Development	Child Psychiatry	Counseling	Parenting	Speech Therapy	Occupational Therapy
1. Salaries						
2. Benefits						
3. Travel						
4. Office • phones • postage • etc.						
5. Program etc.						
Total budget for each program						
Total budget for agency						

The written plan documents the planning and budgeting process. Final plans vary considerably. Some organizations produce very extensive and complex plans which may run to 100 or more pages with charts, action plans, and other support materials. Other organizations prefer a slender plan in which timelines and even goals and objectives are done in chart form. The style of the plan should reflect the culture and needs of the organization. If an outside consultant has been guiding the process, and continues to be involved through the writing of the document, the product may be in a format standard to that consultant.

Required Ingredients of the Completed Plan

Whatever the length or complexity of the document, it must have the following elements to be effective:

1. An executive summary which introduces the document and can be shared with potential donor-investors or volunteers;
2. A summary budget as well as the detailed budget;
3. A list of the goals for the plan, organized by Program (including facilities), Organization (board and staff), and Development (fund raising, marketing, public relations);
4. Measurable objectives, keyed to each of the goals, stating task, person(s) responsible, and date by which the task will be completed;
5. Action plans keyed to each of the objectives, giving details about how the particular objective will be accomplished;
6. A statement describing the plan evaluation process that will be used (e.g., quarterly reviews, who is involved, who is responsible); and
7. A summary timeline which plots all objectives.

SUMMARY

It is impossible to be effective in development and fund raising without an institutional plan to inspire and justify the reasons for inviting community support. When accompanied by a budget which has been developed in a concurrent or companion process of analysis, preparation and validation, the plan both stabilizes and stretches an organization. Plans which are developed using the TRI-POD method, described in this chapter, are inclusive of program, organization, and development goals and objectives, all of which are based on a careful assessment of marketplace needs and institutional capacity.

Ultimately, the process and the resulting document must reflect the organization so the resulting level of ownership and commitment is the highest possible. Success in development and fund raising will ensure the achievement of the organization's long-range plan. Likewise, the vision and wisdom of the long-range plan will help ensure success in development and fund raising.

12 ▼ Implementing the Principles

Life beyond fund raising is a tantalizing proposition. Those who succeed in transforming their organizations understand both the requirements and benefits of moving away from an urgent array of isolated fund-raising activities to an integrated cycle of fund raising positioned as the mutually beneficial product of the development process.

Organizations whose volunteers and staff members have mastered the theories and strategies advanced in this book find that fund raising is easier and more rewarding. They understand the interrelationship of philanthropy, development, and fund raising (Chapter 1). Fund raising is viewed by the volunteer and staff leadership of these organizations as the process of enabling people to act on their values. Asking for an investment is something they end up wanting to do, because they see it as the most appropriate way to continually affirm the relationship between the donor-investor and the organization.

These leaders also readily confess that there are basic steps to implementing a development program, each of which is to a large degree dependent on the institutional behaviors and resources described in this book.

This chapter describes the required behaviors and resources, offers ten steps which will take organizations beyond fund raising, presents two organizations that have begun their journey, and concludes with a review of emerging trends in the nonprofit sector which will affect development and fund raising.

IMPLEMENTING THE PRINCIPLES OF THIS BOOK IN YOUR ORGANIZATION

Certain behaviors and resources are essential if organizations are to go beyond fund raising. Earlier in this book, chapters on the philanthropy/development/fund-raising relationship, development of the investor attitude (putting away the tin cup), institutional planning for development, the strategic role of stewardship, and the urgency of adherence to mission traced the critical paths organizations must follow to achieve vigorous development practices. There were secondary requirements as well: commitment to building and maintaining relationships, sound governance practices including board self-assessment and rotation, honest evaluation of systems and personnel, partnerships between board and staff and throughout the organization, a solid business approach to budget preparation and financial management, and an integrated approach to annual and capital fund raising.

The purpose here is not to elaborate on these strategies or requirements, but to restate and underscore their importance and provide some tips to get things started. The intent of this book has been to convince organizations that they can attain the power and capability to fulfill their mission and engage their communities if they are diligent in developing the behaviors and resources they need to go beyond fund raising.

FIVE BEHAVIORS REQUIRED TO MOVE BEYOND FUND RAISING

Organizations determined to implement development practices must continually reinforce the following principal behaviors among board, staff, and committee members, and in all education or training about donor and fund development.

1. *Acceptance of the values basis of philanthropy, development and fund raising.* Threading its way throughout all activities of healthy nonprofit organizations is a belief in the institution's core values. Often affirmed through published mission-vision-values declarations, these inspiring statements have an internal impact on employees and vol-

unteers and an external impact on prospects, donors, and other community partners. They are context for institutional pride and for community relationship-building, and provide impetus for inviting and retaining investment. Volunteer and staff partners in a successful development process take those statements one step further: they master the ability to "tell the story" of the organization and its impact, and tie those stories back into the core values of the organization. In telling the story of one child who benefits from a therapeutic day care program for emotionally disturbed youngsters, they intimate the impact those benefits have on all 600 children and their families served by the organization and convey the organization's belief in children and their potential for growth. In describing the long-term impact of a scholarship program on one student whose life was changed, the core educational values of an independent school are understood in the implicit larger imprint on all scholarship students. Translation of core values into actual program benefits is a key behavior. Organizations must continually articulate and reinforce those values through the following activities:

- Annually, at the board retreat, reaffirm the core values of the organization through brainstorming and discussion;
- Reflect those values in all written materials to the extent possible and appropriate;
- Coach board members and other volunteers in how to "tell the story" of the impact the organization is having on the lives of those they serve;
- Insert the values as the foundation of all practices;
- Prevent the erosion of values into hollow statements not reinforced by practices; and
- Reflect the accomplishments of the organization within a values context that reinforces the donor-investor's motivation.

Adherence to a belief in the importance of core values in donor-investor motivation leads to an increased respect for each contributor. Donor-investors are understood to be acting on their values when they make a gift. The gift, the giver, and the process of inviting investment are more esteemed. Phrases like "arm twisting," "hitting him up," and others that imply an aggressive organization and an unwilling donor, disappear from the development vocabulary of the organization. Instead, it is remembered that each gift represents a reflection of the donor's values and is a piece of the giver's self. This realization creates and maintains a higher level of regard. This regard, when mutual between the donor-investor and the organization, leads to the solidifying of the relationship.

2. *Adoption of an investor/investment attitude and retirement of the tin cup in fund raising.* As an outcome of values-based development and fund raising, the investor/investment attitude (Chapter 2) influences all interaction with donor-investors. It is also extended to volunteers who participate in program and development activities. When regarded and treated as investors, donors and volunteers view themselves increasingly as important partners in the long-term capacity of the organization to provide and perform.

Fund, donor, and volunteer development are most effective when the invitation to give or join is extended without apology or desperation. Unfortunately, the posture of organizations which still conduct an array of separate fund-raising activities without the larger context of development and philanthropy is one of "urgency": not the urgency of the need that is being met (children's services, school scholarships), but the organization's compelling need for money or volunteers. This latter philosophy leads to a tin cup approach and an implicit apology for "needing" money or volunteers. Nonprofit organizations do need both, but only because of the community needs they are meeting. Nonprofits provide donor-investors with a vehicle for investing in community programs. Retirement of the tin cup requires a reversal in traditional attitudes about fund raising and volunteer involvement.

It is up to organizations to educate their volunteers and donors about "tin cup free fund raising." While many board and staff members still admit to feeling like beggars when they ask for a gift, the movement towards an investment attitude is growing. Volunteers and staff are helped in their efforts to put away the tin cup by a similarly changing attitude among individual and institutional donors. Those seeking funds are no longer viewed by potential funders as "needy;" instead, they are viewed as partners in meeting needs and as excellent investment opportunities for thoughtful citizens.

3. *Willingness to operate at three levels: philosophical, strategic, tactical.* This behavior (Chapter 5) boosts the organization's capacity to go beyond fund raising because volunteers and staff examine nonprofit planning, governance, and development as complex processes. The philosophical level, too often ignored by organizations rushing to raise a

dollar, provides the values analysis needed to create a solid platform for board and fund development, a compelling case for support, and for general planning. Thoughtful evaluation of the organization's beliefs isolates core values and assists organizations in presenting their case to potential donors. Philosophical commitment to volunteerism and stewardship are translated into strategic goals and tactical plans which build the organization's capacity to implement strong development practices.

Strategic planning, conducted in an environment where philosophical issues have been clarified, is more productive. The strategies which emerge are solidly grounded in shared beliefs, and the common understanding of volunteers and staff members leads to ownership and implementation. Finally, at the tactical level, there is energy and commitment to get the job done. Action plans, derived from strategies based in philosophical consensus, are inspired and driven by a sense of commitment to mutual goals.

This trilevel framework, applied to crucial management areas of the organization, contributes to the overall institutional stability which funders seek for their investments.

4. *Belief in donor-centered development and fund raising.* Collateral with the freedom of putting away the tin cup is another behavior: the realization that the donor, not the institution, is the center of all development transactions. Development and fund-raising practices should be developed with this in mind, especially cultivation, solicitation, and stewardship. This belief is reflected in every transaction with prospects and donors beginning with the initial personal contact. Even direct mail, if properly segmented to target specific constituencies for acquisition or renewal, can show a donor-centered focus. However, it is in the establishment of personal relationships with donors and volunteers that this emphasis on the donor becomes so important. The definition of "donor" extends to volunteers as well. They are major donors of time, even when their gifts may be lower than the major gift level.

As an institutional philosophy, the view of the donor as the center of all development transactions is one of the most important. As an institutional strategy, it is vital. And, at the tactical level, it is constantly evaluated by the best test market of all, the donors themselves. Their excitement and commitment increases as their sense of partnership and importance grows. Cultivation, solicitation, and stewardship of donors are most effective when the equation is balanced in their favor.

5. *Commitment to mission.* This behavior influences the first four. Commitment to mission is a given in the nonprofit sector. We often speak of our sector as mission-based. We discuss programs within the context of *consistency with the mission,* and we applaud organizations that are able to raise the funds to fulfill their mission.

The mission statement expresses the organization's mission, and the initial creation and occasional revision of the statement is a priority function for board and staff leadership. Mission statements may be agreed to or quarreled about, and sometimes remain unfinished due to lack of consensus and highly charged emotions. What is ultimately more important than the statement itself is a commitment to the institution's understood mission by the board and staff and its integration into practices. For development to flourish, the understood mission should reflect the institution's core values and clearly state what needs the organization is meeting in the community.

Keeping the commitment to mission fresh is the true challenge in going beyond fund raising. Meet this challenge by doing the following:

- Plan a time at every board meeting for recipients or beneficiaries of services to give a ten-minute talk about the impact of those services on their lives and/or on the community;
- Reach agreement on a statement of mission which is clear, crisp, and compelling;
- Ensure that all printed materials for general or fund-raising purposes reflect the core values and mission of the organization;
- Engage board and staff leadership in strategic discussions at least annually about consistency of mission and program and how well the two are aligned;
- Use the understood or written statement of mission as the basis for making key new program decisions;
- Inform constituents through publications and personal interaction about the mission and core values, and how their support enables the organization to advance the mission; and
- Keep key decision-makers in the community, including civic leaders and funders, informed of the importance of the mission to the community and why investment in the organization is an investment in a better community.

These five key behaviors are the foundation for a strong development program. When complemented by the following resources, organizations are able to go beyond fund raising.

THREE RESOURCES REQUIRED TO GO BEYOND FUND RAISING

The resources required for a successful development program are people (internal and external), adequate budget, and institutional plan.

Seemingly simple, these three resources are broadly inclusive.

1. *People.* Ours is a people business. They are an essential component in the development equation and include board and other volunteers, staff at all levels and in all departments, prospects, donors, community members, and all those who have a stake in your mission or organization. Chapter 4 explores the development partnership and its inclusiveness.

   For development programs to work effectively, people have to be involved. Attracting and maintaining their involvement, and growing their commitment, depends largely on the degree to which the behaviors discussed above are manifested in the organization. The commitment of people both inside an organization and in the community grows when they perceive:

   - The institution's core values and the role these values play in decision-making;
   - An investor/investment attitude towards donors and volunteers, and the partnership that attitude implies;
   - A comprehensive three-level approach to planning and to the analysis and resolution of issues;
   - A sincere focus on the donor or volunteer in all development transactions; and
   - A commitment to mission which influences all program and development decisions.

2. *Adequate Budget.* Organizations cannot implement a true development program without adequate resources to fund long-term prospect, donor and volunteer relations. As observed in Chapter 11, budgeting for development is always more difficult than budgeting for fund raising. Fund-raising activities (annual and major gifts, capital campaigns, fund-raising events) are easily tracked by revenue, expense, and net gain (or loss) analyses. Development activities (cultivation, stewardship, recognition, and acknowledgment) are often not quantifiable. The cause and effect is more difficult to relate. When budgets are trimmed, the dollars assigned to activities

without immediate measurable impact are the first to be cut. To ensure the most successful fund raising, organizations must invest in development. It is the function that broadens the impact of the organization over time. More importantly, development is the function that builds lasting relationships with people whose time and financial resources ensure the future of the organization.

3. *Institutional Plan.* Development planning can only be effective if there is a larger institutional plan in place. Chapter 11 focused on institutional planning. Not enough can be said about the importance of having a solid plan in place. Funders are not nearly as interested in an organization's development plan as they are in the institutional vision, goals, and objectives. Fund raising and development do not drive programs; programs drive fund raising and development. A development plan without an institutional plan guiding its priorities may have tactical value, but its strategic and philosophical structure will be frail. Funders invest in organizations because they see ways to partner in the solution of a problem or in providing a service or enhancement to the community. Only the institutional plan can convey that bigger picture.

Volunteers and staff responsible for the development function in an organization must persuade reluctant administrative or board leadership of the importance of institutional planning, and ensure that a document for which there is ownership emerges. Sometimes, getting a plan done where there is initial or lingering opposition takes a fair dose of courage (Chapter 3). The quandary often distills to questions that are both troublesome and enlightening: Is it more important to keep a job, or do a job? Is our behavior more mission-oriented or job-oriented? There are several known instances of development staff and volunteers who eventually separated from an organization because of staff executives or board leaders who simply refused to plan.

The process of planning is a healthy catalyst for organizations as they resolve institutional priorities and goals. However, it is the plan itself which provides concrete guidance for staff, volunteers, and funders about how their investments of time and money will advance the organization's mission and meet the community's needs.

These behaviors and resources are the tools for creating a high-impact development program. They are the foundation for successful implementation of the ten steps organizations must take to go beyond fund raising.

PREPARING TO TAKE AN ORGANIZATION BEYOND FUND RAISING

Education is the key to successful implementation of the steps which will take your organization beyond fund raising. There is a need to market the development function internally to staff and board, and to market the impact of your nonprofit among your community constituencies.

Internal marketing of the development function should be a primary task for all development professionals and board leaders. Organizations benefit greatly when internal education through presentations at meetings, "good newsletters" circulated to staff, special mailings to board members and other volunteers and diligent reporting of progress and results, leads to the following levels of understanding and advocacy for development:

- Program staff who understand the impact of development and fund raising and their role in it;
- Board members who realize there is a role for them to play in development even if they are still reluctant to make a face-to-face ask;
- Nonprofit executives and administrators who honor the function of development by guaranteeing budget allocations for cultivation and stewardship activities that are often unmeasurable in their impact until long after that budget has been retired, and who convey to all staff that development is an institutional priority;
- Nonboard volunteers who view development as a highly rewarding activity in which they can play many supportive roles; and
- Major donors who feel like participants and investors, and who readily see and can explain their "return on investment."

External marketing of the impact of your nonprofit in the community is also an essential step in going beyond fund raising. Until potential and actual donor-investors realize they are investing in results, not needs and that their investment in your organization is really an investment in the community, they cannot fully know the power of partnering with an institution to act on common values. We must be consistent in our message. We must be relentless in letting people know the impact of what we do, how their time and gifts have made those accomplishments possible, and why their continued role as donor-investors is the one sure way to guarantee the continued value of their involvement.

On the strong foundation of an educated internal and external constituency, nonprofits can build organizations that will go beyond fund raising.

10 STEPS TO TAKE YOUR ORGANIZATION BEYOND FUND RAISING

The following ten steps are provided with an implicit understanding that the above-noted behaviors and resources must be present. The responsibility for carrying out the steps belongs to the partnership of volunteers and staff which is the basis of all successful development endeavors.

The 10 steps that will enable organizations to go beyond fund raising are:

1. Assess
2. Evaluate
3. Plan
4. Recruit
5. Inspire
6. Persuade
7. Engage
8. Involve
9. Retain
10. Renew

1. *Assess.* A perceived need for change must exist before a commitment to evaluate and possibly redesign systems for fund raising and development can occur. Assess board composition, communication, function, practices, and understanding of fund raising and development. Excellent self-assessment instruments are available through The National Center for Nonprofit Boards in Washington, D.C. Their board self-assessment sets the standard in the field. In 1996, a self-assessment for board attitudes and understanding about development and fund raising was developed by NCNB as part of the user's guide for their video, "Speaking of Money." Both of these surveys provide excellent baseline data for volunteer and staff leaders who want to plan and implement long term development practices.

Assess materials and community image. Conduct client, donor, and community surveys to obtain feedback about programs and messages. Surveys and focus groups are valuable tools for gaining this information. Thankathons and phone appeals also provide opportunities to ask donors and prospects a few key questions. Volunteers who make personal calls to enlist or solicit community members often receive feedback which should be passed along to the organization. A form or other mechanism for easily transmitting that information helps ensure that it is conveyed.

2. *Evaluate.* When the assessment is complete, evaluate it. Figure out what it means. What are the implications for board recruitment? Board training? Capacity of the organization to convey the investor attitude? How inclined is the board to move into a development program? If there is reluctance to fund raise, what will the organization do to overcome that? Assessment without evaluation of the results is virtually meaningless: it is the assessment that provides the data for the plan, but it is evaluation which makes those data useful.

Use information obtained from focus groups or surveys to enhance programs, materials, client services, or outreach. Are our donors satisfied? Is our stewardship working? Are our programs meeting critical needs? Do our publications convey our mission and values? Are our fund-raising letters and materials free of apology and do they project accomplishment and results? Does our mission statement really convey our mission? Does our mission project our values, and why we exist?

Evaluation feedback is less threatening to staff and volunteers when both the content and methodology of assessment and reporting is explained beforehand, and when the use of the data is made clear.

When setting out to gather information, be sure to have a system developed prior to the assessment that will guide the evaluation of the feedback. If the data are to be computerized, set up the program before the data start coming in. If there is to be a board, committee, or staff report with manually-prepared data presentation, familiarize people with the format and purpose of the presentation before it is made.

3. *Plan.* Chapter 11 addresses the process of institutional planning as well as its relationship to the development and fund-raising process. Planning is vital to successful organizations. There are too many sad examples of leaders within organizations who felt planning was not essential: it is disastrous for the organization's programs, fund rais-

ing and future. Vision, goals, objectives, and action planning depend on strong assessment and evaluation for their development. The institutional plan is a tool for building community support and investment. It inspires the plan for development and fund raising, which is a largely internal document that focuses on ways to bring the community into partnership with the institution's vision and goals.

4. *Recruit.* With assessment and evaluation informing a solid institutional plan, the recruitment of board, other volunteers and staff is conducted with much more knowledge of the community, the organization, and the needs of both. Recruitment of volunteers and staff needs a well-understood framework. Policies and procedures for recruitment, job descriptions which convey desired behaviors as well as responsibilities, and the capacity to clearly communicate expectations are the three key aspects of successful recruitment.

Recruitment is the first step in building a development team: it is a step involving mutual exploration on the part of the organization and the potential employee or volunteer. It is a function to similar recruitment—or cultivation—of prospective donors. It is a time of inquiry and investigation which may or may not result in a hire or an enlistment. To the degree it can be systematized with solid policies and procedures, it will be more effective. Recruitment should never feel rushed. Decisions should not be made in haste, nor procedures set aside for fear of losing a candidate. The old adage about acting in haste and repenting at leisure is particularly true in nonprofit organizations that find themselves with board members or staff managers whose organizational fit or commitment is lacking, or with donors who were solicited prematurely. Acting under pressure, too many organizations end up having to de-enlist, or endure, board members; buy out contracts of key staff people who were hired in haste because of a sense of urgency; or know disappointment from a solicitation that missed the mark. Be patient with the recruitment (and cultivation) process, and be sure the process is not compromised.

5. *Inspire.* Expose recruited board and staff candidates, and potential donors, to the inspirational aspects of your organization. Arrange tours. Let them observe programs if appropriate, or see a video that describes the programs. Introduce them to staff people. Set up meetings with those who have benefited from the services of the organization. If they are equally inspired by financial stability (and if you are financially stable), schedule a time for meeting with the business manager or investment consultant. Bring them to board meetings. If

your board meetings are not inspiring, alter the format and emphasis so they become more interesting not only to recruits, but to those already enlisted or hired. With potential donors, involve them on committees which have a mission-related purpose (marketing, program, development). Be prepared to answer tough questions, but make the mission manifest through opportunities to intersect with inspirational people and programs.

6. *Persuade.* Once recruited and inspired, excellent donor, volunteer, and staff candidates need to be persuaded. Nonprofits cannot assume that their mission, integrity, or values are obvious. Those involved in donor, board, and staff development must explain, listen, present, respond to objections, and be well-equipped with compelling evidence of the organization's impact. Board members and other volunteers involved in enlistment and solicitation must be able to tell the story of the organization in a way that relates to the perceived needs of the potential staff member, volunteer, or donor. Persuasion is not manipulation. It is based on a real connection between values and opportunities. Persuasion is not deliberately forceful: it becomes powerful when like minds link around shared values and goals. Strong boards, energized staffs, and solid ranks of donor-investors share one principal motivation: they are persuaded of the value and impact of the organization to which they offer their time, careers, and money.

7. *Engage.* A more powerful function than enlistment, engagement implies a deeper involvement. When organizations truly engage a volunteer, employee, or donor, they are adding another partner to the development process. Informed, inspired, and aware of the role they can play in advancing the organization, the engagement is entered into with standards that are taken seriously. Expectations are clearly stated. Implications for sustained involvement are conveyed. This is a powerful moment for the individual, and for the organization.

8. *Involve.* Once engaged, the involvement deepens. While some involvement is the natural result of increased exposure to the organization, there needs to be deliberate involvement as well. Continual matching of skills and interests with opportunities leads to a growing sense of involvement with an organization. Understanding the motivation of staff, volunteers, and donors, is a key component in successful deployment for development. Listening is the key strategy for identifying motivation and increasing involvement. Find out what ignites a person's enthusiasm. Connect people with other people and programs which will encourage their motivation. Get

people involved in projects and programs which provide satisfaction. The benefits will astound you.

9. *Retain.* Carefully recruited, properly persuaded, strongly engaged, and appropriately involved people will stay with your organization. They will continue their employment, serve their board or committee terms, and keep renewing their gifts. The formula is simple; its implementation is sometimes difficult. Changes in leadership, problems within the organization deriving from shifts in external or internal priorities, and the impact of major campaigns or programs on organizational stability can interfere with even the best-intentioned desire to retain the people who are key to the organization. One way to head off devastating loss of employees, volunteers, or donors in times of change is to maintain open, honest, and direct communication. Talk about the issues as they arise. Meet with employees, board members, and donors. Hear their ideas about strategies for getting through difficult times. Listen to their concerns. Mobilize their energy towards positive solutions. Be willing to implement their suggestions. Honor their efforts to resolve the problem even if their ideas are not used. Give feedback on progress towards solution of the problem. Be accessible. Trust is a crucial element in retention of employees, volunteers and donors. Trust them, and be trustworthy. Organizations which survive crises are those that take time and effort to maintain relationships with their partners and investors. They are also the organizations which allocate resources to sustain development practices even in times of perceived financial urgency.

10. *Renew.* Beyond the obvious need to renew gifts to nonprofits is the need to renew relationships. Development is the process of uncovering shared values and growing relationships. These relationships must be continually renewed through outreach, recognition, stewardship, and appropriate involvement. In the quest to renew gifts and relationships, volunteers, and staff should not forget the importance of self-renewal. Taking time to attend a conference, meet with other volunteers or staff, observe a program at a similar organization, read a relevant book, or just revisit the programs at your own organization can be very renewing. Combined with enough exercise and sleep (often neglected during busy times), these renewing activities can help ensure that the other kinds of renewal stay on track.

These 10 steps will set your organization solidly on the path towards development. Two brief case studies illustrate the mechanism and benefits of implementing a development program.

TWO CASE STUDIES:
GOING BEYOND FUND RAISING

The first case involves a social service organization which successfully completed an ambitious capital campaign in spite of the fact that, at the outset, they had few volunteers, little board involvement, a largely undeveloped donor base, no major donors, and a very small staff.

The second involves a cultural organization which has just begun its development program, but is doing a great many right things which will eventually take it beyond fund raising.

The San Francisco Food Bank

A venerable but largely unknown organization, this nearly invisible supplier of food to more than 300 meal-providing agencies in San Francisco needed a new warehouse. The first significant behavioral shift by board and staff was the realization, with coaching, that the *food bank* did not need a new warehouse: a new warehouse was needed by the *community* to help solve the problem of hunger in San Francisco. The food bank was the vehicle for meeting this community need. The existing warehouse could no longer adequately supply the 300+ meal-providing agencies. Further, available food was going to waste because of the inadequacy of freezer, refrigeration, and shelf-storage space. Although nearly four million pounds of food were processed each year, a larger warehouse would permit the storage and distribution of eleven million pounds a year.

Principal visibility for the food bank was among corporations whose employees participated in seasonal food drives. Several prominent professional athletes had also lent their name and endorsement for food drives. The barrels for collecting food were visible at major grocery stores and events, particularly at holiday times. An excellent newsletter, "Give and Take," related stories of the impact of the food bank on agencies and individuals.

Financially, the organization was stable. Fiscal management was prudent, drawing admiration and support from corporations and individuals. It was the rigorous financial management which drew the initial investor in the campaign, and it was the integrity of the staff leadership which drew the volunteer who leveraged several very large gifts. An executive director and a development director, with lean staffs, worked with a dedicated program staff and array of volunteers, many of whom were beneficiaries of feeding programs supplied by the food bank.

The board experienced high turnover during the planning and early phases of the campaign. It was a time of sorting out priorities, and many felt a campaign for $5 million would be too significant a drain on their time and financial resources. For a period of time, board membership was low. Care was exercised in the recruitment of new board members, and the board is still slowly being rebuilt, using policies and procedures based on a recruitment matrix.

The campaign steering committee, comprised principally of board leaders with key staff, other community volunteers, and the consultant, planned the campaign. A feasibility study, funded at great sacrifice by the organization, was a good investment. It identified potential funding sources, provided information for building the case statement, marketed the program for the first time to several corporate, foundation and individual constituency groups, and provided the basis for initial discussions with the eventual lead funders. The lead funder had been identified prior to the feasibility study: a corporation which provided its CEO as co-chair of the community committee for the campaign, an outright six-figure gift, and in-kind services in site identification, preparation and project management.

The campaign got off to a slow start. Difficulty in identifying the right site was finally resolved through the donation of a suitable piece of land, perfectly located. The donation was nearly a year in coming, during which time groundwork for soliciting other gifts was prepared. A community committee was enlisted, and an informational (and inspirational) meeting of the committee was held at the food bank on a fortuitously rainy day which revealed clearly the leaky roof and the generally inadequate facility.

Significantly, in support of the principles of development, a key action in that first year was the connection of the agency with an individual in the community who had no previous knowledge of or involvement with the food bank. Identified early in their planning as someone who might be interested or helpful, he was persuaded, engaged, and became involved. His efforts resulted in the leveraging of more than $1.2 million from corporations and foundations, and he and his wife also made a significant gift to the campaign. The relationship was based on mutual respect, on the expertise the volunteer could provide in several areas, on the volunteer's respect for the integrity and impact of the organization, and on the enthusiasm of the steering committee leadership. They sought the volunteer's advice long before they asked for his assistance in raising money, and they listened to his cautions.

Once the land was secured, and the community committee in place, the campaign got underway. A campaign manager was added at that time, who worked under the direction of the development director and monitored aspects of training, stewardship, cultivation, donor relations, and fund raising. Large gifts from corporations, local government, and foundations, and an anonymous gift from an individual rocketed the total from under $500,000 to nearly $4.5 million in one year. The remaining funds were generated with the help of a challenge grant, and involved many more individual and smaller donors, including the regular donors to the food bank's annual giving programs.

Elapsed time for the campaign was more than three years, with the highest activity during the last 18 months. The campaign had, as its goals, the successful accomplishment of the financial target *but also* increased visibility and an expanded donor base. All the goals will be met.

A campaign is not necessarily the best vehicle for going beyond fund raising. Usually, the pieces must be in place before a campaign begins. In this case, the food bank successfully assembled the bicycle while riding it, and integrated the behaviors and resources suggested in this chapter while taking the steps. They followed all ten steps in the process, and were successful in involving people internally and externally in the project. One of the major gifts was brought in through the connection of a program staff person, who felt like a part of the development team and wanted to see the project succeed. The co-chair of the community committee leveraged the donation of the site. The co-chairs solicited numerous corporate gifts. An accounting firm in San Francisco "adopted" the food bank and vowed to leverage its $25,000 gift into $250,000 by soliciting other companies and individuals.

Budget for the campaign, while kept modest, was well-placed. The precampaign study by the consultant led to her continued involvement on an ad hoc basis. Materials were kept to "desktop" format until the campaign went public. At that time, an advertising agency provided pro bono services for theme and materials development. The theme was based on an assessment done by the food bank, known as the hunger study. The study showed that one of the biggest problems in resolving hunger was food distribution: having a warehouse that was adequate for processing. Materials for the campaign have this enticing opening: "People are hungry. There's plenty of food. So, what's the problem?"

Volunteers and funders alike perceived the core values of the organization. An investor/investment attitude pervaded all transactions with volunteers and donors, and any sense of tin cup fund raising was dispelled when they found the eager acceptance of the impact they were having in the community. They could speak with conviction about their results, and invite investment in a future that would address the issue of hunger even more powerfully.

In the process of designing and implementing the campaign, they wrestled with philosophical issues around the involvement of volunteers, the necessity of training and planning, and the allocation of resources to this fund-raising effort. Resolved, these were the backbone of the eventual campaign plan, the public announcement of the campaign, and the kinds of stewardship and recognition provided. The needs, expertise, and involvement of potential and actual donors became the focus of planning strategies and events. And, in all, the commitment to mission was the motivation.

The campaign was a success, but the people of San Francisco were the true winners. In the summer of 1997, they will have a facility that adequately provides food for programs which can help meet the needs of its hungry citizens.

The American Library in Paris

Although it celebrated its 75th birthday in 1995, the American Library in Paris had no significant record in fund raising. Founded by the American Library Association and a dedicated group of post-World War I Americans in Paris, it had fluctuated in size and site over the years. A board of mostly U.S. corporate and community volunteers, there was high turnover and not much involvement in fund raising or development. Occasional over-the-transom gifts and bequests of money, books, and materials were supplemented by a modest annual campaign and member fees. A small campaign for internal expansion in the early 1990s raised enough money for the project, but was not used to leverage long-term support. Little was done to keep those donors involved.

Although an American library, more than half of its members are French. It operates as a private library providing public library services to Americans and French, including children and teenagers. With a just-recently expanding concept of philanthropy, fund raising within France has always been challenging, even among American individuals and corporations. Many U.S.-based corporations and foundations are prohibited from investing their philanthropic dollars overseas. The Library's growing need for annual giving to support programs for an expanding membership and an anticipated capital need for further interior expansion caused the organization to think sharply about how it could position itself more effectively.

A first-ever board of directors retreat was well-attended. The board had not previously dedicated so much focused time to address issues of mission, values, purpose, and the future. A new director, hired just before the retreat, provided her vision and conveyed her expertise and enthusiasm. A campaign was discussed, and an early commitment made to proceed with the planning. The planning process involved the 10 steps it takes to go beyond fund raising. That process, however, revealed some real needs in the areas of behaviors and resources. A strategic institutional plan now exists, where there was none before. Budget for critical program personnel was allocated so the rationale for donor investment would be easier to convey. The children's program increased 500 percent in attendance and programming, and the Evening with Authors community program also saw great increases with the addition of a full time director of development who assumed outreach responsibilities with the director.

Still in process, but strongly led by several board members and the director, is the integration of the required behaviors recommended in this chapter. Philanthropy is understood, but not yet widely practiced in Europe, and much education is underway by and with the board. Stewardship practices have been implemented in a major way since the festivities commemorating the 75th anniversary. During a gala week of events in Paris, Giverny, and Versailles, many individuals and organizations never previously involved were linked with the library. Care is being taken to sustain those relationships. Among those at the celebration were a number of Americans who made the trip over especially for the week of events. Efforts are being made to keep them involved. The board is expanding, with more French citizens joining to reflect the composition of the library's membership. A belief in donor-centered development and fund raising is emerging, and the director's stewardship and cultivation with individuals has had some very positive gift and volunteer involvement results. The campaign for further internal expansion is inching forward, but until these other pieces are in place and further relationship building occurs, it will be slow.

In an environment in which philanthropy is just now being identified as an aspect of citizenship, this small but sturdy organization is advancing towards development. The opportunity to work within another culture, and to advance tested principles of development and fund raising is unique. The American Library is capitalizing on that opportunity.

These case studies are the tip of the iceberg. Other stories could be told about museums in the U.S. southwest; independent schools in the northwest, east, and west; religious organizations in the midwest and California; symphony orchestras across the United States; a museum in Prague; a university in England; and a leukemia foundation in Australia. It is happening everywhere. It needs to happen.

But the path is not known, nor will it be straight. There are emerging trends which will affect all organizations in the immediate and long-term future.

TRENDS TO ANTICIPATE IN NONPROFIT DEVELOPMENT AND FUND RAISING

1. *The nonprofit sector will play an increasingly important role as a community builder, filling in for important government functions that will be unfunded and building strong and financially solvent coalitions of mission directed organizations that are worthy of community in investment.* There are 1.2 million registered nonprofits in the United States. As resources and donors are tapped increasingly, there will be mergers and coalitions. Some organizations will find they no longer have a viable base of support and will be forced to merge or close. These mergers and coalitions are occurring at a rapid rate. Two museums in southern California have merged and will invite others to join them. Two Catholic universities in Minnesota are sharing facilities, curriculum, and essential student services. A number of American independent schools have merged to provide coeducational programs and consolidate financial operations. Community issues must be addressed, and the sector is finding the best ways to organize to solve problems and provide services.
2. *Because of the first trend, organizations will find themselves increasingly in an educational role with communities.* They will have to define philanthropy and the role they play. This will require new paradigms and new commitments from professional and volunteer staff, to be leaders not only within the organization but in the community. Both internal and external marketing will require new messages, and new energy.
3. *Donors will focus on fewer organizations but make larger gifts.* Donors want to make an impact with their giving, and will give larger gifts to selected organizations. It will become increasingly important to practice excellent stewardship to retain donors.
4. *Combined fund raising campaigns in corporations and communities will continue to be questioned and their results decline.* Donors want more participation in the allocation of their contributions, and a stronger relationship with organizations they fund. United Way and other combined funding programs will face continued challenges. Com-

munity foundations, with their donor-designated funds, will be an increasingly attractive option for those who still want to give funds as a block for distribution by an organization. Administration costs at community foundations are lower, and donor-designated funds are encouraged.

5. *Organizations must be more and more mission focused, with a high results orientation.* Donors are increasingly seeing themselves as investors, and want to see substantial return on their investment by understanding what their dollars are doing. Annual reports, solicitation materials, and all outreach must be based on the impact of gifts on the long term needs of the community.

6. *Volunteerism will continue to be a major force in the success of large gifts programs, in partnership with increasingly professional staff.* Emphasis will be on partnerships between board and staff to increase the amount of personal contact with donors. As more demands are placed on volunteers, and more professional skills are available to nonprofits from volunteers, nonprofits need to be diligent about making the best use of volunteered time. Whether on a volunteer-to-volunteer level, or a staff-volunteer level, respect must undergird all requests for time and energy. Volunteers must have a return on their time investment: an affirmation of their values, a sense of satisfaction, the feeling of a job well done, the visibility of results. Appropriate reinforcement and rewards will keep volunteers interested and loyal, but the best tool for forging a long-lasting relationship is not wasting a volunteer's time.

7. *Donors will increasingly feel and express a need to belong: not only through their gifts but by offering their opinions, ideas, counsel.* Organizations must be prepared to embrace the donor not only as a source of money, but as a source of guidance. Only then will true partnerships be forged, and the magnitude of the investor role be realized.

8. *Technology will play an increasing role in solicitation practices.* More sophisticated methods for prospect research will raise ethical questions. Solicitations over the Internet will be promoted, but will make a difference mostly in smaller gift solicitation programs. Organizations need to be very mindful of the issues of ethics, and the potential for technology to invade privacy.

9. *Countries throughout the world will increasingly emphasize the philanthropic responsibility of its citizens.* Decline of government support in most of the world, and the dismantling of infrastructure in eastern Europe, and parts of South America, Africa, and Asia, has created an awareness of the need for education about philanthropy. A full two-page advertisement in *Paris Match* in May, 1996, stated (translated):

"Foundation of France: Not to forget each form of exclusion; to transform each donation into action." It goes on to say that the Foundation of France is working against forms of exclusion, isolation, and suffering, and that "to give to the Foundation of France, is to have the certainty that each gift is transformed into action." It then summarizes its programs including assistance with a dignified death and help to surviving families, providing opportunities for ill children to take holidays, and helping families of those with dependent elderly adults or handicapped children. The Foundation's slogan is "We help those who wish to be helped." The photograph shows an elderly man alone, eating soup. There is sure to be increasing response and participation, not just at major gift levels, but among the citizenry of these countries.

10. *The sector will become more vital, more professional.* Professional development and training through organizations like The Fund Raising School (Center on Philanthropy, Indiana University), CASE (Council for Advancement and Support of Education), and the National Center for Nonprofit Boards (NCNB) are guaranteeing the strong partnership between boards and staff. The certification programs of the National Society of Fund Raising Executives (NSFRE) and the Association for Healthcare Philanthropy (AHP) have now merged, and overseas organizations like Fundraising Institute Australia (FIA) are bringing new standards and performance to the sector. They are welcome and respected.

11. *Increased emphasis on responsible regulation and legislation of nonprofit activities.* At the federal and state levels, there is more scrutiny of the nonprofit sector. Nonprofits, their umbrella organizations, and professional associations must be ready to work cooperatively to address these concerns. The profession, and volunteers associated with it, need to be watchdogs for their own organizations' compliance with regulations, and take a leadership role in the community.

SUMMARY

It requires new commitments and new paradigms to go beyond fund raising. We are reminded by sages to dream no small dreams, and to hitch our wagons to stars. Ultimately, we are confronted with the reality of the needs we are meeting and our capacity to meet them. It is the gap between the desire and the reality that we strive to close.

There are two bottom lines in all of fund raising: the money raised and the values secured. And there are two more key benefits as well: the joy of asking, and the joy of giving. Both are essential emotions in the advancement of our sector. When people are moved to ask and give in the context of investment and results, they know they have made a difference. They have touched lives. They have made it possible for the hungry to be fed, the religious to be served, children to be educated, seniors to be comforted. When people give in that knowledge, they give part of themselves.

We must be stewards of the gifts we receive: the gifts of money, and the gifts of heart. Build those relationships. Curry your passion so it is inspiring to others, remembering that commitment is sustained passion.

You will then travel beyond fund raising, and know the value and results of development.

References

Grace, Kay Sprinkel. 1991. "Can We Throw Away the Tin Cup?" in *Taking Fund Raising Seriously: Advancing the Profession and Practice of Raising Money*, ed. D. Burlingame and L. Hulse. San Francisco, CA: Jossey-Bass, Inc.

Grace, Kay Sprinkel. 1995. "Towards Passionate Pragmatism: Building and Sustaining Board Commitment" in *Taking Trusteeship Seriously*, ed. R. Turner. Indianapolis, IN: Indiana University Center on Philanthropy.

Payton, Robert L. 1988. *Philanthropy: Voluntary Action for the Public Good*. New York: Collier Macmillan.

Rosso, Henry A. and Associates. 1991. *Achieving Excellence in Fund Raising*. San Francisco, CA: Jossey-Bass, Inc.

Index